GEORGE PADMORE'S **BLACK INTERNATIONALISM**

GEORGE PADMORE'S
Black Internationalism

Rodney Worrell

The University of the West Indies Press
Jamaica • Barbados • Trinidad and Tobago

The University of the West Indies Press
7A Gibraltar Hall Road, Mona
Kingston 7, Jamaica
www.uwipress.com

© 2020 by Rodney Worrell
All rights reserved. Published 2020

A catalogue record of this book is available from the
National Library of Jamaica.

ISBN: 978-976-640-810-7
978-976-640-811-4 (Kindle)
978-976-640-812-1 (ePub)

Set in Sabon 10.5/15 x 27

Cover photograph: George Padmore, ca. 1950. W.E.B. Du Bois Papers (MS 312). Special Collections and University Archives, University of Massachusetts Amherst Libraries

Cover and book design by Robert Harris – roberth@cwjamaica.com

The University of the West Indies Press has no responsibility for the persistence or accuracy of URLs for external or third-party Internet websites referred to in this publication and does not guarantee that any content on such websites is, or will remain, accurate or appropriate.

Printed in the United States of America

CONTENTS

Acknowledgements | *vii*

List of Abbreviations | *ix*

Introduction | *1*

1. The Making of a Pan-Africanist | *8*
2. Early Marxism | *21*
3. A Black Internationalist within the Comintern | *48*
4. Radical Pan-African Activism | *91*
5. Radical Anti-imperialist Critiques | *118*
6. Pan-African Theorizing | *144*

Conclusion | *175*

Notes | *185*

Bibliography | *219*

Index | *249*

ACKNOWLEDGEMENTS

THIS BOOK BEGAN AS A PHD DISSERTATION at the University of the West Indies, Mona. I wish to express my gratitude to Rupert Lewis, Neville Duncan, Anthony Bogues, the late Fitz Baptiste, Brian Meeks, Susan Pennybacker, Robert Hill, Leslie James, Horace Campbell, Ian Boxhill, Carol Polsgrove, Jermaine McCaplin, Maziki Thame, Viola Davis, Richard Goodridge, Tennyson Joseph, Hugh Thompson, Alexandria Jules, Christopher Oliver, Andy Taitt, Wynel Applewhaite and Archirri Adams for providing encouragement and assistance in completing this book. Special thanks to the helpful staff of the University of the West Indies, Mona Library; Sidney Martin Library, the University of the West Indies, Cave Hill; Alma Jordan Library, the University of the West Indies, St Augustine; Troy Belle at the Schomburg Center for Research in Black Culture; Angela Cannon and the staff of the Library of Congress, Washington, DC; and Chris Naylor and the staff at the National Archives and Records Administrations, Maryland. I am indebted to you for your patience and kind assistance. I wish to thank my pan-Africanist brothers, sisters and comrades in Barbados: Joy Workman, Angela Brandon-Hall, Trevor Prescod, Anthony Reid, David Denny, Kofi Akobi, Charles Odell, Lloyd Jones, Michael Cummins and David Commissiong for their support. Finally, I wish to express my appreciation and heartfelt thanks to Kwame and my family for their patience and tolerance. Without their support I could not have completed this project.

LIST OF ABBREVIATIONS

AFL	American Federation of Labor
ANLC	American Negro Labor Congress
BSCP	Brotherhood of Sleeping Car Porters
CPUSA	Communist Party of the United States of America
Comintern	Communist International
IASB	International African Service Bureau
ICC	International Control Commission
ICU	Industrial Commercial Union
ILP	Independent Labour Party
ITUCNW	International Trade Union Committee of Negro Workers
KUTV	Communist University of the Toilers of the East
NAACP	National Association for the Advancement of Colored People
PAC	Pan-African Congress
PAF	Pan-African Federation
RILU	Red International of Labour Unions
TUUL	Trade Union Unity League
UNIA	Universal Negro Improvement Association

INTRODUCTION

THIS BOOK'S PRIMARY PURPOSE IS TO EXPLORE George Padmore's social and political thought. Padmore was an engaged Marxist and pan-Africanist activist and theoretician who made an outstanding contribution to the liberation of Africa and the Caribbean from European colonial rule – he was fully dedicated to this objective. Padmore was one of the leading black operatives in the Communist International (Comintern) in the early 1930s, where he served as the chairman of the Negro Bureau of the Red International of Labour Unions (RILU), the executive secretary of the International Trade Union Committee of Negro Workers (ITUCNW) and the editor of its journal, *Negro Worker*. After he severed his connections with the Comintern in 1934, he was one of the leading pan-African activists and theorists until his death in 1959. Padmore was one of the foremost figures within the International African Service Bureau (IASB) and the Pan-African Federation (PAF). He played a major role in organizing the fifth Pan-African Congress (PAC) in Manchester, in 1945. Padmore was also a prolific writer, having authored or edited many books, pamphlets and newspaper articles. In his writings, he systematically attacked colonialism, particularly in Africa and the Caribbean, and championed self-determination for colonial territories. He was also the political advisor on African affairs to Kwame Nkrumah, the first prime minister/president of Ghana.

This work began as a dissertation at a time when there was a glaring lack of scholarly material available on Padmore's social and political thought. As someone with more than a passing interest in pan-Africanism, I felt that a study of Padmore's enormous contribution to pan-Africanism was long overdue. In his book *The Coyaba Chronicles*,

Peter Abrahams, a former comrade of Padmore familiar with his contribution to the African anti-colonial struggle, lamented the insufficiency of knowledge on his life and work.[1] It is my hope that this book will contribute to spreading the word on Padmore, given his enormous contribution to pan-African thought and activism, engaged Marxism and anti-colonial thought.

The book is largely concerned with Padmore's utilization of the ideologies of Marxism-Leninism and pan-Africanism in his quest to free Africa and the Caribbean from European colonial control. I have sought to excavate, examine and bring to the attention of readers some of Padmore's main ideas with the view to add to the scholarship on this revolutionary, as well as on pan-Africanism, black internationalism, black radicalism, anti-colonial thought and the Caribbean intellectual tradition. This work seeks to comprehensively, critically and analytically discuss his social and political thought, while exploring how he was able to negotiate and manoeuvre the various ideological shifts from black nationalism, to Marxism, to black internationalism, to radical anti-colonialism and to radical pan-Africanism.

BLACK RADICAL TRADITION/BLACK INTERNATIONALISM

This book situates Padmore firmly within the black radical and black international traditions. I see black internationalism as a branch of black radicalism. Cedric Robinson, a leading black radical theorist, describes it as evolving from "the first organized revolts in the slave castle in Africa" when African captives sought to gain their freedom.[2] The struggle for freedom continued aboard slave ships as captives sought to return to their African homeland. It was also evident in their attempts to flee plantations and establish independent communities.[3] Anthony Bogues, another notable black radical theorist, adds that the black radical tradition in the Western Hemisphere "spans anti-slavery and anti-colonial struggles, labour struggles, socialist movements and democratic and civil rights campaigns".[4] He identifies four major strands in the tradition: the reclamation of humanity, the redefinition and reclamation of history and the establishment of sovereignty, pan-Africanism, and a humanist approach.[5]

Michael West and William Martin, two distinguished black internationalists, posit that black internationalism "is a product of consciousness, that is, the conscious interconnection and interlocution of black struggles across man-made and natural boundaries – including the boundaries of nations, empires, continents, oceans and seas".[6] They argued that from its inception, black internationalism "envisioned a circle of universal emancipation in time and space".[7] The struggle against enslavement was the major issue that united black people in the Caribbean and the Americas for over two centuries. The Haitian Revolution was the central event in the evolution of the black radical and black international traditions. It was the only revolution in the Western Hemisphere where enslaved people defeated the colonial power to abolish slavery and declare their independence. Haiti became an inspiration for all enslaved people in the Caribbean and the Americas.

In the wake of the success of the Bolshevik Revolution, the Comintern expressed its support for oppressed Africans and people of African descent worldwide. The fourth Congress of the Comintern (1922) established a Negro Commission and discussed the Theses on the Negro Question. This congress recognized the need for "supporting every form of the Negro Movement which tends to undermine capitalism and imperialism". The Comintern gave its support to the "fight for race equality of the Negro with the white people, for equal wages and political and social rights".[8]

Padmore, like many black intellectuals who became important figures of the black radical tradition and black internationalism during the 1920s and 1930s, began his political journey as a Marxist and though initially he was attracted to black nationalism, became a communist. He joined the Communist Party of the United States (CPUSA) in 1927 because he felt that this organization would assist him with his political objective of liberating Africa from the grip of European colonial rule. Michael Dawson informs us that "a section of the black activists turned to Marxism as a way to identify potentially progressive allies outside of the black community".[9]

Padmore, like the other few blacks who were Marxist, was attracted to Marx's critique of capitalism and the hope that the destruction of capitalism would bring into being a more just, humane, socialist society. They blamed capitalism for racism and the brutal exploitation and oppression of people of African descent. Black Marxists were impressed by the developments in the socialist experiment in the Soviet Union especially when it came to the race question, self-determination and its support for anti-colonial and labour struggles in the colonies.

Padmore became a devoted and enthusiastic communist and rose to be an important figure within the Comintern. He became the executive secretary of the ITUCNW and the editor of the *Negro Worker*, two of the main tools created by the Comintern to spread its black internationalism. The main duties of the ITUCNW were "to help build strong contacts with the trade unions and working class organizations of Negro workers, to strengthen these contacts and to support the establishment of revolutionary trade union organizations of industrial and agricultural workers".[10] The *Negro Worker*'s mission was to "discuss and analyse the day to day problems of the Negro toilers and to connect these with the international struggles and problems of the workers".[11] Brent Haynes Edwards informs us that Padmore and Tiemoko Kouyatè, a leading black Marxist, were "involved in a discourse of black internationalism" that was "aimed at a race-specific formation that rejects the Comintern Universalism, adamantly insisting that racial oppression involves factors that cannot be summed up or submerged in a critique of class exploitation".[12] With the rise of fascism during the 1930s, the Soviet Union began to change its position on black internationalism. Padmore felt that the black internationalist project was being threatened, given the policy shifts taking place in the Soviet Union, leading him to become more critical of the class-versus-race strategy that was employed by the Comintern in its efforts to end colonialism. He also began to lose faith in the viability of proletarian internationalism to liberate Africa and the Caribbean from colonial rule. Bogues explains that black radical intellectualism began as an "an engagement and dialogue with Western radical political ideas and then moved on to a critique of their ideas as their incompleteness was revealed".[13] Padmore was forced to sever his ties with the Comintern, although he remained a Marxist.

After Padmore left the Comintern, he turned to pan-Africanism as the vehicle to liberate Africa and the Caribbean. Robinson notes that some black radicals who left socialism logically sought to "resurrect Pan-Africanism as a radical theory of struggle and history. From the early 1930s on, a radical Pan-Africanism emerged."[14] The Italian invasion of Abyssinia in October 1935 led to international outrage among black people. Ethiopia, as the only truly independent territory on the African continent, held great symbolic, historical and psychological significance to black people. The Ethiopian struggle became the central issue of pan-Africanism at this juncture. Padmore, as a journalist and a pan-African activist within the International African Friends of Abyssinia, became very involved in this struggle. Later, he played an important role in the pan-African struggle in Britain as a member of the IASB and the PAF. Padmore, who played a key role in organizing the fifth PAC in Manchester in 1945, became a staunch advocate of continental pan-Africanism and the organic unification of the African continent and the leading proponent of pan-African socialism.

CARIBBEAN INTELLECTUAL TRADITION

This work also positions Padmore within the Caribbean intellectual tradition. Paget Henry makes the point that the Caribbean intellectual tradition "emerge[d] from the discursive attempts by Africans, Amerindians and Indians to de-legitimate European colonial rule" and to safeguard "traditional identities and to legitimate their attempts at racial and national liberation".[15] He adds that the Caribbean intellectual tradition can be viewed as "a series of contentious dialogues between Europeans and the above groups", exchanges that were set in motion from the arrival of the Europeans in the "sixteenth century and continue into the present".[16] Although Padmore wrote extensively on Africa, he was very much part of the Caribbean intellectual, pan-Africanist tradition of Edward Blyden, J.J. Thomas, Henry Sylvester Williams and Marcus Garvey. C.L.R. James argued that Padmore was one of the Caribbean intellectual descendants of J.J. Thomas.[17]

In an attempt to fully explore the social and political thought of Padmore, this book is divided into six chapters. This chapter introduces the reader to the main content of this work. Chapter 1 focuses on the Trinidadian environment in order to show the reader some of the individuals and issues that played a critical role in Padmore's pan-Africanist development. It provides biographical data on Padmore and briefly outlines the main ideas of Edward Blyden, J.J. Thomas and Henry Sylvester Williams, whose ideas had a major impact on the Trinidadian landscape. Finally, the chapter examines the social, economic and political ferment that took place in Trinidad in the immediate post–World War I period.

Chapter 2 shifts the focus from Trinidad to the United States, where Padmore migrated to pursue a university education. The chapter discusses Padmore's student activism at Fisk University and Howard University. In addition, it examines why Padmore joined the CPUSA and the tension between the primacy of race or class as the main vehicle for black liberation. Chapter 2 also explores his attraction to the Bolshevik Revolution and the impact of the Russian Revolution and Lenin on Padmore and analyses his critique of the "Black Belt Republic" thesis. Finally, it looks at the reports Padmore prepared during his time in Russia on the significance for black people of the formation of the Trade Union Unity League (TUUL) convention and the Gastonia affair.

Chapter 3 looks at Padmore's career within the Comintern. The chapter explores his rise in the Comintern and the role he played in making the first International Conference of Negro Workers in Hamburg in 1930 a reality. Moreover, the chapter examines *The Life and Struggles of Negro Toilers*, the most significant anti-colonial and black internationalist text he produced as a member of the Comintern. Chapter 3 also analyses Padmore's roles within the Comintern and explores his utilization of his positions as executive secretary of the ITUCNW and editor of the *Negro Worker* in promoting a "red" black internationalist anti-colonialism. The chapter sheds some light on Padmore's break with the Comintern. Finally, it examines the charges brought by the International Communist Commission, the ITUCNW and other leading communists against Padmore.

Chapter 4 explains how Padmore brought his skills in political organizing that he had developed as a member of the Comintern into the service of pan-Africanism. The chapter examines his role in the aborted Negro World Conference of 1935 and looks at the Italian invasion of Abyssinia and the reaction of pan-Africanists. Chapter 4 also discusses at great length the activities of the IASB and the PAF. Additionally, it looks at Padmore's correspondence with W.E.B. Du Bois in relation to planning the fifth PAC. Lastly, it discusses the fifth PAC.

Chapter 5 examines Padmore's radical anti-colonial critique of imperialism and the administrative colonial devices that facilitated the exploitation of Africans: the mandate system, trusteeship, direct rule/crown colony government and indirect rule. The chapter provides a full explanation of Padmore's conception of colonial fascism and concludes with a discussion on the case he makes for African and Caribbean self-determination.

Chapter 6 explores Padmore's theorizing on pan-Africanism in his work *Pan-Africanism or Communism*. The chapter examines some of the major issues raised by him: the tension between communism and African nationalism, non-alignment, continental pan-Africanism, political and social objectives of pan-Africanism, tribalism, reparations and pan-African socialism.

The book concludes by examining Padmore's contribution to the advancement of Marxist and pan-African thought and investigates his contribution to anti-colonial thought. Finally, it looks at his political praxis.

1. THE MAKING OF A PAN-AFRICANIST

GEORGE PADMORE, CHRISTENED MALCOLM NURSE, WAS BORN to Anna and James Nurse in Arouca, Trinidad and Tobago, on 28 June 1903. In 1927, when he became a revolutionary, Nurse adopted the name George Padmore, by which he was known throughout his life, following the common practice of revolutionaries of using pseudonyms to conceal their identity from the authorities. There are two stories surrounding his name selection. Biographer James Hooker posits that this name was a combination of a friend's surname and Padmore's father-in-law's first name.[1] Hermie Huiswoud, a comrade of Padmore, tells us that when Nurse was looking for a nom de plume, she suggested the name Padmore after a Liberian minister. Nurse accepted this suggestion and then added George.[2]

Padmore's grandfather, Alphonso Nurse, had been enslaved on the Belle plantation in Barbados until emancipation (1834). In 1860, he migrated to Trinidad. Throughout his life, Padmore would repeat to his audiences that he was the grandson of a former slave.[3] It was a practice he inherited from his father, who habitually reminded his listeners that he was the son of a former enslaved man. Neither man was ashamed to let all and sundry know of a heritage that had fostered in them the desire to struggle for the liberation of black people from racial and colonial oppression. James Nurse had been a teacher before he was seconded to the Department of Agriculture, where he worked as a botanist. Although a teacher was not paid a large amount in late-nineteenth-century Trinidad, teaching was viewed as a respectable profession. Given the existing class structure of the period, Nurse would have been classified as a member of the lower middle class.

James Nurse was a black nationalist/pan-Africanist and an ardent disciple of Edward Wilmot Blyden, the leading black nationalist/pan-African intellectual of the nineteenth century. Nurse read widely and had an expansive library of "books packed from the floor to the ceiling".[4] It was said that Blyden's book *Christianity, Islam and the Negro Race* had a profound impact on Nurse to the extent that he began to describe himself as a Muslim, which was uncommon for a black man in Trinidad and Tobago at that time. Nurse often engaged in discussions about the evils of enslavement in the Caribbean and he regularly attacked the Christian church for its role in the enslavement of Africans in the Caribbean and the Americas.[5]

Padmore attended Tranquillity School and then went on to attend the Catholic St Mary's College, one of the few schools that provided secondary education in Trinidad and Tobago, at a time when this was not readily available there for the general populace. (The other leading secondary school in Trinad was Queen's Royal College.) The educational system taught "both the spoken and written English and the verities of the British Empire", as well as offering a Cambridge Senior Certificate, which was required to get a good job within the civil service.[6]

Eric Williams, a historian and prime minister of Trinidad and Tobago, argued that the staff and the curriculum of Queen's Royal College and St Mary's College were of the same calibre as any of the leading secondary schools in Britain. Moreover, he contended that these schools "produced a number of outstanding scholars that could have competed with any school within Britain or her colonial empire".[7] The available evidence does not suggest that Padmore distinguished himself at St Mary's College. He labelled himself an average student who loved to play cricket, the most popular sport of Trinidad and Tobago at the time. However, he successfully completed the Cambridge Senior certificate, which allowed him entrance to the civil service.

Padmore as a boy was exposed to his father's vast library of progressive books. He also read Marcus Garvey's *Negro World*, which was widely disseminated in Trinidad. As a young man, Padmore engaged in debates with his friends about some of the burning issues of the day such as Marxism, the labour movement, racism, Marcus Garvey and the Universal Negro

Improvement Association (UNIA), as well as colonialism and imperialism.[8] Padmore resented the fact that the prevailing racism denied many young black men the jobs to which their abilities and qualifications entitled them. He felt that "there should be no prejudice in the world and that every man should be judged and treated according to his character and ability and not according to race".[9]

In 1921, Padmore became a reporter for the *Trinidad Guardian*, the country's largest newspaper. However, he did not enjoy his two years there, given that there was no possibility for the kind of analytical writing that he was interested in, and he despised the editor, Edward J. Partridge, an Englishman whom Padmore described as "one of the most arrogant agents of British Imperialism".[10]

He married Julia Semper in 1924, and the union produced a daughter, Blyden, who was named after the great pan-Africanist Edward Wilmot Blyden. It is important to note that Padmore instructed his wife to name their baby Blyden regardless of its sex. The high esteem in which Padmore's father held Blyden was shared by his son, who posited that "Blyden was the greatest West Indian".[11] Padmore's assessment of Blyden demonstrated that he was well acquainted with Blyden's outstanding contribution in asserting the dignity and humanity of African people globally. Shortly after his marriage, Padmore departed for the United States in pursuit of higher education.

EDWARD WILMOT BLYDEN

Edward Wilmot Blyden was born in the Danish West Indian island of St Thomas in 1832. He migrated to Liberia in 1851 and became a prolific writer who exposed many of the racist myths that were prevalent about Africa and people of African descent. His espousal of pan-Africanism in his writings had a tremendous impact on a small section of the Trinidadian black middle class, including James Nurse, J.J. Thomas and Henry Sylvester Williams, who distinguished themselves as outstanding pan-Africanists.

Blyden rejected the standard argument of the period that Africans had no culture or monuments of historical significance. He noted that the Greek historians wrote extensively about the great achievements of Africans.

Homer was so impressed with their accomplishments that he referred to them as "the blameless Ethiopians" and suggested that Ethiopians were chosen by the gods "as a people fit to be lifted to the social level of Olympian divinities".[12] To buttress his claim about African monuments, Blyden noted that the Great Pyramid was located in Africa and that many scholars regarded the pyramid as central to providing answers to some of the mysteries of the universe. He contended that Africa was the birthplace of human civilization and that all the sciences and the two great religions of Christianity and Islam originated and were nurtured in Africa.[13] Blyden felt that anyone who was writing the history of modern civilization would be "culpably negligent" if they did not acknowledge that Africans had made a noteworthy contribution to the economic development of "America and Western Europe".[14]

Blyden recognized that Africans on the continent and in the diaspora had little or no political or economic power: if they remained "scattered and divided", they would be "weak and . . . ruled by other races".[15] Blyden was convinced that the African race would never be respected unless it created a "powerful nationality". He called for the creation of strong African states that would fashion and administer their own laws, have self-rule, create a navy, develop a relevant school curriculum, and control the press and thus aid in shaping the opinions and guiding the destinies of humankind.[16]

As someone fiercely proud of his race, Blyden was dismayed to discover that a section of the emerging African middle class had so assimilated into European culture that they insisted that the African personality be "lost, if possible, in another race".[17] Blyden castigated them and felt that this position was as foolish as to utter "let us do away with gravity, with heat and cold and sunshine and rain". He encouraged all blacks "to love and honour your Race. Be yourselves, as God intended you to be or he would not have made you thus."[18]

J.J. THOMAS

Like many Trinidadians at this time, Padmore was familiar with the work of J.J. Thomas, whom Carl Campbell described as "undoubtedly the most famous black man in the history of Trinidad in the second half of the nineteenth century".[19] Thomas took on James Anthony Froude, Regius Professor of Modern History at Oxford University and one of the leading intellectuals of the time in Great Britain and a disciple of Thomas Carlyle, well-known for his virulent racism. Froude visited the West Indies in 1887 and wrote *The English in the West Indies*. The contents of this book provoked anger and indignation throughout the West Indies. J.J. Thomas, a Trinidadian educator, was recuperating in Grenada when he read the book, and he responded with a series of critical articles in the *St George's Chronicle* and *Grenada Gazette*. He subsequently published *Froudacity: West Indian Fables by James Anthony Froude* as a rebuttal to Froude's *The English in the West Indies*.

Thomas described Froude's book as "the dark outlines of a scheme to thwart the political aspirations in the Antilles".[20] He recognized that one of the main objectives of the book was to persuade colonial authorities not to grant crown colonies an elected local legislature, arguing that if blacks were given universal suffrage they would elect blacks to the legislature "who would pass vindictive and retaliatory laws against their white fellow colonists".[21] Thomas argued that the crown colony system was "a degrading tyranny, which the sneers of Mr. Froude cannot make otherwise". He predicted that the system as it was constituted at that time was doomed, and while Britain continued to deny Trinidad and the other colonies autonomy, it would have to seriously alter the system of choosing and employing governors.[22]

Thomas accused Froude of being racist and raised the question, "Does Mr. Froude's scorn of the Negroes' skin extend, inconsistently on his part, to their intelligence and feeling also?" He felt it was inexplicable that Englishmen at the time should still be using racism to impede the "life careers and aspirations" of black people. Therefore, he asked, "Are we to be grateful that colour difference should be made the basis and justification of the dastardly denials of justice, social, intellectual and moral, which have characterized the régime of those who Mr. Froude boasts were left to the representatives of Britain's morality and fair play?"[23] Thomas noted that in the previous twenty-five years, blacks in the United States and West Indies had several outstanding achievements to their credit that should have persuaded those who accused blacks of being lazy to desist from that charge. The repetition of the accusation of laziness in the fading days of the nineteenth century, according to Thomas, was "a discredited anachronism, which, however, has no deterring features for Mr. Froude".[24]

As a pan-Africanist, Thomas recognized that Africans on the continent seemed powerless as they struggled against imperialism. However, he wondered whether Africans in the diaspora, "apt apprentices in every conceivable department of civilized culture", would unite in a "grand racial combination" and come to the assistance of Africa.[25]

Froudacity, according to Denis Benn, marks the tentative starting point of a systematic intellectual tradition of nationalist protest in Caribbean.[26] Selwyn Cudjoe contends that *"Froudacity* can be read as a part of that concern for the way members of the indigenous population were treated and their quest for empowerment".[27] Although Thomas was not a militant anti-colonialist, he attacked the ideological pillars of colonial rule that rested on the assumption that blacks were incapable of ruling themselves. It was noteworthy that Thomas was heavily influenced by Blyden's black nationalism.[28]

HENRY SYLVESTER WILLIAMS

Ras Makonnen, a close friend of Padmore, related that Padmore spoke extensively about Henry Sylvester Williams.[29] Incidentally, Williams came from Arouca, the same village as Padmore, and Padmore claimed that they were related.[30] Williams was the main catalyst behind the creation of the African Association formed on 24 September 1897. The main objective of this group was to promote solidarity and friendly intercourse among all African and people of African descent. This organization issued the call for the first pan-African conference in London in 1900. According to Padmore, the idea for this conference "arose as a manifestation of fraternal solidarity among Africans and peoples of African descent". He attributed the initiative to Williams, who had close contacts with "West Africans in Britain and later acted as legal advisor to several African chiefs and dignitaries who visited the United Kingdom on political missions to the colonial office".[31]

Padmore gave three reasons why the first pan-African conference was called: (1) to combat the aggressive imperialist policies of Britain, (2) to protest against the aggression of white colonizers and (3) to appeal to the missionary and abolitionist traditions of the British people to protect Africans from the destructive policies of empire-builders.[32] Over thirty delegates from Africa, United States, Canada, West Indies and the United Kingdom attended this historic conference. It is significant that three of the delegates came from Trinidad: Henry Sylvester Williams, R.E. Phipps and A. Pulcherrie Pierre.[33] The African Association became the Pan-African Association in 1900, with Williams becoming its general secretary.

In the wake of Williams's trip to Trinidad in 1901,[34] several branches of the Pan-African Association were established in Trinidad. The *Mirror* editorialized that "Williams was moving the masses and the middle class to a sense of responsibility to themselves and to the greater body of the African race".[35] However, this enthusiasm was ephemeral, and several members quickly left the Pan-African Association. By the time Williams returned to Trinidad in 1908, there were no functioning Pan-African Association branches. Marika Sherwood noted that "the Rate Payers Association had attracted many members of the local branches of the Pan-African Association when these declined".[36]

AGITATION FOR CONSTITUTIONAL CHANGE

Throughout the latter half of the nineteenth and early twentieth centuries, Trinidadians agitated for constitutional reform. Trinidad was a typical Caribbean crown colony, and from the mid-1880s there were calls to modify this form of government. Williams was a sharp critic of the crown colony government, attacking the white-only legislative council as well as its anti-democratic tendencies, given that none of the council members were elected.[37] According to Padmore, before World War I, West Indian leaders in Trinidad, the Leeward Islands and British Guiana had insisted on constitutional reforms and representative government. However, the colonial office resisted any change "because the sugar planters, merchants and other plutocrats were opposed to representation of the common people".[38] After the outbreak of World War I in 1914, calls for reform and representative government ceased as West Indians supported the war efforts of the imperial powers.

RACISM IN THE BRITISH WEST INDIES REGIMENT

Initially, the British government refused to consider any requests for black West Indians to serve in the British Army. Following lobbying, the intervention of the colonial office, and with the tacit support of King George V, it was agreed to form the British West Indies Regiment, an independent unit apart from the British Army.[39] Padmore noted that racism was prevalent within the armed forces at this time, where darker-skinned men were separated from the lighter. The darker-skinned West Indians were assigned to the Public Contingent under the command of English and local-born white officers, while the whites and the near-whites were attached to the Merchants' and Planters' Contingent in England and incorporated into various regiments. The brazenness of this racism "created extreme resentment among the Negroes, who were debarred by the King's Regulation from holding a commission in the army".[40]

The British West Indies Regiment replicated the racist colonial system existing in the West Indies. Throughout the war, the vast majority of the members of the West Indian contingent were based in Egypt performing "labour services", though some were involved in direct combat in Palestine and Sinai. A few of the battalions served in Europe as ammunition carriers and labourers, but they were never given the opportunity to take part in combat. It was clear that the military authorities at every opportunity sought to "humiliate and degrade the black soldiers".[41] Officers, who came from the ranks of the "colonial plantocracy", with a history of "exploiting and ill-treating Negroes, naturally brought their slave-driver mentality into army life", Padmore wrote.[42] The degrading treatment was forcefully captured by a Trinidadian soldier in a letter: "We are treated neither as Christians nor as British citizens, but as West Indian niggers without anybody to be interested in or to look after us."[43]

The racist, exploitative practices exploded at Taranto, Italy, at the end of the war. Members of the British West Indies Regiment, on top of being segregated in inferior canteens, cinemas and hospitals, were made to wash the linen and clean the toilets of the Italian Corps. The racist South African commander of the camp, Brigadier General Carey-Bernard, felt that members of the British West Indies Regiment were "niggers" and should be treated like "niggers".[44] This level of racism led the members of the regiment to openly revolt, resulting in a number of them being court-martialled. For W.F. Elkins, the revolt at Taranto witnessed "the modern advent of mass resistance by West Indians to British rule".[45]

THE IMPACT OF WORLD WAR I

On their return home, soldiers brought a new militancy to a growing explosive industrial and racial climate in Trinidad and Tobago. The memories of the ill-treatment, humiliation and racial discrimination they had suffered during the war continued to affect them. Many of them had been exposed to Marcus Garvey's black nationalism, Marxism-Leninism or some other variant of socialism. Captain A.A. Cipriani, the head of the Trinidad Workingmen's Association, was of the view "that the workers who had gone abroad had come back emancipated from old prejudices and superstitions which hitherto had posed stumbling blocks to effective social action".[46] E.F.L. Wood, the undersecretary of state for the colonies, noted that the war and experience abroad had emancipated and enlarged the minds of British West Indians about their rights as British subjects.[47] Padmore concurred with Cipriani and Wood that "World War I certainly marked a definite turning point in the ideology of West Indians". He observed, "Most of the men who served abroad came back more racially and politically conscious."[48]

World War I had a major impact on the development of political organization and political protest in Trinidad and Tobago. During the war, deteriorating economic conditions resulted in tremendous hardships throughout the colony. There was a steep rise in the cost of living but there was no corresponding increase in the wages of the people.[49] This led to demands for higher wages, and when these demands were not met, workers protested. In 1917, oil and asphalt workers mounted the first major protest action, going on a five-day strike at Fyzabad and Point Fortin. At the Trinidad Lake Asphalt Company, some striking workers sabotaged the company's storage and refining sheds. The flotilla and members of the British West Indies Regiment were called in to restore order and to prevent any further escalation of the protest.[50]

In 1919, a succession of strikes occurred throughout Trinidad and Tobago. There can be no disagreement that the exorbitant cost of living was at the root of this industrial ferment, but racial feelings played an important role in heightening tensions in 1919. The contents of the *Negro World*, the organ of Marcus Garvey's UNIA, made the Trinidadian authorities jittery, and the governor considered passing the Seditious Publications Ordinance to ban the *Negro World* and other progressive literature.[51]

In addition to the *Negro World* raising the consciousness of the people, the pan-Africanist C. Loughton, a Garveyite from Canada, visited Trinidad and gave a lecture to a "well attended crowd".[52] About two weeks later in September 1919, another pan-Africanist, F.E.M. Hercules, the secretary of the Society of Peoples of African Origin and editor of the *African Telegraph*, arrived on the island to give a series of lectures. Hercules, a Trinidadian living in England, was an activist at the forefront of protests against racial discrimination and the ill-treatment of black West Indian World War I veterans in England.[53] Before Hercules came to Trinidad, he visited Jamaica, and the authorities accused him of causing strikes and unrest.[54] In Trinidad he spoke to large crowds and many people joined his organization.[55] The newspaper *Argos* hoped that the three main points of Hercules's lectures would be echoed throughout the black world: that people of African descent should become race-conscious, they should unite, and they should struggle to acquire economic independence to redress their present economic disabilities.[56] Hercules was banned from re-entering Trinidad after going to British Guiana.

The ideology of race pride was also actively promoted by *Argos*. The paper was owned by George Aldric Lee Lum, a Chinese Trinidadian, but its main commentaries were written by blacks who were accused of being anti-white.[57] The white oligarchy, headed by G.F. Huggins, "accused the paper of spreading all kinds of revolutionary, seditious and mischievous literature",[58] and Huggins wrote to the colonial secretary expressing alarm at the widespread hostility shown by the black population towards the whites. They also called for the suppression of *Argos*, the arming of white folk and the need to station a regular British force in Trinidad.[59]

The industrial foment, which manifested itself in the dockworkers' strike of December 1919, had been festering for a long time given the high cost of living, low wages, high unemployment rate and racial discrimination. The unrest was expressed in several strikes across the island. The political scientist Selwyn Ryan notes that this was "the nearest thing to a general strike the colony had yet seen". Crowds "marched up and down the city streets forcing merchants to close".[60] The American consul in Trinidad reported to the US State Department that "the *Negro World* was responsible for the rapid growth of race and class feelings and of anarchistic and Bolshevik ideas among the ignorant population here".[61] The leaders of the strike in Port of Spain were said to "be imbued with the idea that there must be a black world controlled and governed by the black people of our own race".[62] The strikes combined industrial grievances with radical political demands.[63]

In response to this development, the colonial government in Trinidad and Tobago passed the Seditious Publications Ordinance, which was aimed at curbing the publishing of *Negro World*. Kelvin Singh has remarked that with the possible exception of the Habitual Idlers Ordinance of 1918, the Seditious Publications Ordinance was the most comprehensively repressive piece of legislation passed in this period by the colonial government.[64] The governor claimed that "propaganda of a seditious character aimed at exciting racial animosities was being spread on the island by persons who, for the most part were not Trinidadians". This led to the deportation of some of the Garveyite leaders, including Ven Edward Seiler Salmon and the veteran activist John Sydney de Bourg.[65]

In the wake of the disturbances, Major Edward Wood was sent to Trinidad to investigate the causes. As a result of Wood's findings, Trinidad moved from crown colony government to a modified system with provisions for seven elected representatives in the twenty-six-member legislative council. However, the franchise was extremely limited, based on income and property qualifications, and power remained in the hands of the merchant/planter oligarchs. This constitutional reform did not benefit the working class or the black middle class. Padmore claimed that the number of enfranchised people was still small, numbering about 6.5 per cent of the population of Trinidad. He stressed that "the merchants, planters and other capitalists secured additional representation".[66] The constitutional changes, "while providing a partially elected legislature, left legislative control firmly in the grasp of the elite representatives of capital, imperial and colonial".[67]

There is no evidence to connect Padmore to the industrial and political agitation that took place in Trinidad. One might speculate that he had not reached political maturity at this time. However, Ras Makonnen relates an interesting discussion he had with Padmore as to why individuals avoided radical activity in their homeland. Padmore said that in order to protect one's family from harassment and embarrassment, one tended to stay away from radical activity.[68] The severity of the repression that Padmore would have seen in Trinidad in the aftermath of the 1919 disturbances would make anyone hesitant about being involved in any form of radicalism. Many of the agitators were imprisoned, some were deported, houses were searched, ordinances against striking were passed and the Seditious Publications Ordinance was instituted.[69]

Padmore's description of Edward Partridge, editor of the *Trinidad Guardian*, demonstrated that he was not immune to developments taking place in Trinidadian society and that he had started to develop an anti-imperialist perspective. Partridge had a reputation for ill-treating his subordinates. On the margins of a clipping of Partridge's obituary in the *Trinidad Guardian*, Padmore wrote, "The Passing of a Slave Driver" and added: "I worked as a reporter on the staff of the Trinidadian Guardian under Partridge for years. Well he was one of the most arrogant agents of British Imperialism I have ever encountered. I held him in utter contempt and hoped to use my pen in exposing his role before the colonial workers and peasants whom he oppressed through his dirty sheet the Guardian."[70]

The *Trinidad Guardian* joined forces with the *Port of Spain Gazette* and forced the *Catholic Standard* to apologize for paying tribute to the "organizing ability of the proletariat" during the dockworkers' strike. The *Trinidad Guardian* and the chamber of commerce complained that the police did nothing "while the strikers were beating the people".[71] One can thus conclude that the *Trinidad Guardian* served as a pliant instrument for Partridge and the conservative and reactionary chamber of commerce, and one can see why Padmore's criticism of him was so severe. C.L.R. James, Padmore's boyhood friend, claimed that Padmore "joined the labour movement in Trinidad before I did".[72] However, I have found no evidence to substantiate this assertion, but it is clear from Padmore's critique of Partridge that he was on the side of the oppressed labouring people in Trinidad and Tobago.

The Trinidadian environment exposed Padmore to many of the issues that would concern him for the rest of his life: pan-Africanism, race and racism, socialism, self-determination, colonial rule, imperialism, social justice and trade unionism. It also provided Padmore with a solid education, both formal and informal, and journalistic skills that would stand him in good stead. It was also evident that Padmore had begun to hate racism and injustice.

2. EARLY MARXISM

GEORGE PADMORE LEFT TRINIDAD IN DECEMBER 1924 with the intention of attaining higher education in the United States. In pursuit of his dream, he enrolled in 1925 at Fisk University, an all-black institution located in Nashville, Tennessee that was surrounded by a "sea of anti-Negro prejudice and restrictions".[1] At this time the atmosphere at Fisk University was "reportedly troubled" because of the intensification of student activism on the campus, with students involved in a protracted struggle with campus administrators, resulting in regular militant student protest.[2]

While the available evidence demonstrates that Padmore was a bystander in the industrial and political ferment that had rocked Trinidad a few years before, he quickly became involved with the student protests at Fisk University. Winston James provides us with a perspective that helps to explain why many West Indians were drawn to radical activity in the United States. He argues that conditions there were more favourable for political action: "while they had to endure the everyday unfreedom of racism", they "had fewer restrictions on political activity".[3] Moreover, they could pursue political agitation without having to worry whether their families would be harassed or embarrassed. The effect agitation had on families was the rationale advanced by Padmore to explain why Caribbean nationals were reluctant to be politically active in their homelands.[4] Many West Indians were aware of the subtle racism existing in the Caribbean, but they were taken aback when they were confronted with the overt racism of the Jim Crow system in the United States. Padmore first encountered the Jim Crow system while travelling on the train from New York to Nashville. When he got to Columbus, he was forced to leave the carriage that he was in and "go to a Negroes-only carriage".[5] Padmore then experienced Jim Crow in Nashville soon after arriving at Fisk, when he attended a concert where the whites sat on the main floor and blacks sat in the balcony. It was reported that Padmore could not stand the sight of blacks singing spirituals for white folks, while the other blacks – the educated blacks – "were sitting upstairs listening joyfully".[6] These experiences heightened his deep hatred of the system of racism and served to radicalize Padmore.

At Fisk, Padmore wrote for the student paper the *Fisk Herald*. Padmore claimed that he and four other students organized the "biggest student strike ever pulled off in the South".[7] He became well-known on and off the campus as one of the leading student anti-colonial speakers. John Dillingham, one of the organizers of a conference held at Kings Mountain, North Carolina, wrote a letter to a Mr W.C. Craver in response to a request to have foreign students speak at the conference. He recommended that George Padmore of Fisk University and Jeremiah Moore of Morristown Normal School be selected. Dillingham was impressed with Padmore's oratorical skills and intellectual ability and described him as "one of the outstanding students in Nashville". He admitted that he had heard Padmore speak on several occasions and noted that "his service is in great demand". Dillingham added that Padmore, who was from the British West Indies, would make an important contribution to the conference. Moreover, he made it abundantly clear that if there was going to be only one foreign student at the conference, they should ensure that it would be Padmore.[8]

In April 1927, while still attending Fisk University, Padmore wrote to Benjamin Azikiwe, the Nigerian pan-Africanist, who was attending Storer College in West Virginia, and sought his assistance in establishing a pan-African student organization. This action was significant as it represented Padmore's first attempt at establishing a pan-African organization. Padmore's letter was also a manifestation of his embryonic pan-Africanist sensibilities. Padmore wrote to Azikiwe "on the basis of our racial kinship, with respect to a matter that I feel is of mutual interest to us". He explained that the objective of such an organization "will be to foster racial consciousness and a spirit of nationalism aiming at the protection of the sovereignty of Liberia".[9] It was not accidental that Liberia was the object of Padmore's attention. In 1847, when Liberia became a republic, it became important in the psyche of many blacks living in the diaspora. A number of blacks from the United States and Caribbean migrated to Liberia, and the republic was promoted as a place where the skills and resources of blacks from the diaspora and the African continent would be employed to create a great civilization. Edward Wilmot Blyden, who was a powerful influence on Padmore at this stage, migrated to Liberia and became a leading advocate of repatriation to Liberia. Many of the leading pan-Africanists of the nineteenth and early twentieth centuries (Alexander Crummell, John Brown Russwurm, Bishop Henry McNeal Turner and Robert Campbell) repatriated to Liberia and promoted Liberia as the "African utopia". Marcus Garvey wanted to establish his headquarters in Liberia. It was of great significance that Liberia and Ethiopia were two independent black territories on the African continent, surrounded by a sea of European colonies.

One of the major resolutions passed by the delegates at the historic first pan-African conference in 1900 called on the imperialistic nations to "respect the integrity and independence of the independent African States of Abyssinia, Liberia and Haiti".[10] Liberia continued to be an important space in the imagination of pan-Africanists in the early twentieth century as the African territory rich with possibilities to launch the renaissance of the African continent and its people globally. However, because of Liberia's financial woes, it appeared to be a neo-colony of the United States. Notwithstanding these challenges Liberia remained an important symbol to global Africans and this was why Marcus Garvey expressed his intention of relocating his headquarters to Liberia and initiated talks with governmental officials to realize this dream. Unfortunately, the Liberian government refused to grant Garvey permission to transfer his headquarters to Liberia in 1924. It was believed that the French and British imperialist governments pressured the Liberian government in arriving at this decision. Therefore, Liberia's autonomy was brought into sharper focus.[11] In 1926, when the Firestone Plantation Company was given permission to set up rubber plantations, along with lavish concessions, it was felt that Liberian independence was being further compromised. This became more apparent when the Finance Corporation of America, a subsidiary of Firestone, "agreed to pay a forty-year loan of five million dollars to refund the 1912 loan held by the European and American bankers and to promote development".[12] As part of the loan agreement, Liberia was given eight new administrators, led by a financial advisor chosen by the American president. Five other officials were to supervise its financial affairs, and two were placed in charge of the Liberian army. In light of the terms of the loan and the attendant governmental reform, some Marxists and pan-Africanists and African nationalists felt that Liberia's autonomy was severely compromised. A US foreign service inspector informed them that the receiver viewed the loan as "necessary to give [the receivership] control" of Liberia and his associate confessed that he was working "with the idea of making this an American colony".[13]

His concern for the independence of Liberia led Padmore to establish the pan-African student organization. Padmore was not overly optimistic about receiving support for the creation of the student pan-African organization from African American students because in his opinion they were not concerned with developments in Africa. However, he was still hoping that some of them would join the organization. Padmore stressed that the protection of the sovereignty of Liberia was "a matter of most concern to us who are looking forward to going back to the fatherland".[14] This statement locates Padmore within the pan-Africanist tradition of Blyden and the advocates of repatriation to Africa. It was clear in Padmore's thought and action that Liberia and the African continent loomed large in his consciousness.

Phillip Davies, a student from Liberia and one of the other founding members of the student organization, informed Azikiwe that Padmore was "acting on my advice; in fact, he and I had planned to make this a working organization". The objectives of the organization were "to stimulate interest among African students that they may determine more with a 'dark Africa' ever before their minds and to hasten the renaissance and to do our part in preparing our people for the inevitable factors of history".[15] Davies added that "somebody must make a start and I think it is our duty as students, who have the opportunity to observe the world's economic struggles and the motives of man".[16]

STUDENT ACTIVISM AT HOWARD UNIVERSITY

After two years at Fisk University, Padmore terminated his studies. It is not clear what prompted him to leave Fisk, although there has been speculation that he left because of threats from the Ku Klux Klan. He enrolled at New York University in 1927 to study law but never attended any classes.[17] He subsequently headed to Howard University to pursue studies in this same area "in order to practise law in Liberia".[18] Howard University had a large concentration of foreign students, the bulk of whom came from British colonies.

At Howard, Padmore continued to be actively involved in radical student anti-colonialism/anti-imperialism activism. It was while attending Howard that he joined the Communist Party. He became the secretary of the International Anti-Imperialist Youth League and was the principal organizer of the demonstration against the visit of the British ambassador, Sir Esmé Howard, to Howard University to open the International Club on 5 December 1928. Padmore viewed the opening of the club as a positive development since it would allow African Americans, Africans and students of African descent "to get together in order to understand each other and to unite in common struggle for the full and complete emancipation of our suppressed race".[19] He recognized that as long as African people were divided, the "imperialist oppressors will be able to hold us in subjection". Padmore warned his fellow students that the imperialist "forces which have been our historic enemies will try to invade your ranks and poison your healthy attitude of militant struggle for complete emancipation". He excoriated all the mediators of imperialism who were responsible for the oppression and exploitation of millions of black men, women and children in the United States and throughout the world.[20]

Padmore confronted the university's leaders, who failed to consult or solicit the approval of the student body before deciding to invite the British ambassador and "other imperialist lackeys to officiate" at the opening of the International Club. He stressed that Sir Esmé Howard was no friend of black people; he "merely condescends to hob-nob" since this was part of his job. According to Padmore, Sir Esmé's major objective was to secure the allegiance and collaboration of the future colonial leaders, so that when they return home they will abandon the masses of the peoples "who are beginning to revolt against their inhuman exploiters".[21] Padmore condemned Sir Esmé and his allies for the role they played in the deportation of Marcus Garvey from the United States in November 1927 and Canada in October 1928. Garvey was expelled from the United States after his sentence was commuted. Garvey subsequently embarked on a European tour and stopped in Canada, where the authorities arrested him to prevent him from addressing a meeting in Montreal. Garvey was deported from Canada under "regulations prohibiting political agitators".[22] Padmore opined that the main reason Garvey was deported was because these officials of the US government and British colonial officials were "determined to prevent all champions of freedom from arousing the consciousness of the Negro masses and organizing them to fight against the social, political and economic outrages".[23] At this time the relationship between the communists in the United States and Garvey was not as hostile as in 1925, at the time of Garvey's imprisonment. The CPUSA appeared to be sympathetic to Garvey's plight; it opposed his deportation and urged black and white workers to call for his release from prison.[24] Padmore, in an article, indicated that the communists "were among the first to point out to the Negro masses and to the working class of the world that Garvey was a victim of a nefarious frame-up system".[25] Padmore predicted that Sir Esmé and his minions would be the adversaries whom the upcoming leaders of the nationalist political parties and trade unions would have to fight in the battle for national freedom and independence.[26]

The British ambassador was stung by Padmore's attack and requested information from the US authorities about him and the International Anti-Imperialist Youth League. The authorities discovered that Padmore was a field organizer of the American Negro Labor Congress (ANLC) and on the editorial staff of the *Negro Champion*. However, they were unable to unearth any information about the Anti-Imperialistic Youth League and it was assumed that the organization was a branch of the League against Imperialism and Colonial Oppression, a section of the All-American Anti-Imperialist League, which was formed in 1924 under the auspices of the Workers Party of America, or an organization formed by the Young Workers' League of America, which was the American section of the Communist International of Youth.[27]

Padmore was described as extremely popular among the student body and faculty. He was considered to be "bright and industrious". Metz Lochard, a member of the faculty at Howard, opined that Padmore had much more "drive" than most African Americans because he was a "product of the British system which did not completely silence their grievances at home".[28] Ivar Oxaal stated that "the West Indian colored colonials had educational and social advantages far superior to those attained by the Negroes suffering under the American caste system or under the cruder, less 'enlightened' British trusteeship in Black Africa".[29] Padmore, like many of his counterparts from the West Indies, understood the importance of "book learning and education" because of their part in facilitating upward social mobility in British colonies.[30]

In addition to being intelligent, Padmore was known as a "militant" at Howard. According to Ras Makonnen, Padmore "did not hesitate to take action against any interference with the college from outsiders".[31] Moreover, he informs us, Padmore viewed "the university as a place of consciousness, not just a place where you subject yourselves to individuals because they are professors". He maintains that Padmore felt that the students had the right to question their professors because the professors "are merely consulting text books here and there and you and I have access to the same books and we may come to different conclusions".[32] Makonnen affirms that Padmore was continually pushing students to be watchful and critical of faculty members like Kelly Miller, a sociology professor with a reputation for insulting his students with statements such as, "Are you from Africa? I thought so, can't expect anything great from you."[33] Padmore, like many other students, may have had issues with this teaching style, but the criticism of Miller transcended the lecture room and was an attack on Miller's political orientation, described as "conservative, anti-labour, pro-big business and a supporter of segregation, if the facilities were equal".[34] Miller was the chair of the Negro Sanhedrin, a united front of black organizations that met in Chicago in February 1924. It was believed that Miller sought to marginalize the contributions of black communists and was castigated by them for this action. He was also attacked for his position that "capitalist stands for an open shop which gives every man the unhindered right to work according to his ability and skill. In this proposition the capitalist and Negro are one."³⁵ Padmore's critique of Miller was in keeping with the position of the communist spokespersons who attacked Miller. Miller, with his pro-capitalist and anti-labour stance, did not ingratiate himself to Padmore.

In contrast, Padmore had a high opinion of philosophy professor Alain Locke and felt that "as long as the students had Professors like Locke they would be safe".³⁶ Professor Locke had an endearing teaching style that made him popular among his students in his interdisciplinary course on race relations. Locke was also instrumental in the propagation of the Harlem Renaissance with his editing of the *New Negro*, an anthology of poetry and plays by black artists. In his article "Negro Art in America", Padmore noted that the *New Negro* had been "acclaimed as one of the finest of its kind". He felt that "*The New Negro* deserves a place in the library of every student of Negro history and art, as it represents a master piece in modern American literature".³⁷ According to Robin Kelley, "the Comintern's new position on the Negro Question compelled Black Communists to call upon African-American writers, artists and historians to focus their work on the age-old tradition of Black rebellion".³⁸ Kelley added that "most Communist theoreticians assumed that genuine Black folk culture was at least implicitly, if not explicitly, revolutionary".³⁹ The position of the Comintern on the role of writers like Locke heightened Padmore's respect for him and he viewed Locke as a positive influence on the students.

AMERICAN NEGRO LABOR CONGRESS

In 1927 Padmore became a member of the ANLC, an auxiliary of the CPUSA.⁴⁰ The ANLC was formed in 1925 in response to RILU's plea for agitation among black workers in the United States. The ANLC was "an organization uniting Negro Workers and class-conscious white workers in a common struggle against racial, social and economic oppression".⁴¹ Its mission was to be a centralized movement of black protest led by labour, cleanse labour of racial prejudice, lay the groundwork for industrial unionism, turn the black masses away from bourgeois misleaders and advance the "hegemony" of the working class, and be black America's contribution to training and providing leadership for the worldwide anti-imperialist movement.⁴² Within the ANLC, Padmore worked closely with the Barbadian Richard B. Moore, who became the head of the organization in 1927. Padmore worked as an organizer and also wrote for and edited the *Negro Champion*, the organ of the ANLC.

From the outset, the publication suffered from a lack of monetary resources that made it difficult to publish on a consistent basis. In an article titled "An Appeal to Negro Workers! Help Build Your Paper", Padmore called on African Americans to support the newspaper financially on the basis that the paper always fought the battles of the oppressed masses. Padmore stressed that the *Negro Champion* was the only paper of its kind in the United States. It was a labour paper "dedicated to the task of fighting for the Negro workers" and the black "race as a whole, against exploitation, segregation, Jim Crowism, lynching and other social abuses".⁴³

At this time Padmore was concerned not only with developments taking place in the United States but also had a keen interest in the political events taking place in the Caribbean. This was evident in an article in the *Negro Champion* entitled "A Federated West Indies". Padmore noted that one of the most debatable subjects in West Indian political life was the question of the federation of the West Indies.⁴⁴ After World War I, the idea of a West Indian federation began to take root among a section of the people, championed by Captain Andrew Cipriani in Trinidad and T.A. Marryshow in Grenada. They felt that the political organizations in the West Indies should make a concerted demand on the colonial office because it was thought that the islands could not become self-governing entities unless they were federated. The idea of a federation also resonated with the colonial office and sections of the merchant and planter class who felt that a federation would reduce the cost of government. In 1920, the Barbados Chamber of Commerce, the Trinidad Chamber of Commerce, the Jamaican Imperial Association and the Associated West Indian Chambers of Commerce called for serious consideration to be given to the federation of the British West Indies colonies.⁴⁵ Notwithstanding the discussions taking place about a federation, Major Wood in 1922 stated that it was "both inopportune and impractical to attempt amalgamation of existing units of Government into anything approaching a general federal system".⁴⁶

The question of a federated West Indies was also discussed in 1926 at a conference in London where the secretary of state for the colonies proposed a standing committee, a purely advisory body with no executive powers. Although Padmore's idea of a West Indian federation differed significantly from that of the undersecretary of state for the colonies, he was firmly in support of a federated West Indies. He believed that with the development of the labour movement in Trinidad, Jamaica, British Guiana and Grenada, it should not be too difficult to get the leaders of the working class to take a decisive stand on working for a federation and argued that such a federation would lead to the development of a nationalist movement. Padmore stressed that the *Negro Champion* stood ready to give its full support to a radical movement for the federation and freedom of the West Indies.[47] He favoured the Soviet Union's model of federation that stated that "federation is a transitional form toward complete union of all the workers of all countries".[48] As a young Marxist, he appeared to be familiar with V.I. Lenin's pronouncement that the "aim of socialism was not only to bring the nations closer together but to integrate them".[49]

HARLEM TENANTS LEAGUE

Padmore was also a member of the Harlem Tenants League, another auxiliary of the CPUSA. This body included a number of West Indians, including Richard B. Moore, Cyril Briggs, Wilfred Domingo, Grace Campbell, A. Elizabeth Hendrickson, Cecil Hope, Otto Huiswoud and Edward Welsh. It led rent strikes, protested against evictions and rent gouging, and lobbied for housing codes to improve conditions, such as inadequate heat, that were the responsibility of the landlords.[50] It is important to note that during the first three decades of the twentieth century, Harlem had a large influx of immigrants of African descent from the British Caribbean, a number of whom played important roles in socialist organizations in Harlem. Mark Solomon contends that they brought "a sensitivity to the social stratification of their Caribbean homelands" that had "engendered a sharp class awareness and assertive psychological makeup, heightened by their majority racial status in the islands and their relatively extensive colonial schooling".⁵¹ He added that "these colonial roots made them fiercely anti-imperialist and hostile to capitalism".⁵²

COMMUNIST PARTY OF THE UNITED STATES

Padmore officially became a card-carrying member of the CPUSA in 1927. He strongly believed that communism presented the best available programme for the liberation of the black working class in the United States and the working masses globally. Padmore admitted that "he entered socialism and communism because the communists were in the forefront for racial equality in the United States".⁵³ He strongly believed that the evils of this world emanated from the capitalist system, and "only by abolishing this nefarious system will the oppressed races and classes be emancipated and the brotherhood of man established".⁵⁴ Padmore abandoned his dream of getting a degree and dropped out of university in order to become a full-time revolutionary so that he "could render in a fuller way some aid to my Negro brothers in Africa".⁵⁵ He attended the New York Workers School and "had the dubious distinction of being the school's first Negro graduate".⁵⁶ Padmore was an enthusiastic member of the CPUSA and was described as "active, devoted and fearless".⁵⁷

It is important to note that Padmore would have been exposed to all of the radical ideas floating around Harlem at this time. Harlem was fertile with radicalism being spread by the *Emancipator*, edited by W.A. Domingo, and the *Crusader*, edited by Briggs, the founder of the African Blood Brotherhood. He would also have been exposed to the black nationalism of the Garveyites in Harlem. During the early 1920s, Garvey's UNIA "was proportionately the most powerful mass movement in America".⁵⁸ However, by the mid-twenties, Garveyism as a political force had started to wane. Padmore wrote that "Garvey's anti-communist tirades had a demoralizing effect upon neophyte Negro party members" like himself who were seeking to poach members of the UNIA to join the ranks of the communists. He noted that Garvey, by stressing "the proud tradition of the African past and race pride, helped to put steel into the spine of many Negroes who had previously been ashamed of their colour and their identification with the Negro group". Padmore admitted that it was not until Garvey's imprisonment and subsequent deportation back to Jamaica that communism was able to make any sizeable headway among African Americans and immigrants from the West Indies who had settled in New York.[59] However, like many Marxists of his day, he sought to reduce the Garveyite programme to "Back to Africa or Negro Zionism".[60] While there was a repatriation component to the movement, the scope and depth of the movement was much more extensive. The UNIA worked to raise the self-esteem of black people, create employment for black people through the Negro Factories Corporation, started a shipping line for the basis of pan-African trade, fought for the dignity and humanity of all African people, sought to build a spirit of nationhood and worked to redress all the disadvantages facing Africans. Therefore, to reduce the UNIA to the slogan "Back to Africa" was disingenuous, reductionist and erroneous.

Padmore would also have been exposed to the programme of the National Association for the Advancement of Colored People (NAACP), articulated through its *Crisis* magazine edited by W.E.B. Du Bois. However, the communist programme held the greatest attraction for him.

RACE OR CLASS

It is important to note that the tension between race and class that concerned Padmore has been an area of fierce contestation for those involved in the black struggle for racial equality. Black nationalism/pan-Africanism has historically placed the emphasis on race because black people were oppressed as a race under the Jim Crow system, South African apartheid and colonial systems in Africa and the Caribbean. For Marxism, class considerations took precedence over all other factors because the class struggle was seen as the motivating force of history. According to Marxism, workers under capitalism are oppressed and exploited as a class, not as a race. Therefore, racial oppression is subordinate to class oppression.

As a Marxist, Padmore felt that class considerations should take precedence over racial considerations. He doubted whether "any race will be united under capitalism, where there is rich and poor, exploiters and exploited". Padmore blamed black leaders for creating the false impression that all black people, "whether they belong to the capitalist or working class, have the same interests". He was clear that in all capitalist countries, "whether the population happens to be white as in Europe, yellow as in Japan and China, brown as in India, or black as in Liberia and Haiti, it is not colour that counts but class".[61] Moreover, he asserted the problems of imperialism were "fundamentally economic" and could only be resolved by eradicating capitalism, which fostered and took advantage of racial and religious disagreements in the interest of those "who live by rent, profit and interest".[62]

While Padmore argued for the primacy of class, he felt that race was also extremely important and should not be entirely incorporated into a rigid class analysis. In his writings and pronouncements, the race question always featured prominently given the fact that black people in the United States, the Caribbean and Africa were exploited and oppressed as a class and as a race. Given this reality, Padmore felt that communist leadership never fully "understood that the Negro Question had racial connotations which demanded special consideration by the party".[63] It was felt by some members of the CPUSA that Padmore had certain black nationalist predispositions that made it difficult for him to adhere to orthodox communist doctrine. This outlook created tension between Padmore and some sections of the CPUSA, but it in no way diminished his commitment to communism. According to C.L.R. James, Padmore stated that when a black man speaks constantly about his race he is not trying to create the impression that the African is better. His intention is "to establish equality, to make up for the humiliation and historical degradation which his race has suffered".[64]

ATTRACTION OF THE BOLSHEVIK REVOLUTION

Briggs, a West Indian from Nevis and one of the founders of the black nationalist African Blood Brotherhood and a member of the CPUSA, confessed that blacks who joined a communist party did so not because they were socialists, but because they felt that the party was working on their behalf. He admitted that he was converted to communism because "of the solution to the national question in the Soviet Union and he was confident that the American party would in time take its lead from the Soviet Party which is what it eventually did".⁶⁵ Another important black Marxist, Harry Haywood, stated that what impressed him about communism was its "political identity with the successful Bolshevik Revolution".⁶⁶ Padmore found the communist programme to be attractive for several reasons:

> The Communist Party advocated the doctrine of racial equality and fought militantly for the full social, political and economic rights of all races and peoples, irrespective of skin colour.
> The CPUSA was the only political organization in the United States that championed the cause of black people, the most exploited section of the American working class.
> The communists were the only ones who opposed and struggled against imperialism, which had resulted in the enslavement of the colonized peoples in China, India, Africa, Latin America and other parts of the world.⁶⁷

Although the communist programme was comprehensive in tackling the disadvantages of people of African descent, Mark Naison asserted that to become a member of the CPUSA in the early 1920s was not the easiest decision "for black intellectuals, it was a leap of faith that seemed to go against the direction of black political life".⁶⁸ Incidentally, not for white intellectuals either, given that the membership of the party numbered fewer than ten thousand at this time. By 1927, when Padmore joined the party, the black membership was estimated at "a little over two dozen blacks". Three other West Indians, Cyril Briggs, Richard B. Moore and Otto Huiswoud, were also members.⁶⁹ Michael Dawson attributes the paucity in numbers to "black suspicion of whites in general and white workers in particular". He adds that hostility "on the part of white workers towards blacks and the perception that the political economy was racialized and racist made traditional socialist organizing ineffective among blacks".⁷⁰ The majority of the leading political institutions in Harlem deemed "capitalism as a fact of life, if not a positive good". These organizations were convinced that the Bolshevik model of revolution "was impossible or undesirable – in the United States, they viewed the white working class as an enemy and a competitor".⁷¹ Padmore, in speaking to the small number of blacks within the CPUSA many years later, attributed this development to the "tactical mistakes and psychological blunders which the communist parties of the Western World have made in their approach to the darker peoples".[72] However, it was evident that the CPUSA expended much time and financial resources to win over blacks to the party. Notwithstanding the reluctance of blacks to join the party, Marxism was attractive to some black intellectuals because "its promise of a hidden truth, its open opposition to an insidious social order, its alternative mapping of the historical origins of the ruling classes, which they came to despise and its identification with the under classes, made it an almost irresistible companion".[73]

Padmore, like so many other progressives around the world, was impressed with what the Bolshevik Revolution stood for. It was the first successful socialist revolution in history. This development set in motion the transformation of Russian society from capitalism to socialism. Padmore observed that the total transferral "of power from the capitalists to the working class was the essential prerequisite for the solution of the National and Colonial Question".[74] The Russian Revolution "cracked open the foundations of imperialism and pointed the way forward to the millions of oppressed and exploited colonial peoples around the world".[75]

LENIN'S IMPACT ON PADMORE

While Padmore was a Marxist-Leninist, it could just as easily be said he was a Leninist-Marxist. Leninism was centred on the vanguard party, overthrowing imperialism, national self-determination and the role of the state in society. For many, Leninism became the Marxism of the day, since it contributed to a Marxist theory capable of organizing people and seizing state power.[76] Although Padmore was not a proponent of the "great man" philosophy of liberation, he was a big fan of Lenin and felt that Lenin was the greatest revolutionary of all time. In his view, Lenin was "a unique and profound thinker and an organizer and inspirer, tactician and strategist of incomparable stature".[77] Padmore reasoned that Lenin's role in the Russian Revolution was an "outstanding example of the role of the individual in history". Indeed, he argued that without Lenin there could be "no Bolshevik Party, or no social revolution".[78]

What impressed Padmore about Lenin was that "he refused to follow blindly Marx's theories; he bent theory to the facts not facts to the theory".[79] Kevin McDermott and Jeremy Agnew, in a similar vein, made the point that Lenin's thought was neither static nor inflexible. According to them, Lenin's Marxism evolved in response to a rapidly changing world and hence should be placed firmly in the specific historical contexts in which it was shaped.[80] Marx predicted that the proletarian revolution, which would result in communism, would take place in highly developed capitalist countries. The class struggle between the bourgeoisie and the proletariat would lead to a revolution in which the proletarian masses would be victorious. This revolution would remove the ruling class and establish a new mode of production that would culminate in the achievement of an egalitarian society.[81] According to Padmore, Lenin recognized that the workers in advanced capitalist countries were not ready "to perform the historic role which Marx assigned to them"; therefore, he decided to reach out to those in Africa and Asia who "yearned to break the fetters of imperialist domination".[82]

In Padmore's view, Lenin saw clearly what Marx was unable to see: "the gradual corruption of the European socialist movements through their bourgeoizification".[83] Lenin recognized that the super-profits that capitalists extorted from workers in the colonies made it possible to pay off labour leaders and the higher echelons of the "labour aristocracy". He accused capitalists in advanced countries of bribing the "labour aristocracy" in "a thousand different ways, direct and indirect, overt and covert".[84] The financial and military power of the great powers rested upon the continued exploitation of the coloured races, and the mega-profits the governing classes derived from exploiting colonial workers enabled them "to corrupt the white workers and blunt their revolutionary ardour".[85] Given the revolutionary inertia among European workers, Lenin argued that "the Western domination of the world could only be broken by stirring the coloured colonial and semi-colonial peoples of Asia and Africa to achieve their independence".[86] This forced Lenin to seek allies among the colonized and semi-colonized peoples in an effort to weaken the "colonial foundations upon which the great western powers rested". Lenin saw the growth of colonial nationalism as a means of weakening the strength of the colonial powers and as a means of obtaining assistance "for his new and relatively isolated regime".[87]

Padmore contended that Lenin's thrust with respect to Asia and Africa was a strong deviation from conventional Marxism. He remarked that "Marx never envisaged" that colonized peoples in Asia and Africa would be "more revolutionary than the white workers of Europe". This neo-Marxist position was linked with the national and colonial question as a strategic weapon in the advancement of "Communism in backward and undeveloped countries".[88] Padmore strongly asserted that Lenin was concerned not only with the emancipation of Russian workers but with the social freedom of all workers and oppressed peoples throughout the world. Lenin demonstrated his internationalism by stressing to the workers of Europe and America "that their freedom [was] inextricably bound up with the freedom of the colonial masses of China, India, Africa and elsewhere", telling them that they "must render every support in their fight to liberate themselves from the yoke of imperialism".[89]

It was reported that Lenin, in his correspondence with American communists, was astonished that their reports to Moscow made no mention of the CPUSA's work among blacks and suggested that they should be acknowledged as a "strategically important element in Communist activity".[90] At the second congress of the Comintern in 1920, Lenin presented his Draft Theses on the National and Colonial Question. Lenin's position on the national question and the interest he took in regard to American blacks further endeared him to Padmore. In his theses, Lenin stressed that the Comintern must seek to bring about a union of the proletarian and working classes of all nations for a joint revolutionary struggle leading to the downfall of capitalism and support the revolutionary movement among the subject nations in all colonies and in the less-developed countries.[91]

Lenin's theses were subsequently modified after a robust debate with M.K. Roy, an Indian Marxist intellectual. Due to the influence and inspiration of Lenin, the fourth congress of the Comintern in 1922 established a Negro Commission that adopted the Theses on the Negro Question.[92]

Lenin's position on anti-Semitism, racial chauvinism and self-determination had a great impact on Padmore. He noted that the Soviet Union was the only country in the world where racial discrimination was prohibited.[93]

This was a significant departure from the Jim Crow laws that existed in the United States and the racist colonial system that Padmore had been exposed to in Trinidad. As a product of colonial Trinidad and someone whose objective was the liberation of African people from colonial rule, Padmore was profoundly affected by Lenin's call for self-determination. For Lenin, self-determination meant "the political separation of those nations from alien national bodies and the formation of an independent nation state".[94] Padmore was also deeply influenced by Lenin's conception of imperialism. According to Lenin, "imperialism is the monopoly stage of capitalism".[95] Therefore, Padmore consistently applied the Leninist model of imperial plunder in analysing African and Caribbean societies.

CRITIQUE OF THE BLACK BELT THESIS

At the sixth Comintern Congress in Moscow in 1928, the colonial question occupied a significant part of the deliberations. After evaluating the revolutionary movements in Asia and Africa within the context of the international political environment, the congress asserted that Lenin's Theses on the National and Colonial Question adopted by the second congress were still relevant and should serve as the blueprint for all communist parties.[96] This congress passed the resolution on the famous "self-determination for the Black Belt" in relation to the US South, which Padmore acknowledged was influenced by Garveyism. He believed that since Garvey had mobilized popular support by "promising to establish a 'National Home' for blacks in Africa, the American Communist should go one better and offer the Negroes their own Black Belt".[97]

Padmore posited that to make "theory fit his plan", Kuusinen "rejected all the findings of all the acknowledged sociological experts in America, that the Negroes suffered disabilities as a racial minority".[98] According to Padmore, Kuusinen insisted that the "Negro problem was a national minority one" and "its solution called for the application of the Stalinist formula". Therefore, the doctrine of self-determination, with the right of secession and the establishment of an independent black nation, was declared applicable to blacks in the Southern United States.[99] Theodore Draper has pointed out that Padmore wrongly identified Kuusinen as the genius behind this scheme and explained that "Kuusinen was no doubt entrusted with the management of this operation", but the mastermind "was undoubtedly Stalin, whose bidding Kuusinen unfailingly obeyed".[100] Harvey Klehr remarks that as the Soviet expert on the national question, Stalin was the obvious instigator in applying his theory to the United States.[101] Cedric Robinson makes the point that for years the true origin of this position was a mystery to the members of the CPUSA as well as to its historians.[102]

Padmore described the Black Belt thesis as "Marxist sociology turned upside down". Many blacks wanted to know how "a poor down-trodden and unarmed racial minority were going to establish an autonomous self-governing Black Belt within the Republic of the United States".[103] Naison contends that in defining self-determination, the resolution was ambiguous: it did not specify whether the Black Belt should become an independent nation or a self-governing region within the United States.[104] Robinson points out that the theoretical basis for the party's classification of blacks as a nation was unconventional in terms of Marxist theory: "Marx and Engels had both distinguished between nations and nationalities, recognizing in the former the capacity for independent existence and, in the latter, an incapacity."[105] Haywood, one of the main proponents of self-determination for the Black Belt, admitted he was the only black attending the congress who supported "the new line on self determination". He revealed that the other blacks insisted that it was a race question, not a national question, implying that the solution lay through assimilation under socialism.[106] Haywood was strongly influenced by the Siberian Charles Nasanov, who viewed "blacks as an oppressed nation with the right of self-determination".[107]

Haywood confirmed that Padmore had deep reservations about the Black Belt thesis while still a member of the Comintern and that he did not develop this position after his break with the Comintern. Haywood stated:

> I first met George Padmore in December 1929, when Foster had brought him to Moscow. I got to know him quite well and on a number of occasions visited him in his room. . . . At the time I sized him up as a pragmatist with only a superficial grasp of Marxist theory. Politically, he appeared to be a staunch supporter of the fight for independence in Africa and the

West Indies, but he was adamantly opposed to the right of self determination for US Blacks, whom he regarded not as a nation, but as an opposed racial minority.[108]

While Padmore had deep reservations about this line, it did not lead to any major falling-out with the CPUSA or the Comintern. However, Padmore became more strident in his criticism of the Black Belt thesis after he broke with the Comintern. Indeed, the Black Belt thesis never garnered any substantial support among black American communists, and Padmore's criticism was not unique among them.

Padmore took a similar position on the application of the "Native Republic" model in South Africa. This model was a carbon copy of the Black Belt thesis. He strongly asserted that South Africans, like their counterparts in the United States, while opposed to all forms of racial discrimination, "have never demanded separatism, either in the form of apartheid or Native Republic". Instead, they had always demanded full citizenship rights within a multi-racial society. They therefore looked with deep suspicion upon the new communist slogan of a "Native Republic", which they construed as an attempt to separate "them into some sort of Bantu state".[109]

PRESENTATIONS IN RUSSIA

In December 1929 Padmore accompanied William Z. Foster, a leading figure in the CPUSA, to Russia, where he was asked to deliver an analysis of the implications of the TUUL convention in Cleveland and the Gastonia strike. Padmore was seen as a hard-working, dedicated and committed young communist. The Cleveland conference of 31 August–2 September 1929 was of great significance as it witnessed the dissolution of the Trade Union Educational League and the founding of the TUUL. At the sixth Congress of the Comintern in 1928, the CPUSA was instructed to "launch revolutionary unions" to oppose the failing "American Federation of Labor [AFL] and to meet the demands of an envisioned revolutionary crisis".[110] It was asserted that the "fascist AFL was incapable of aiding the workers, hence a new dual union movement was needed".[111] The new

Communist Party position had abandoned the "boring-from-within" line that was adhered to in the earlier period. The boring-from-within approach did not realize the results hoped for in penetrating the trade unions, left-of centre-parties and race-based formations like the UNIA and the National Association for the Advancement of Colored People. The new tactic called for the growth of "separatist organizations dedicated to an independent uncompromising assault on capitalism" by inciting proletarian revolutions in the more developed countries and supporting "national liberation movements in colonial areas".[112]

A few months before the Cleveland conference, Padmore suggested that the TUUL convention would "mark a turning point in the history of the labour movement in America and will be a tremendous step forward in the struggle of the emancipation of the working class". In his view, the convention was taking place at a time when the working class was faced with the most brutal expressions of "capitalist rationalizations, wage cuts and intolerable conditions".[113] Padmore had participated in the Cleveland convention, where he spoke against "white chauvinism and black Uncle Tomism".[114] He also authored an article, "Trade Union Unity Convention and the Negro Worker and the Negro Masses", which appeared in the *Daily Worker*.

In his report to the convention, Padmore informed his audience that millions of black workers, the bulk of whom lived in the US South, were not only brutally exploited, but were the targets of the "most vicious attacks of race prejudice which assumes the form of police terrorism, lynching, Jim Crowism, segregation, disenfranchisement and peonage".[115] In addition to these harms, black workers had been betrayed by the AFL, which, despite its declaration of non-discrimination, followed a calculated strategy of racial discrimination. Padmore further charged that the AFL had made no serious attempt to organize the blacks, but had "done everything possible to impede and hamper the development of the growth of unionism".[116] The historian Theodore Kornweibel notes that at "its founding in 1881, the AFL made genuine efforts to implement racial harmony and organize black workers". However after 1900, the AFL "organized blacks in separate locals or indirectly affiliated federal unions, neither of which guaranteed much security for their hapless members".[117] Marc Karson and Ronald Radosh contend that the AFL "had chosen not to become a leader in the fight against segregation but to accommodate itself to and, in fact, incorporate segregation into its own organization".[118]

In light of the discriminatory practices of the AFL and the "reactionary position" of the Brotherhood of Sleeping Car Porters (BSCP), Padmore argued that the black workers would have "to turn to the left wing of the labour movement for leadership".[119] In June 1928, the BSCP, led by A. Philip Randolph, called off a strike against the Pullman Company when it was informed by William Green, the head of the AFL, that conditions were not favourable for industrial action. The members of the CPUSA accused Randolph of "selling out to the AFL, choking the workers' militant spirit and depending on phony bourgeois laws".[120] Kornweibel asserted that the AFL found Randolph's moderate politics palatable and the BSCP a safe instrument for rallying black workers under the influence, if not sponsorship, of the AFL. Moreover, Randolph was frequently advised by William Green.[121] This discredited Randolph and the BSCP in the eyes of Padmore and the members of the CPUSA.

In Padmore's opinion, the leaders of the left-wing labour movement were the "only ones who [could] expose the corrupt policies of those who call[ed] themselves champions of the working class". In this category he specifically mentioned socialists and Musties.[122] The position of the Comintern at this time discouraged any alliances with "progressives" and this line was followed by the CPUSA. The Musties, or Labour Action, led by A.J. Muste, were viewed "as the greatest danger to the working class", since they were a "left social reformist group carrying on the policy of the AFL under the cover of progressive phrases". Furthermore, "any proposals of united fronts with these elements (Musties) must be mercilessly combatted".[123] Padmore sought to educate his listeners about the work of the left-wing unions led by the TUUL. He explained that these unions fight for the admittance of black workers into the trade unions, support the equality of blacks and whites, and insist that blacks should hold positions in the unions in order to be able to formulate policies and protect their rights and fight against the discriminatory practices of separate racial unions which have weakened the struggle of the working class.[124]

According to Padmore, blacks were already occupying leadership positions in some left-wing unions. He cited the example of William Boyce, who was elected vice president of the National Miners Union. In the racist US South, the left-wing National Textile Workers Union was advocating "equality in the union for Negro and white alike". However, the United Textile Workers Union, controlled by the AFL, and unions connected to the Socialist Party of the United States refused to admit the Negro Textile Workers, and when the left-wing faction dared to raise its voice in protest against the policy of racial discrimination, they were expelled as "Reds" and "Nigger lovers".[125]

Padmore laid out the challenges facing the black working class: first they would have to join with the class-conscious white workers to struggle against racism in the trade unions and then they would have to fight against the deceitful "agenda of the petty bourgeoisie Uncle Tom" blacks who would try to prevent black workers from becoming members of the Marxist-oriented trade unions.[126]

GASTONIA

Padmore was also invited to address the importance of the "famous" Gastonia textile strike. On 1 April 1929, twenty-two hundred workers at the Loray Mills in Gastonia, North Carolina, went on strike for better wages and better working conditions. The owners and their representatives used brute force to return the workers to work; strikers were beaten by the police, thugs and gangsters. A group of vigilantes destroyed the strikers' headquarters, and many of the workers were evicted from company housing. The chief of police was killed in the melee. Padmore had previously written the article "Gastonia: Its Significance for Negro Labour", which appeared in the *Daily Worker*, and was quite familiar with the events that took place in Gastonia; therefore, he was able to provide the Comintern officials with a comprehensive report.

Although this was an inconsequential, failed strike in the eyes of the populace, for the CPUSA this strike was significant because it was "able to transform a failed strike into a symbolic victory".[127] The party received "an important psychological boost" from its involvement in the Gastonia strike: "for however brief a moment, the Party had led American born workers from the South".[128] A party plenary meeting declared: "the struggle in the South symbolized by Gastonia is the best proof of the growing radicalization of the working class in the Third Period".[129] Mark Solomon argues that the party insisted on making Gastonia a testing ground for the solidarity of black and white labour.[130] At the TUUL convention, twelve rank-and-file members were chosen to attend the trial of some of the strikers who were arrested as a workers' jury and render a verdict to the working class. Moreover, the convention sent a telegram of solidarity to the Southern textile workers who were on strike and the defendants who were being tried. The cable "commended the stand of the strikers in defending their union headquarters from the attack of the mill operators and the police, demanding unconditional release".[131] The delegates left the Hotel Inn and Kennard Hotel after these hotels denied black delegates entrance. A decision was taken to picket the hotels, and Padmore was one of the main speakers at the mass meeting where this decision was taken.[132]

The Gastonia affair, according to Padmore, was not simply the expression of another stage "of the class struggle on the American battle front of world capitalism". It epitomized "in a far reaching and significant way events making for the emancipation of millions of oppressed and brutally persecuted Negroes in the South".[133] He felt that Gastonia was the first of many class battles that were going to take place in the recently "industrialized South". These clashes would be increased because of the process of capitalist restructuring produced by the crisis of capitalism. Padmore contended that Southern workers' standard of living was the lowest among the black working class. He posited that the living conditions of the poor whites and blacks in the South were akin to those of workers in China, India, Africa, the West Indies and Latin America.[134]

Padmore felt the class struggle would compel black and white workers to understand "that despite their racial differences, they are both members of the proletariat". Only when they became aware of this would "they be able to fight effectively in the common struggles of the working class against the capitalist overlords". He was optimistic that "this unity of purpose [would] be the most powerful force in breaking through the age-long prejudices between the workers of both races".[135] Wilson Record informs us that according to the thinking of the communists, the unity of the proletariat was assured by common suffering under capitalist oppressors; as the exploitation increased, workers would come to realize that the enemy was not members of any particular racial group, but capitalists.[136] In Will Herberg's words, "the white heat of class war will burn out the corruption of race prejudice".[137] Padmore, while treading the line of interracial solidarity, was honest enough to admit that the abolition of racial discrimination would not take place instantaneously.[138] He observed that for a long time the "capitalist oppressors" had used the race card as their most valuable medium to preserve their "privileged position". White workers had been taught that their impoverishment was caused by blacks. This idea was deeply ingrained in white workers, making it easy to "incite them into lynching mobs". However, the Gastonia conflict demonstrated that the working class would no longer be misled by the "deceptive propaganda of their oppressors".[139]

Padmore maintained that the Gastonia textile strike presented tangible evidence of the viability of proletarian interracial solidarity. He used this example as the basis for predicting greater interracial solidarity between the white and black working classes. Padmore insisted that several valuable lessons could be learned from Gastonia in relation to the working class in general and blacks in particular:

> (1) The struggle immediately brings on the order of the day the right of workers to defend themselves. This must be the central issue for us, for as indicated, the workers will engage in more and more class battles in the near future, during which the fascist elements such as the "committee of one hundred" would be mobilized against the strikers. We cannot surrender the right of self defense otherwise we will be simply inviting wholesale massacre of the working class.
>
> (2) Race prejudice is not a geographical feature of American capitalist society. It is everywhere, although more bitterly entrenched in the South, because of its semi-feudal remnants. As the process of industrialization proceeds and the Negroes and poor whites are drawn from the rural communities into the industrial centers they will be forced to discard the ideology of the past and to orientate themselves to their new environment. This process of urbanization will bring them together and out of these contacts they will learn to recognize that both groups are the slaves of the bosses. They will further learn that through their everyday experiences that the

employers foster race prejudice in order to keep them apart and thereby exploit them more easily.

(3) The new class battles which will increasingly break out will necessitate the application of new methods of class warfare. We have already realized that the antiquated Jim Crow craft unions fostered by the AF of L must be displaced by new industrial unions under the militant leadership of the Communists and the left wing TUUL. Every battle will present us with new lessons in class tactics and methods of struggle. We must therefore be always on the alert to recognize our weak and strong points. Rigid self-criticism must be indulged in, in order to immediately correct our mistakes and steel our fighting forces so that all advantageous positions gained by the workers will be consolidated.

(4) A systematic ideological campaign against white chauvinism must be carried on among the workers as well as within the Party ranks. There is still a tremendous underestimation of Negro work among some of our comrades. Up till now too little serious attention has been given to this phase of our activities. The TUUL convention marks a new effort, which, however, must now end merely in resolutions. The large Negro delegation shows the two are capable of winning the black workers to our banner if we ourselves carry on systematic work among them. These Negro workers, as pointed out by the Comintern over and over again, represent revolutionary potentialities which it will be criminal for us to neglect for the social revolution. We must therefore intensify our work among them, and draw them not only into the new unions but into the ranks of the Party.

(5) We must popularize our slogans of full social, political and economic equality for Negroes more than we have done in the past. The most effective means of doing this is through our press, especially the "Negro Champion", which should be developed into the mass organ of the Negro workers. In districts and centers where large groups of Negroes are employed especially in the centers of the basic industries special leaflets and bulletins dealing in a concrete way with their everyday problems should be distributed at regular intervals. The Negro press can also be utilized to a greater extent than some of our comrades recognize.[140]

Padmore's analysis of the TUUL Convention and the Gastonia affair were cast within the Comintern's third period framework. The tenth executive committee of the Comintern plenum in 1929 on the Theses on the International Situation and the Immediate Task of the Communist International characterized the third period as one of increasing growth of the general crisis of capitalism, the accelerated accentuation of the fundamental external and internal contradictions of imperialism leading to imperialist wars, to great class conflicts, to an era of development of a new upward swing of the revolutionary movement in the principal capitalist countries and to great anti-imperialist revolutions in colonial countries.[141] Padmore made a positive impression on the members of the RILU hierarchy and lived up to his growing reputation as a bright and committed young communist.

Padmore was a militant student activist at Fisk and Howard universities. He joined the CPUSA because he felt that it would allow him to work for the liberation of his brothers and sisters in Africa. Padmore was profoundly influenced by Lenin and the achievements of the Bolshevik Revolution, and Lenin's positions on the national question, imperialism, self-determination and socialist federation had a fundamental impact on him.

3. A BLACK INTERNATIONALIST WITHIN THE COMINTERN

SOON AFTER GEORGE PADMORE DELIVERED HIS REPORT to the RILU officials in Russia in December 1929, he became the manager of the Negro Workers Committee based in Moscow.[1] Between 1930 and 1933, Padmore was one of the leading black operatives of the Comintern. He held several important positions, including lecturer at the Communist University of the Toilers of the East (KUTV), chairman of the Negro Bureau of the RILU and executive secretary of the ITUCNW.[2] He was also the editor of the *Negro Worker* and was a member of the high-powered Comintern Commission that was created to investigate the charges of ultra-left deviation levelled by Mao Tse Tung against Li Li San.[3]

Padmore was also elected to the Moscow City Soviet in 1930 to demonstrate that the Soviet Union had blacks in its government.[4] He was the first black to be selected as a deputy to the Moscow Soviet, and he was nominated by the Stalin Ball Bearing Works as their representative.[5] If Padmore had been living in his home country of Trinidad and Tobago at the time, he would not have been eligible to sit in the legislature of the crown colony government, as it comprised only white men. For Padmore, this clearly illustrated the difference between the "ethnic democracy" of the USSR and the racist, anti-democratic systems of the British Empire.[6]

In relating the narrative of his election to the Moscow Soviet Council, Padmore was initially reluctant to stand for office, because he did not speak Russian and he was not sufficiently knowledgeable about Russia's internal politics. However, he was persuaded and subsequently elected, although he was never given any major responsibilities.[7] In 1931, when a group of British people visited Russia, among them George Bernard Shaw, they were told that Padmore, a black man, was a representative of the Moscow Soviet. The British visitors were reminded that during the many years of Britain's empire, never once had a black person been elected as a member of the British Parliament.[8] As a representative of the Moscow Council, Padmore was accorded many of the privileges usually reserved for the top bureaucrats in the Soviet Union.[9]

THE HAMBURG CONFERENCE

In the face of the savaging of workers in Africa and its diaspora during the Great Depression (known as a crisis of capitalism to communists), an International Conference of Negro Workers was held in Hamburg, Germany in July 1930. The Great Depression was the longest, most destructive and profound economic crisis that capitalism had ever known.[10] It was also the gravest period during the twentieth century for workers, with millions of people globally being made redundant. Economist Arthur Lewis estimated that the number of people who were unemployed during the lowest point of the Depression was about thirty million, with about fifteen million in the United States.[11] In Padmore's estimation, black workers in Africa, the West Indies, the United States and South America were among the hardest hit by the crisis.[12]

The idea of a black world conference had initially been mooted by the Comintern in 1928. The International Conference of Negro Workers was slated to be held in London, but the Ramsay MacDonald Labour government refused to grant the organizers the required permission to hold the conference on British soil. The vision for making this summit a reality gathered momentum at the second conference of the League against Imperialism held in Frankfurt, July 1929. James Ford, one of the main organizers of the conference, explained that the black delegates who had come for the congress of the League against Imperialism "discussed the problems and questions of trade union organization amongst the Negro Workers and decided that an international Conference of Negro Workers should be called".[13] Padmore explained that "a committee of Negro Workers in America decided to call a Conference of the representatives of the Negro workers from different parts of the world for the purpose of discussing ways and means of improving their conditions".[14] A provisional committee of the ITUCNW was created to plan the conference. It comprised James Ford, William Burroughs, Johnstone Kenyatta, Henry Rosemond, M. Ali, Lucas Prentice, Isaac Munsey, Otto Hall, W. Thibedi, M.E. Burns and George Padmore. Padmore represented the Negro Trade Union Committee of the RILU. Ford, the chairman, was assigned to take care of visa applications and logistics while Padmore and the Negro Bureau handled political and operative planning.

Padmore, in Moscow, was intimately involved with the operational planning of the conference. He also travelled to Africa to recruit delegates to attend the conference, visiting Sierra Leone, Gambia, Senegal, Liberia, Nigeria and the Gold Coast. Padmore stated that he knew Dakar and the adjoining territories well.[15] In a letter to his friend Cyril Ollivierre, he noted that he had been up and down two continents and he was on his way back to Africa.[16] Padmore returned to Germany with four delegates from West Africa. In his journeys, Padmore had encountered "white capitalists" who sought to prevent blacks from attending the conference; they "refused to grant passports to the delegates and threatened to arrest and imprison those who attended the conference".[17] The South African government denied passports to delegates from South Africa, France refused to grant visas to delegates from Paris, and the British customs authorities did their utmost to prevent any African from entering or leaving British ports.[18] Padmore also experienced some challenges with sourcing food and other vital support for the delegates he brought from West Africa because of the bureaucratic inertia of the Comintern officials. He wrote a letter expressing his frustrations: "It is now one week since I have had these Negro workers in Berlin during which period I have not been able to provide them with a penny for food. As a result of this the men are entirely demoralized."[19]

At this conference, seventeen delegates from Africa, the United States, West Indies and Latin America discussed trade union issues and "the most vital problems affecting their social and political conditions".[20] They spoke about the appalling conditions under which black workers laboured in the colonies: starvation wages, long hours, bad food and the unsanitary conditions under which black workers and children were compelled to work and live.[21] Ford felt that the conference produced a thorough analysis of the economic and political situation of black people, drew a clear picture of capitalist imperialist oppression, laid down a programme of trade union organization and took up the problems of black workers with the national liberation struggle.[22]

Padmore, in a similar vein as Ford, hailed the conference as "a great success" because it "passed a number of resolutions and decided to establish a permanent organization so as to enable the Negro trade unions and other working class organizations in the different countries to keep in contact and help each other".[23] The Negro Workers Committee was formed at the conference, which Padmore insisted "is not a race, but a class organization, organizing and leading the fight in the interests of Negro workers in Africa, the West Indies and other colonies".[24]

THE LIFE AND STRUGGLES OF NEGRO TOILERS

The fifth RILU Congress was held in August 1930. In the wake of this meeting, the Negro Trade Union Committee was reorganized and renamed the RILU Negro Bureau. Padmore was made chairman of this body. Its main objective was to popularize the decisions and resolutions of the RILU Congress and the Hamburg Conference. The RILU Negro Bureau was to spearhead the international work among black workers by stimulating trade union work, challenging white chauvinism and working at solutions to the problems of the black labour and peasant movement.[25] As chairman of the bureau, Padmore envisioned and delineated a black international to direct the organization of black workers in Africa, the Americas and the West Indies and to closely cooperate with and give advice to the American, British, French, Belgian, Latin American and South African sections of the RILU.[26] Padmore, Grigorij Naumovic Slavin and Sandalio Junco were tasked with the responsibility of writing investigative reports for the Social Economic Department of the RILU on the social and economic conditions of black workers in the United States, South Africa, West Africa, Latin America and the West Indies.[27]

Padmore's report to the RILU was titled *The Life and Struggles of Negro Toilers* and was subsequently published. In it, he extended the discussion of the Hamburg Conference and fashioned a pioneering text of black internationalism that examined the conditions of black workers in Africa, America, the Caribbean and Latin America and the potential of these workers to effect revolutionary change during the crisis facing capitalism. It was a scathing critique of colonialism and the civilizing mission of imperialism. Some socialists and a number of Marxists were still ambivalent about colonialism. In fact, the second International Stuttgart Congress of 1907 demonstrated the contradictory attitude of many socialists toward colonialism, when the congress concluded that the brutality of colonial exploitation should be condemned, but not the entire project of colonialism. Moreover, the congress stated that the "task of the socialists should be to improve and reform colonialism, rather than to carry on a futile and purely negative struggle against it".[28] Some Marxists also supported this position and viewed colonialism as a progressive development bringing modernization to so-called backward societies. Padmore was not swayed by this line of reasoning. For him colonialism was savage, barbaric, exploitative and horrific, and he wanted to see an end to it. He therefore used Lenin's idea of imperialist plunder to characterize the exploitation of black workers in Africa, America, the West Indies and Latin America under colonialism in general and during the crisis of capitalism in particular.

Padmore argued that the "oppression of the Negroes takes two distinctive forms: on the one hand, they are oppressed as a class and on the other, as a nation".[29] Although Padmore was a dedicated Marxist who argued for the primacy of the class struggle, he was cognizant that blacks were oppressed not only as a class but also as a race, and he sought to remind his comrades of this important, but overlooked, reality. Bill Schwarz argues that Padmore, in his analysis, revived the classic Marxist interpretation of imperialism, though he positioned racial oppression at the analytical heart of his critique of capitalism.[30] *The Life and Struggles of Negro Toilers* was not a standard Marxist text but one tailored to address the concerns of black workers and to aid in the organization of a black international.

Racial oppression, argued Padmore, had its origin in the "social-economic relation of the Negro under capitalism". This form of oppression was most conspicuous in the Black Belt of the United States and in South

Africa. However, Padmore opined that the general "conditions under which Negroes live, either as a race or as a class, form one of the most degrading spectacles of bourgeois civilization".[31] Padmore noted that the crisis of world capitalism had exacerbated the stark economic, political and social status of black workers. He recognized that the imperialist powers, in their quest to resolve their problems occasioned by the crisis of capitalism, had intensified the level of exploitation of white workers by the implementation of wage cuts, abolition of social insurance and layoffs. In addition, they were turning their interest "more and more" towards exploiting Africa and the supposedly independent black territories of Haiti and Liberia that were then controlled by US imperialism.[32] The idea of African territories being viewed as the means to overcome the challenges facing the metropolis was nevertheless given new life in the 1930s by the shift of the colonial powers towards new protectionist trade policies.[33]

Padmore felt that he had a duty to educate metropolitan workers about the methods used by European colonizers to "enslave the black colonial and semi-colonial peoples". He opined that this information would allow the "revolutionary working classes in Europe and America to realize the danger ahead of them".[34] Padmore believed it was essential for metropolitan workers to "understand that it is only through the exploitation of the colonial workers, that the capitalists are able to get super-profits from the colonies". These super-profits enabled imperialists "to bribe the reformist and social-fascist trade union bureaucrats" and allow them to "betray the struggles of the workers".[35]

THE CONDITIONS OF BLACK WORKERS THROUGHOUT AFRICA

Padmore noted that there were about two hundred million blacks in the world, the majority being workers on the African continent. With the exception of Ethiopia and Liberia, the entire continent had been colonized by Great Britain, France, Belgium, Portugal, the Netherlands, Spain and Italy. In all African colonies, "Negro toilers" were oppressed; many of them had been removed from their land and placed in reserves, brutally exploited, and a system of forced labour and slave labour was used extensively across the continent. The "Negro toilers" were paid starvation wages and subjected to high taxes. A large section of them lived in subhuman conditions, and they lacked economic and political power.

Padmore estimated that some fifty million black people lived in the African diaspora. In the United States they had to cope with race prejudice, lynching, slavery, peonage and poverty. In the Caribbean, black workers had no political power, and starvation and poverty were widespread. In Latin America, blacks encountered racism and rampant unemployment. Throughout Africa and her diaspora, the stark, exploitative conditions of black workers were exacerbated by the crisis of capitalism.

THE RESPONSE OF BLACK WORKERS TO THE CRISIS OF CAPITALISM

Padmore was more than satisfied with the ferment taking place throughout Africa as a direct result of the crisis of capitalism. This turmoil was manifested in demonstrations, strikes, marches, revolts, uprisings and other forms of protest. He argued that these strategies were a counteroffensive against imperialism and "demonstrated the tremendous revolutionary potentialities of black workers" and revealed their willingness "to wage a relentless struggle against European and American imperialism" as well as their own local collaborators, who were the representatives of the white imperialists.[36] It is important to note that within the Comintern at this time, "every strike, every demonstration was to become an integral component of the immediate struggle for revolution, for socialism".[37] Therefore, Padmore sought to highlight the potential for revolutionary activity given the widespread discontent taking place among black workers globally.

Padmore felt that class-conscious white workers should bring the black workers into the ranks of the revolutionary unions and the labour movement. This would give them the "opportunity of actively participating" and influencing the programmes of the "workers' organizations" in the united front of the working class against capitalism. He firmly believed that if this approach was not followed, the black population would not be won over to the cause of revolutionary struggle. Padmore asserted that there must be no retreat in the face of white chauvinism and only by active engagement would they be able to remove the mistrust that existed between blacks and whites.[38]

Padmore reminded white workers that in the current crisis of capitalism, imperialists were trying to find a way out of their economic predicament on the backs of black workers, particularly in the colonies. As a consequence, "the struggles of the Negro workers against capitalism must be made part and parcel of the common struggle against imperialism". He insisted that the liberation of white workers from the oppression of capitalism could only be achieved by making a definite break with all reformist tendencies and supporting the programme of the Comintern and the RILU.[39]

Padmore also recommended that black workers should take a "more active part in the revolutionary struggles of the working class as a whole". He made the point that black workers must make a decisive break with all bourgeois and petty bourgeois reform movements. It should be noted that after the Comintern abandoned the strategy of "boring from inside" in 1928, non-communist black leaders were condemned as "social fascists", "mis-leaders of labour" and "betrayers of the Negro people".[40] Padmore enthusiastically embraced this new directive and went on the attack against the foremost black leaders in the United States, some of whom he had supported before he became a communist through his pamphlet *What Is the ITUCNW?* and his articles "What Is the ITUCNW?" and the "Bankruptcy of Negro Leaders" in the *Negro Worker*.

He stressed that black workers should not allow themselves to be misled by reformist leaders like W.E.B. Du Bois, Robert Moton and Oscar De Priest. According to Padmore, these "mis-leaders are only office seekers and demagogues paid by the ruling class to trick the Negro masses in order to direct their attention away from the revolutionary struggle into reformist channels".[41] Padmore charged that Du Bois, the editor of the *Crisis*, the mouthpiece of the NAACP, and the leading pan-Africanists who had organized the 1919, 1921, 1923 and 1927 pan-African congresses were trying to take the lead away from the revolutionary movement by playing with "left" phrases on the question of unemployment. Du Bois was an unaffiliated socialist at this time who held the view that the "Marxist class analysis to people of colour had limited validity". Moreover, he argued that it would be imprudent to desert the pragmatic programme for

African American liberation "laid down and thought out by the NAACP by seeking to join a revolution that we do not understand".[42] According to Padmore, Du Bois was telling unemployed blacks to spend their money where they could get employment. This position clearly demonstrated to Padmore that Du Bois and the NAACP were bankrupt and had no programme to lead the people out of their current circumstances.[43] Padmore not only attacked Du Bois, but he also criticized the NAACP, the leading civil rights organization in the United States. Till 1929, the Comintern regarded the NAACP as a reform organization and, while in the recent past some of the leading black communists had worked with the NAACP, according to the new Comintern approach this would no longer be possible. As a student at Fisk University, Padmore had thought highly of Du Bois as an important leader of black people and felt that black youth and students should look to him for guidance and inspiration. Padmore had even reprimanded the students at Fisk who did not attend a lecture given by Du Bois when he visited the campus.[44] Later, after Padmore broke with the Comintern, his assessment of Du Bois changed considerably. In his book *Africa: Britain's Third Empire,* which Padmore dedicated to Du Bois and J.E. Casely Hayford, he described Du Bois as the "father of Pan-Africanism, scholar and Uncompromising Fighter for Human rights".[45] Padmore corresponded regularly with Du Bois when he was organizing the fifth PAC and continued long after the congress. It should also be noted that after his separation from the Comintern, several of his articles were carried in the *Crisis,* the organ of the NAACP.

Padmore berated Robert Moton, "another of the black misleaders", the principal of the Tuskegee Institute, a historically all-black technical institute that trained African Americans mainly in the field of agriculture and industry. Tuskegee was previously headed by Booker T. Washington from its founding in 1881 until his death in 1915. Washington became renowed for his conservative politics and anti-trade union posture. Moton continued in the tradition of his predecessor as being politically conservative and continuing to depend on white capitalist philanthropy. The CPUSA consistently dismissed Tuskegee as a "Jim Crow technical school", and they asserted that Moton asked his students "to slavishly accept the degradation heaped upon them by American imperialism".[46] Padmore also assailed Oscar De Priest, the first African American to be elected to the US Congress, in 1928. De Priest, who was seen as the leader of all African Americans, was a staunch opponent of communism. Padmore accused De Priest of opposing a bill that demanded relief for the unemployed because he considered it "un-American" for the government to provide assistance to the unemployed. Padmore felt that by taking this stance, De Priest clearly demonstrated his support for the "policy of President Hoover and the capitalist rulers of America that the unemployed must starve or depend on the charity of the Salvation Army and other private institutions".[47] De Priest was opposed to federal grants for the states to be used for relief purposes and only changed his position in 1932 because of circumstances in his congressional district in Illinois.[48] Communist leaders stated that De Priest must be disgraced for his anti-communist position and the reactionary position that he took on many issues that affected African Americans and his constituents. Padmore's condemnation of De Priest was in keeping with communist dictates.

Padmore stressed that black workers had to carry out an unrelenting struggle against the leadership of black trade unions, whose main goal was to mislead the "struggles of the Negroes on the economic front". He remarked that the BSCP had once been the largest mass organization among black workers but because of the unscrupulous strategies pursued by A. Philip Randolph and his supporters, the organization was on the brink of ruin.[49] Randolph, constantly under attack by Padmore and the CPUSA for his conservatism, was a socialist and used the pages of the *Messenger*, which he edited with Chandler Owen, to attack communism and the American Negro Labor Congress.[50] After leaving the Comintern, Padmore referred to Randolph as one of "the most distinguished Afro-American socialists".[51]

Padmore compared the BSCP to the Industrial Commercial Union (ICU) in South Africa and asserted that "Negroes in South Africa must conduct a sharper struggle" against the strategies of Clements Kadalie, A.W.G. Champion and William Ballinger, "the chief splitters of the working class movement among the blacks".[52] Kadalie founded the ICU in Cape Town in 1919, and by 1927, the ICU had over one hundred thousand members. The misuse of funds, mismanagement and factional fighting, however, reduced the membership of the union.⁵³ Champion was the national secretary of the ICU and president of the Transvaal Mine Clerks Association and led the splinter group of the ICU in Natal.⁵⁴ Ballinger was a trade union organizer who was sent to South Africa by the British Independent Labour Party (ILP) in 1928 to advise the ICU. However, Ballinger ended up leading a section of the ICU.⁵⁵ The communists within the ICU wanted a more militant policy of industrial engagement to curb the power of the leaders and to control the finances of the organization.⁵⁶ Kadalie was led to believe that if he expelled the communists, the government would recognize the organization. The ICU would become a member of the International Federation of Trade Unions, also known as the Amsterdam International because the Constituent Congress had been held in Amsterdam in July 1919. The Amsterdam International was made up of social democratic trade unions and not Marxist-Leninist trade unions. In 1926, Kadalie sponsored a resolution that excluded all communists from holding office in the ICU. This led to communists leaving the ICU, "which weakened the workers' resistance to capitalist attacks". Padmore accused Kadalie of having "an unparalleled record of betrayals of the struggles of the natives of South Africa".⁵⁷ It must be mentioned that after Padmore broke with the Comintern, he constructed new, healthy relations with these black leaders and sought to present Kadalie as "an able organizer", the "uncrowned King of the black masses" and the "greatest challenge the white man has yet faced in South Africa".⁵⁸

Padmore argued that the struggle against Garveyism represented one of the major tasks of the black workers in America, Africa and the West Indies. His position on Garvey had changed considerably from his days in Trinidad and when he had led a protest at Howard University, where he had referred to Garvey as a champion of freedom. Additionally, his position had shifted from the more measured critique he had written a few years before in his article "Marcus Garvey, Misleader of His Race: Negro Workers Vote Communist". In that article Padmore confessed that "Garveyism has done much to arouse the consciousness of the Negro masses in America and other parts of the world". He contended that Garvey was "persecuted by the American capitalist class and lackeys because he dared to attempt to organize black workers, whose labour power represents untold wealth and profit for the Wall Street exploiters in America".[59]

Padmore's attack on Garvey was largely motivated by the sixth Congress of the Comintern in 1928, which declared open war against the UNIA because its leaders rejected communist overtures in their attempt to exploit the organization. The directive stated that

> Garveyism, at one time the ideology of the American Negro petty bourgeoisie and workers, and still with a certain influence over the Negro masses, today impedes the movement of these masses towards a revolutionary position. While at first advocating complete social equality for Negroes, it turned into a kind of 'Negro Zionism' which instead of fighting American imperialism advanced the slogan 'Back to Africa'. This dangerous ideology without a democratic feature ... must be vigorously resisted for it does not promote but hampers the struggles of the Negro masses for liberation from American imperialism.[60]

At the fourth Congress of the Comintern (1922), the Surinamese Otto Huiswoud, the first black member of the CPUSA and one of its delegates, addressed the gathering on the condition of black people in the United States and recommended that communists form a common front with the radical rank-and-file of Garvey's movement.[61] The delegates of the CPUSA acknowledged the "Negro Question" as an important issue of the world revolution. The Comintern had praised the UNIA for its wide base and its anti-colonial stance. Although the delegates from the CPUSA were critical of its strategy and rhetoric, they expressed the hope that communists could infiltrate the UNIA and "transform it into an organization fighting for the class interests of the Negro workers in the United States".[62] Communists also felt that Garveyism could become a vehicle for carrying the communist revolutionary message to Africa. But with the new policy, Garveyism was seen as a reactionary force no longer fit for Comintern support. This directive re-energized communist attacks on Garvey, and Padmore became one of the foremost critics of Garvey, as evident in his writings. It is strange that Padmore and the CPUSA would spend so much energy discrediting Garvey when the UNIA was in decline by this time. The answer lies in Padmore's awareness that even though the UNIA movement had splintered during the imprisonment and deportation of Garvey from the United States, Garveyism was still strong among sections of black workers in the United States and the Caribbean.

Henry Kendal, a Garveyite from British Guiana, was outraged at Padmore for his constant vilification of Garvey. Padmore's disparagement of Garvey in the article "What Is the International Trade Union Committee of Negro Workers?" so incensed Kendal that he wrote a letter to Padmore expressing his annoyance and bewilderment at the way Padmore described Garvey.[63] Kendal credited Garvey with "speaking about a free Africa and nationalism for Africans at home and abroad". Kendal asked Padmore: "Why as a leader of the race should you count a man like Garvey among the crooks of the world?" He told Padmore that the black people of British Guiana "do not like your constant attacks on Garvey", and because of these criticisms, "your work will not get as much hearing as it ought to get". Kendal told Padmore to stop criticizing Garvey and "strike your blows at one side and leave Garvey on the other".[64] He, however, wanted to be a representative "for the *Negro Worker* and the good books which are showing the wrongs done to our people in Africa and all over the world". He stressed his love for the ITUCNW's work but insisted that "for God Allmighty's sake leave the African's leader, the Hon. Marcus Garvey alone, the first man who put Africa before us".[65]

After leaving the Comintern, Padmore stated that Garvey most definitely made a marked contribution to the struggle for African awakening and that this fact was recognized by even his bitterest opponents. He further sought to vindicate Garvey by pointing out that "nobody really believed that Garvey was an unscrupulous demagogue" out to defraud the black working class. "Garvey was born poor, lived moderately and died even poorer than he was born."[66] Padmore admitted that Garvey was undoubtedly "one of the greatest Negroes since emancipation, a visionary who inspired his race in its upward struggle from degradation of centuries of slavery".[67] He called Garvey the greatest black leader since Toussaint L'Overture.[68] For Padmore, Garvey put steel into the spine of many blacks who had previously been ashamed of their colour and their association with the black race by emphasizing the rich tradition of their African past, racial pride and the virtue of blackness.⁶⁹ While Padmore's characterization of Garvey changed considerably, it was unfortunate that C.L.R. James and Padmore, two of the leading anti-imperialists in Britain, heckled Garvey at a meetings in London in the mid-1930s and "expose[d] him particularly to people who might have been misled by his great reputation" because they believed him guilty of lauding British imperialism for civilizing the inhabitants of Africa.⁷⁰

ITUCNW/HAMBURG COMMITTEE

The objectives of the ITUCNW were as follows:

1. To carry on propaganda and agitation, calling upon the Negro workers to organize themselves into revolutionary trade unions in order to fight for higher wages, shorter hours and better conditions.
2. To help the millions of Negro workers who are now unemployed organize councils in order to demand relief from the government, free rent and non-payment of taxes.
3. To agitate and organize the Negro Workers against the approaching imperialist war and the intervention in Soviet Russia, in which the white capitalist exploiters intend to use black workers as cannon-fodder as they did in the last war.
4. To promote and develop the spirit of international solidarity between the workers of all colurs and nationalities, calling upon them to support the Soviet Union which fights for the freedom of the working class and all oppressed peoples, as well as the Chinese, Indian, South African and all other revolutionary liberation movements of the colonial toilers.
5. The Committee also fights against white chauvinism, (race prejudice) social-reformism and the reformists programmes of the Negro capitalist misleaders, like Marcus Garvey, Du Bois, Pickens and Walter White of the National Association of Colored People in America; Kadalie and Champion in South Africa, the white trade union faker, Captain Cipriani, in the West Indies; and the missionaries, preachers and other agents of imperialism.⁷¹

In October 1931, the RILU Negro Bureau and the RILU Secretariat reorganized the ITUCNW/Hamburg Committee. The Negro Section of the Eastern Secretariat in its January 1931 resolution envisioned the ITUCNW becoming the assembling body for all areas of the African Atlantic, including Africa and the United States. However, the RILU Secretariat proposed a much more restricted role for the organization. It felt that the ITUCNW/Hamburg Committee should concentrate its work on Africa and the Caribbean. The Political Commission sought to arbitrate the discussion and rejected the suggestion that the ITUCNW should become an international black organization with a focus on African and Caribbean colonies.[72] James Ford was removed as the executive secretary and Padmore was installed as the new one. According to Jan Valtin, a former Comintern operative, "a more efficient colleague, one George Padmore arrived from Moscow to take charge of the Negro Committee".[73] Valtin was clearly not impressed with Ford's work. He opined that Ford was too "much of an intellectual to be a revolutionary activist".[74] Although the idea of transforming the ITUCNW into a black international that would concentrate its work in Africa, the Caribbean, the United States and Europe at the time of Padmore's transfer was rejected, it seems that privately Padmore still harboured thoughts of making the organization the vanguard of black internationalism globally. Hakim Adi states that "Padmore continually attempted to direct some of the Negro work in the United States, France, Britain and elsewhere even though this was not his responsibility".[75] It was clear that Padmore's vision was larger than that of the ITUCNW mandate. He wanted a black international that was not restricted geographically. The ITUCNW furnished Padmore with the infrastructure to promote the black international of the Comintern and to achieve his objective of attacking and undermining colonial rule in Africa.

EDITOR OF THE *NEGRO WORKER*

Padmore was one of the most prolific pamphleteers for the ITUCNW. During the early life of the committee, Padmore wrote six of the organization's twenty-five published pamphlets, and many of his essays were reprinted in journals. He wrote *What Is the International Trade Union*

Committee of Negro Workers?, *The Life and Struggles of the Negro Toilers*, *Negro Workers and the Imperialist War*, *Forced Labour in Africa*, *American Imperialism Enslaves Liberia* and *Labour Imperialism and East Africa*. However, his most important contribution as a propagandist was his editorship of the *Negro Worker*, to which he was appointed in November 1931. Between 1928 and 1929 the *International Negro Workers' Review* was edited by James Ford and it was rebranded as the *Negro Worker*. The *Negro Worker* was the principal medium the Comintern used to try to win Africans to its revolutionary cause. It was the main weapon Padmore used to attack the colonialism in Africa and the Caribbean, and it was one of the main vehicles that facilitated the spread of black internationalism between 1931 and 1934.[76]

Lenin, in *What Is to Be Done?*, affirmed that "a newspaper is not only a collective propagandist and a collective agitator; it is also a collective organizer".[77] As a disciple of Lenin, Padmore clearly understood the power of political journalism and the benefits that could be derived from using this medium. In the report he gave to the Comintern officials in Russia on his first visit in 1929, he put forward the idea of creating a mass organ for black workers and creating special leaflets and bulletins to deal with their everyday problems. Padmore argued that "without a fighting paper we cannot build a real revolutionary movement".[78] Theodore Kornweibel makes the point that journalism for oppressed people anywhere in the modern world has proven to be a potent weapon.[79] Theodore Vincent argues that "the press is an organizing device. It orders, shapes and directs the consciousness of its readers", and "creates a community among that readership, who are all simultaneously exposed to the same experience its pages provide".[80] The *Negro Worker* provided Padmore with the organizing infrastructure to promote and build a black international.

When Padmore was made editor he was instructed that the *Negro Worker* should be built into a popular journal, the articles should be written in simple style and they should deal with the burning everyday problems of black workers as well as all problems confronting the international working class, such as the threat of war and the defence of the USSR.[81] In his first editorial Padmore noted: "This journal is the official organ of the ITUCNW." However, it was his intention "not to make this a sort of theoretical journal to discuss resolutions, opinions, etc.".[82] Anyone who is familiar with Marxist writing knows how dense, abstract and theoretical it can be. However, Padmore, as an engaged Marxist, was more concerned with action than abstract theory. In a letter to Ollivierre, he wrote that he was pleased that the articles in the *Labour Monthly* were intellectually stimulating, but "I am not so interested in this kind of highbrow stuff as in getting rid of the damn white blood suckers from the W.I. and Africa."[83] Padmore wanted a paper "to discuss and analyse the day to day problems of the Negro toilers and connect these with the international struggles and the problems of the workers". He felt that this was the only "way that we can build a much needed popular journal, taking up the broad problems of Negro Workers".[84] He invited leading black communists from Africa and the Caribbean to occasionally contribute something to the *Negro Worker* in order to "assist us in popularizing it among the Negro workers". He instructed them to "be merciless in your criticism, with the object of helping us make the *Negro Worker* a popular organ carrying on the struggle against imperialism and for the emancipation of the black toiling masses".[85]

When Padmore became the executive secretary of ITUCNW, the organization had about sixty contacts in Africa and the Caribbean. A year later Padmore reported that he had established thousands of new contacts in Gambia, Sierra Leone, the Gold Coast, Nigeria, South Africa, Belgian Congo, Kenya, Uganda, Tanganyika, Jamaica, Haiti, Barbados, Trinidad, Grenada, St Lucia, the Virgin Islands, Bermuda, British Guiana, Panama and British Honduras. In addition, he claimed that he had established hundreds of contacts in the United States, England and France.[86] These contacts were important for the distribution of the *Negro Worker*. In 1932, Padmore took the decision to distribute the journal for free in order to ensure that it was more widely disseminated and read. The circulation moved from about one thousand copies at the time of Padmore's takeover to about five thousand copies by the end of the year.[87]

Padmore recognized that capitalists were seeking to prevent the paper from being widely distributed in Africa and the West Indies, fearful that if the workers read the *Negro Worker* they would begin to agitate for their rights. According to Padmore, "The systematic persecution of the *Negro*

Worker in the colonies is the best indication that our organ is meeting with popular support."⁸⁸ Valtin disclosed that "since the contents of the *Negro Worker* were very inflammatory, the greater portion of each edition had to be smuggled to its destinations by the maritime couriers".⁸⁹ In British West Africa, vessels arriving from Europe were searched regularly for copies of the *Negro Worker*, and the British government imposed lengthy prison sentences on residents found with it in their possession.⁹⁰ The paper was subsequently banned in Nigeria and Trinidad. Copies of the *Negro Worker* were, nevertheless, smuggled to many colonial ports, evading bans imposed by colonial governments.

According to Edward Wilson, although Padmore contributed numerous articles and editorials as editor of the *Negro Worker*, the general themes of his writings were clearly prescribed by higher Comintern authorities, particularly by the organization's Russian leadership.⁹¹ To support his contention, he states that three features of the Soviet experience were emphasized: the economic system of the Soviet Union was held up as a model that Africans should adopt in order to abolish exploitation and to achieve rapid economic and social progress, the federally organized political structure of the Soviet Union was presented as the answer both to the general problem of obtaining political emancipation and the more specific problem of securing full and equal rights for national minorities and Africans were promised that by following the Soviet example they could achieve racial equality.⁹² Wilson repeated what Ivan Potekin had stated, that "although others edited the paper, we determined its direction because the Comintern had greater experience".⁹³ But while the *Negro Worker* provided a space to highlight the benefits of the Soviet experiment, it also afforded a forum for information about political developments in Africa and the struggles of blacks generally. Therefore, whether Africans wrote the articles or the Comintern, as alleged, readers were informed about global black struggles. The paper also allowed readers to become familiar with the names of important African Marxists – Albert Nzula, Garan Kouyatè, Jomo Kenyatta, Edward Small and I.T.A. Wallace-Johnson – who played important roles in the Comintern's black internationalism. Wilson held the view that while the *Negro Worker* was an instrument for spreading propaganda and revolutionary advice for the Comintern, it also "provided one of the first channels for political communication among Africans".⁹⁴ C.L.R. James stated that the *Negro Worker* gave "information, advice, guidance, ideas about black struggles on every continent" and was of the view that in addition to an ideology the oppressed needed a consciousness that they were not alone.⁹⁵ This was "what the *Negro Worker* gave to the sweating and struggling thousands in the West Indies, in Nigeria, in South Africa".⁹⁶

It must be mentioned that Padmore was responsible for the change in the name of the paper from the *International Workers' Review* to the *Negro Worker*. Padmore, as head of the RILU Negro Bureau, had instructed Ford to change the name. The *Negro Worker* was shorter and therefore more easily made popular among black workers. Furthermore, the title *Negro Worker* communicated "more clearly and definitely" the central objective "of our Committee", that it is only by "the organization and leadership of the workers, that the Negro toilers can successfully carry on the struggle for their freedom and emancipation".⁹⁷ The journal was also given a new design on the cover – a picture of a black worker breaking the chains of enslavement that bound blacks in the United States, West Indies and Africa. The black worker on the cover symbolized the power and strength that lay in the organization of black workers for the class struggle and through which they could join hands with the workers of the world.⁹⁸ Mikah Makalani reminds us that this image was used by the ANLC on its letterhead, pamphlets and flyers.⁹⁹ Padmore felt that the use of the image of the black man breaking his chains "will help to establish a certain familiarity among the workers for our literature and at the same time convey the idea that only the workers themselves can break the chain".¹⁰⁰

The black internationalist project of Padmore, the Comintern and the pan-Africanist mission appeared to be ideologically quite similar and historian Imanuel Geiss argues that while Padmore was the chief editor, the content of the *Negro Worker* was pan-African in the widest sense. He contends that the very title and cover design of the *Negro Worker* point in this direction.¹⁰¹ Geiss explains that communism and pan-Africanism were "opposed to colonialism and imperialism, although with a different intensity and for different motives; this necessarily gave them a certain common ground".[102] The Comintern's black internationalism resembled pan-Africanism in its efforts to explain the exploitation of Africans and people of African descent, the major difference being its emphasis on class and the class struggle rather than race and the racial struggle. Geiss asserts that except for Garvey's journal the *Black Man*, which appeared only sporadically in the early thirties, the *Negro Worker* was the only pan-African organ at the time. It thus fulfilled a pan-African as well as a communist function.[103]

One must remember that Padmore joined the Communist Party because he felt it would provide a place for him to work for the liberation of his people. The *Negro Worker* provided Padmore with a medium to attack capitalism and the colonial system. In his article "Hands Off Liberia", Padmore wrote that "Liberia had become an economic colony of American imperialism and the peasantry the slaves of the Government and Firestone Co.".[104] In the previous chapter, I discussed how Padmore wrote to Nnamdi Azikiwe for assistance in forming a pan-African organization to protect Liberia's independence, which was being threatened by the Firestone Corporation. He also wrote a pamphlet entitled *American Imperialism Enslaves Liberia*. Padmore contended that the conditions of black workers on American plantations and big farms owned by local officials in Liberia were so disgraceful that an investigation should be conducted.[105] In June 1929, the US State Department informed the Liberian government that reports were circulating about the export of Liberians to Bioko, then known as Fernando Pó. The League of Nations sent a fact-finding commission to Liberia. The ensuing report noted that the Americo-Liberians who controlled the government and who had made the agreement with Firestone in 1925 were forcing thousands of Liberians to work without wages under terrible conditions and that slavery and forced labour were pervasive throughout Liberia. The commission recommended that Liberia abandon its "closed-door" policy, re-establish the authority of the chiefs, appoint Americans to administrative positions in the government, declare domestic slavery and pawning illegal, cease the shipment of labourers to Bioko and other foreign places, increase discipline over the military forces and encourage African American immigration.[106]

In Padmore's view, the commission's report exonerated Firestone from the charge that it used forced labour. Padmore argued forcefully that it was common knowledge that thousands of Liberians were "ruthlessly exploited on Firestone plantations". He was adamant that the commission sanitized the "crimes of Firestone" and discredited the already corrupt Americo-Liberian officials, "thereby justifying the American imperialists with the tacit connivance of the League of Nations to openly annex" the only independent black nation in West Africa.[107] The findings of the commission indicted the C.B. King administration and not Firestone for ruthlessly exploiting Liberian workers.

Padmore argued that black workers in Africa, the United States and the West Indies had to realize that the enslavement of Liberia had not only been organized and carried out by American imperialists and their white agents, but by influential blacks in the United States and Liberia. Dr Charles Johnson, a professor at Fisk University, who sat on the commission as a representative of the US government, was excoriated by Padmore for playing the "role of a Judas" in concealing the misdemeanours of "the white American capitalists" and giving the impression that "only President King and his officials were guilty of extorting forced labour out of the indigenous masses".[108] Dr Johnson was selected to sit on the commission because a section of the ruling oligarchs wanted "a suitable black man" to sit on the commission. This was clearly articulated by Undersecretary of State William Castle, who felt that if the inquiry substantiated the existence of slavery and the collusion of the government, "it would make a much better impression among the Negroes of this country if the report were signed by a man of their own race".[109] Padmore was extremely critical of the journalist George Schuyler, editor of the *Courier*, whom he accused of seeking to "white wash Firestone" for its misdemeanours against exploited Liberians. Schuyler, who was sent to Liberia by a number of newspapers, had written some articles on developments in Liberia. These articles, in Padmore's opinion, glorified "Firestone's love and kindness for the Africans".[110] It should be pointed out that Schuyler later became well-known for his anti-communist views. Padmore believed that the US press was trying to absolve Firestone of any responsibility for the pervasive presence of forced labour in Liberia and was supporting "the American capitalists in Africa" by indicating their ethical responsibility as "self-appointed trustees like Great Britain". He sensed that the groundwork was being laid for the enslavement of Liberia, and he predicted that the next step would be the open annexation of the country as a colony of US imperialism under the guise of a mandate.[111]

To support his position, Padmore cited a number of influential spokesmen, including W.G. Ormsby-Gore, member of Parliament and former undersecretary of state for the colonies, who believed Liberia "should be taken over by one of the white nations and put in proper order".[112] R.C.F. Maughan, a former British consul general to Liberia, stated that "the administration" of Liberia should be removed from the jurisdiction of Liberians and administered by either the League of Nations, under the mandatory system, or one "of the great colonizing powers".[113] In Padmore's view, these sentiments exposed the plan of capitalist powers to deprive Liberia of its sovereignty and to intensify the exploitation of the country's working class. He felt that the existing situation in Liberia called for a determined struggle on the part of the international working class, especially the proletariat in the United States, against the ruthless exploitation by US capitalists in Africa. He called on the dockworkers and "seamen to organize themselves into trade unions" as the starting point for the "development of a broad mass anti-imperialist movement". Moreover, he stressed that Liberian workers must "not put their faith in the Americo-Liberian politicians but they must develop leaders from the ranks of their own class".[114]

Padmore, in "How the Empire Is Governed", made the point that for hundreds of years the ruling class of Britain had maintained its control over colonized people through deceit, hypocrisy and corruption. However, when these approaches failed, its only recourse was using "brute force and terrorism" to maintain its authority.[115] In Africa, the British used divide-and-rule tactics, initially using chiefs to this end and when that no longer worked, isolating intellectuals from the people, thereby weakening the nationalist movement and retarding the "anti-imperialist struggle for freedom and self-determination". The British government, Padmore observed, co-opted many of the intellectuals by promising them important jobs in the colonial service, and a number of them who once were opposed to British colonialism and defenders of the people were "won over by the skilful manoeuvring of the white officials and missionaries – agents of the imperialists". In addition to jobs, they were also "given decorative seats on the legislative councils, decorated with some medal or title such as the Order of the British Empire, or given a knighthood".[116]

Padmore observed that in the West Indies the black bourgeoisie and upper middle class were the most "bribable strata of the population". British rulers had used the "colour caste system", an artificial method of dividing the population, to prevent the formation of a dangerous anti-imperialist united front. Economic and political power was vested in the hands of the whites, who employed the offspring of whites and blacks as overseers to keep the black population subjected. Thus, whenever black workers rebelled against oppressive taxation or any kind of "imperialist robbery", they noticed that the individuals who were in the direct line of their ire were the biracial supervisors "who shelter the real blood suckers, the white imperialists".[117]

According to Padmore, British imperialists cultivated "many illusions" among colonized blacks and deceived millions about the real purpose of their presence in colonies. Churches, missionary schools, Boy Scouts and Girls Guides and flag-waving ceremonies, especially Empire Day, were all brought into full play in the service of British imperialism. The most widespread illusion in Africa and the West Indies was that the Union Jack was the symbol of "justice" and "fair play" for all, "white or black, rich or poor". Padmore noted that this was repeated over and over again and that even though blacks were treated like slaves, many of them believed this.[118]

Padmore asserted that blacks in Africa and the West Indies could never free themselves from their colonial masters by themselves. Victory could only be achieved when the workers of India, Ireland, Britain "and other parts of the Empire realize that theirs is a common struggle with ours. That the same rulers who oppress them, also oppress us." He opined that "as long as the British imperialists" were capable of keeping the struggles of blacks separate from other struggles, they would continue their dominance throughout Africa and the West Indies. Padmore made a plea for all oppressed peoples in Britain and its colonies to unite in opposition to the "common Enemy".[119]

In his article "How the Imperialists Are Civilizing Africa", Padmore wrote that "every exploiting class always attempts to create some ideology to justify their oppression" and this is precisely what capitalists were doing in Africa. Capitalists hoped to convince white labourers in Europe that their role in their colonies was not to exploit the inhabitants, "but to carry the blessings of civilization to these benighted masses". Using this rationale, imperialists were suggesting that Africans and other subjected races had no basis for dissatisfaction and no need to revolt. Padmore noted that capitalists and their representatives were trying their utmost to conceal the true extent of their bloodstained tyranny in the colonies and "mobilize the more backward strata of the European workers to support their robber policies by promising them a share in the spoils".[120]

In communist circles during the third period, social democratic parties and reformist trade unions were perceived as the most dangerous enemy precisely because they retained widespread working-class support.[121] The majority of these groups were members of the Labour and Socialist International, which was established in 1923 as the successor to the Second International. Padmore saw social democrats as "traitors of the European workers" and "the greatest enemies of the colonial masses". He argued that Ramsay MacDonald, the prime minister of Britain, and Arthur Henderson, the British foreign minister, were the vilest oppressors of workers in Africa, India and China. He was critical of MacDonald and Henderson because even though they were members of the British Labour Party, a social democratic party with ties to the trade union movement, they had no qualms about oppressing colonial workers. In Padmore's opinion, the British Labour government was an imperialist government that enabled British capitalists to profit immensely from the exploitation of colonized workers. He felt that their record was no different from that of Stanley Baldwin and Winston Churchill, two of the leading members of the Conservative Party, and the "other openly reactionary politicians for suppressing every attempt of the colonial peoples for freedom".[122]

In a similar vein, Padmore denounced French socialists including Joseph Paul-Boncour, the French prime minister, and Léon Jouhaux, a long-serving secretary of the Confédération générale du travail unitaire, whom he labelled not only "the worst types of chauvinists, but the very ones actively helping the French bankers and concessionaries to squeeze millions of francs out of the sweat and blood of the Negroes in Africa and the workers of Indo-China". Like their British counterparts, socialists in France had shown little regard for colonized workers while being seen as champions of the trade union movement at home. To Padmore, socialists in Belgium were in a class by themselves. Led by Emile Vandervelde, the president of the Second International and first member of the Belgian Labour Party to hold a position as a minister (Foreign Affairs), they had not only offered themselves as the "watchdogs" of Belgian imperialism, but they themselves took an active part in the looting of the Congo. They were not satisfied with "grinding super-profits" out of black workers, but "they vote[d] millions of francs in the Belgian parliament for the maintenance of a huge military force in the Congo in order to suppress revolts". The same was true of Dutch socialists in Indonesia and the West Indies.[123] It was clear that while social democratic parties championed trade unionism in metropolises, they turned a blind eye to the exploitation taking place in the colonies. Lenin had described socialists as "chauvinists and lackeys of blood-stained and filthy imperialist monarchies and the imperial bourgeoisie" because of their failure to demand self-determination for the colonies and extend their revolutionary propaganda and revolutionary mass activity directly to the struggle against national oppression.[124]

COMINTERN OPERATIVE

Given the mystery surrounding Padmore's work as a Comintern operative, it is difficult to "determine the nature of his clandestine activity".[125] According to Roi Ottley, "Padmore was a first-class conspirator, a specialist in decoys, codes and stratagems." Ottley claims he was made a colonel in the Red Army and had unlimited funds at his disposal for this secretive work. He adds that Padmore was dispatched to organize in Europe and Africa and "a network of communists in Europe facilitated his movements legal and illegal".[126] There is no evidence to suggest that Padmore was ever made a colonel in the Red Army. It was true that from his base in Hamburg, he attended to Comintern business and was entrusted with funds to recruit agents to go to Moscow.[127] Part of the operation of the Hamburg Committee was to participate in an underground communications network for Comintern operations. Therefore, Padmore in his capacity as the executive secretary of ITUCNW would have provided courier services for the Comintern.

Harvey Klehr, John Haynes and Fridrikh Firsov shed some light on the modus operandi of a Comintern operative. They note that operatives "often travelled on false passports, entered countries illegally and carried large amounts of cash and valuables to distribute secretly to local party leaders and organizations". They add that the Comintern would regularly issue "instructions and pleas to its member parties to form secret units, train cadres to operate illegally and prepare systems of safe houses and fake identification documents to protect its key officials in case of repression by hostile governments".[128]

ARREST AND DEPORTATION

Padmore was arrested by the Altona police in Hamburg in February 1933. He was imprisoned for two weeks before he was deported to Britain (he held a British passport). The police confiscated all of the copies of the *Negro Worker* they found as well as other progressive literature that connected Padmore to the revolutionary movement. From his interfacing with the British Central Intelligence Department, Padmore was able to get a sense of the impact of his work in Africa. He remarked that the officers "made enquiries about the famous G.P., whom I professed not to know, only having read about. They were very bitter in their denunciation of this bastard."[129] The police were unaware that Malcolm Nurse, whom they had arrested, and George Padmore were the same individual. In one of his letters to Ollivierre, Padmore revealed that "the British and French have a reward on my head. They say I am their greatest black enemy."[130] During his short stay in Britain, his friend Arnold Ward of the Negro Welfare Association assisted him financially before he went to France. In France, Padmore lived with Garan Kouyatè, the founder of the Ligue de défense de la race nègre and the editor of *La Race Nègre* and *La Cri des nègres*.

BREAK WITH THE COMINTERN: RESIGNATION OR EXPULSION?

In March 1933, shortly after his arrival in France, Padmore got a letter from Alexander Zusmanovich of the RILU indicating that "as a result of the last events", the committee would be taking on a new name, International Committee for Mutual Aid to Negro Workers. The letter was extremely critical of Padmore's work and suggested that the "former master of disguises, first-class conspirator and specialist in decoys, codes and stratagems" had become sloppy and suggested that he change his modus operandi.[131] The letter stated:

> We cannot allow such a situation as existed before to continue.... [Y]our activities must be based on a skillful combination of legal, semi-illegal and illegal methods of work as the occasion arises. We want to call your attention in a comradely manner to the fact that you must radically change your method of work. Concretely and firstly not to leave so many traces of yourself not in your mass work but on a quite personal basis. Not only should you not speak in open meetings but create an *"active"* around you through which you must work in your present place and in the other place.
>
> It is important to stress here the absolute necessity for collective work and not individualist business relationships. In this respect there is much to be required of you in the way of quitting some of your inclinations in this direction. You have a good opportunity for collective work now.[132]

Valtin reminds us that in Comintern service, to become conspicuous meant to become useless for conspirative work.[133]

The letter was particularly harsh on Padmore in relation to the recruits he was sending for training: "We want to draw your attention to the question of selection of students. It is intolerable for you to send people that you don't know.... As a rule you have no right to send people whom you have not thoroughly investigated from every aspect."[134] The latter charge had some merit. A good example of Padmore's lack of meticulousness was evident in the correspondence between Padmore and Kobina Sekyi, the pan-Africanist from the Aboriginal Rights Protection Society in the Gold Coast. Padmore wrote Sekyi and asked for his help in a "scheme to send African workers from the Gold Coast to study in Europe" where they would be able to assist "the toiling masses of the Gold Coast in organizing themselves for better economic and social conditions".¹³⁵ Padmore's major criterion for the selection of candidates was their commitment to the liberation of Africa from colonial rule rather than an allegiance to the tenets of Marxism-Leninism. Padmore wrote to Sekyi, "I often dream of the day when every black boy and girl in mother Africa will be guaranteed a proper, sanitary home; good, healthy food and every educational opportunity."¹³⁶ According to Samuel Rohdie, Sekyi shared this dream.¹³⁷ In a letter to an unnamed reporter, Padmore stated that "[w]e are waiting for 100% Bolsheviks to come out of Central Africa. No, Comrades, it is our task to get hold of the raw people and send them back 100% Bolsheviks."¹³⁸ Padmore had instructed I.T.A. Wallace-Johnson (editor of the *Nigerian Daily Telegraph*, general secretary of the African Workers Union, executive member of the ITUCNW, member of the editorial board of the *Negro Worker*, and one of Padmore's West African contacts who assisted him in recruiting Africans for training in Moscow) to select young, working-class men who were in good health and able to read and write. He depended on Wallace-Johnson to select students with the right character and dedication to the cause.¹³⁹ The students were to be trained to be revolutionaries and return to Africa to mobilize peasants and workers for the struggle against colonialism.

At the same time, as James pointed out, "conflicts between the Africans who had come to Russia for training and the communists were endless".¹⁴⁰ In early 1933, the students at KUTV sent a petition to the Comintern with a litany of complaints: the appalling conditions at the KUTV, the quality of English spoken by the teachers at KUTV, Russian textbooks, the meagre fee they received for living expenses and the unsatisfactory condition of the food and laundry services.¹⁴¹ There were also ideological tensions between the Africans and the Russian administrators at KUTV because the Africans were more committed to African nationalism than to the tenets of Marxism-Leninism. According to Moscow officials, very few of the African students became committed communists. Some of them never fully accepted Marxism-Leninism, never joined a communist party and were union activists.¹⁴² E.F. Small, the leader of Bathurst Trade Union in Gambia, who assisted Padmore in recruiting students from West Africa, held the view that it "would be a big mistake to have future cadres educated in Moscow with such a limited understanding of the realities of the African masses". He was quite clear that "Africans are exploited as a mass and not a class and the Negro problem can only be solved if it is analysed from a racial rather than a class perspective".[143]

RESIGNATION

Joyce Moore Turner is of the view that Padmore did not take kindly to the accusations raised in Zusmanovich's letter and subsequently resigned as the editor of the *Negro Worker*.[144] One should note that Padmore resigned in August 1933, some four months after receiving this critical evaluation and not immediately after. Zusmanovich had told Rolf Italiaander that the RILU often received complaints from Hamburg concerning Padmore's obstinacy.[145] Padmore's tenacious struggle against the bureaucracy within the Comintern was viewed by some elements in the Comintern as stubbornness. For example, he had to fight hard to get money, food and accommodation for the delegates he brought from Africa to attend the first International Negro Workers Conference.[146] Padmore had several battles with Max Ziese, the head of the RILU Bureau in Berlin and the International Communications Office of the Comintern, and comrades of the International of Seamen and Harbour Workers for funds. He had to struggle against bureaucratic bungling and confusion to have *The Life and Struggles of Negro Toilers* published. Indeed, the comrades at the Negro Bureau wrote a letter complaining that it was taking too long to have the book published.[147] In 1931 Padmore wrote a letter to the Negro Bureau complaining about Ziese's chauvinistic and racist attitudes after he refused to assist two Africans who were stranded in Berlin.[148] The above examples are just a few of the many battles Padmore fought against the various arms of the Comintern bureaucracy that negated the effectiveness of his work in the RILU and ITUCNW and which led to him being labelled as stubborn. Susan Pennybacker has hinted that Padmore's struggles against the Comintern bureaucratic structures frustrated him.[149] I am in agreement with Pennybacker's assessment and strongly believe that these battles with the Comintern bureaucracy played a major role in his severing his ties with the Comintern.

The comradely advice in Zusmanovich's letter added to Padmore's disappointment and frustration with the Comintern. This letter in many ways represented the proverbial straw that led to his resignation as the editor of the *Negro Worker*. However, in reading his letter of resignation ("Au Revoir") that was carried in the *Negro Worker,* not the slightest hint of animosity is present. Padmore wrote with deep regret: "I relinquish my position as Editor of the *Negro Worker.*" In fact, he stated that he hoped that the "magazine would go on forever". Padmore explained that for the three years he was the editor, the *Negro Worker* was faced with serious financial challenges, despite the fact that the journal was well received by blacks in the United States, Africa and the West Indies. The *Negro Worker* was also popular among "the anti-imperialist masses in the Far East and the white proletariat in England and America".[150]

Padmore remarked that anyone who was familiar with the publication of a magazine in the vein of the *Negro Worker* would hardly expect it to be a financial success because its mission was not to make a profit but to advance the principles of revolutionary struggle and expose the atrocities committed in the black colonies day after day. This information would help blacks to organize and take their place in the worldwide struggle against imperialism and work for national freedom and social emancipation. To effectively carry out its mission, "the *Negro Worker* needs the moral support of the black masses and our white class brothers, friends and sympathizers". Moreover, further financial sacrifices would have to be made if this work was to continue.[151] Padmore told black workers not to be discouraged but to do everything in their power to "maintain our militant journal". He requested that the *Negro Worker* family support "the new editor to overcome the present financial difficulties and to carry on the militant traditions of the *Negro Worker*".[152]

Wilson makes the assertion that the Comintern, in order to reorient or to terminate ITUCNW activity, resorted to the well-established practice of undermining a Comintern affiliate by withholding subsidies necessary for operating costs.[153] Valtin's view on this question is reminiscent of Wilson's. He informs us that the technique of "breaking men" within the communist movement starts with the withholding of all subsidies.[154] Based on the economic challenges confronting the *Negro Worker,* it would be reasonable to ask whether this was an attempt to close down the *Negro Worker*. Or was it an attempt to remove Padmore as the editor of the journal? Or a covert attempt to reorient the *Negro Worker*?

Otto Huiswoud, the hierarchy of the French communist party and Padmore held a meeting on 24 August 1933 to discuss the possibility of publishing the *Negro Worker* in France and the future of the ITUCNW. At the meeting, Huiswoud spoke about the financial viability of the *Negro Worker* and the ITUCNW. He raised the questions whether the cost and organization of maintaining the *Negro Worker* could become the responsibility of the Colonial Commission of the Confédération générale du travail unitaire and whether the work of the ITUCNW should be based in Paris or located elsewhere.[155] At the meeting Padmore was critical of the "racist attitudes of the French comrades and the inflexibility and apathy of the RILU headquarters towards his and Kouyatè's work".[156] It was after this meeting that Padmore penned his resignation letter as the editor of the *Negro Worker*. In his report to the RILU, Huiswoud made it clear that the Confédération générale du travail unitaire could not be responsible for the ITUCNW or the *Negro Worker*. He suggested that another individual should be found to head the ITUCNW and recommended that the head office of the ITUCNW be located in one of the Dutch ports.[157]

Although Padmore resigned as the editor of the *Negro Worker*, he remained a member of the Comintern but finally severed his relationship in February 1934. Whether Padmore's departure from the Comintern was a resignation or expulsion has generated tremendous discussion. In a letter to Ollivierre, his close friend and confidant, Padmore wrote:

> Last August [1933] the Communist International wanted us to close down our activities in order to appease the British foreign office. . . . Well the Africans objected. I stood loyally with them and resigned. . . . I am very disappointed in the way our so-called friends have let us down, but today Stalin has given up the idea of support to those who are still under the yoke in order to win capitalist support.[158]

About a decade later, Padmore released the following explanation to the general public for his resignation from the Comintern:

I held a responsible position in the higher councils of the Communist International, which was called upon not only to endorse the new diplomatic policy of the Soviet Government, but to put a brake upon the anti-imperialist work of its affiliate sections and thereby sacrifice the young national liberation movements in Asia and Africa. This I considered to be a betrayal of the fundamental interest of my people, with which I could not identify myself. I therefore had no choice but to sever my connection with the Communist International.[159]

While the above explanation was accepted by Padmore's contemporaries, recent scholars have questioned the accuracy of the statement in light of the unavailability of any document to support Padmore's contention. It is likely that Padmore felt that his removal was the first step in closing down the ITUCNW. The RILU Negro Bureau and the Negro Section of the Eastern Secretariat were amalgamated in the fall of 1933. The ITUCNW was placed under the executive committee of the Comintern Eastern Secretariat and became a leaner entity with a head and a secretary.[160] This restructuring led Padmore to make the assertion that black work was being sacrificed. Mark Solomon posits that Padmore's "break with the Comintern was probably triggered by cutbacks in clandestine funding and perhaps also cuts in the arming of colonial unions and leftist organizations".[161] The financial challenges facing the *Negro Worker* and the unfolding political climate in Europe might also have suggested to Padmore that the days for propagating radical anti-colonialism and building a black international were numbered. Jonathan Derrick explains that "it was quite possible that Padmore had heard some talk about the possible curbing of the Comintern activity relating to the United States in particular". He notes that the issue arose in 1932–33 in discussions about US recognition of the Soviet government.[162] It is clear that the rise of Adolf Hitler and the fascist threat to the Soviet Union would have had some impact on Soviet foreign policy. Padmore recognized that this could cause a de-emphasis of the anti-colonial position of the Soviet Union, and subsequent events proved him correct. In 1933, Stalin actively began to reorient Russian foreign policy and that of the Comintern, a shift that might have suggested to the keen observer that black internationalism and the foreign policy of Russia were on a collision course. On 18 March

1933, the Comintern Eastern Secretariat had "vaguely proposed united front actions with social democratic elements and non-revolutionary trade unions for the purposes of stopping reaction and fascism".[163] The US government decided to recognize the Soviet government in November 1933. Padmore felt that the United States made this decision only when the Soviet Union agreed to tone down its anti-US propaganda. However, the Soviets denied making this promise and communist activity continued in the United States, as did anti-American propaganda.[164] Padmore also strongly believed that in order to appease the United States, the Soviet Union cancelled the film *Blacks and Whites*, which was supposed to depict "racial and labour conflicts in Birmingham, Alabama".[165] The Soviets, in their defence of this decision, stated that the film was cancelled for technical reasons.[166]

The Soviet foreign policy shifts in 1934, involving discussions with France about a mutual defence agreement and subsequently the signing of the Franco-Soviet Treaty in May 1935, gives some credence to Padmore's assertions. Moreover, the signing of the Anglo-Soviet Agreement in January 1935 clearly demonstrated a new direction for the Comintern. Indeed, Britain supported the Soviet Union's entry into the League of Nations, an organization that previously the Soviets had been extremely critical of. These foreign policy initiatives demonstrated to Padmore that the national interests of the Soviet Union were taking precedence over black internationalism and led him to argue that the Comintern did not believe in permanent cooperation. Instead, its aim was to use its allies to advance the party line, and alliances were, therefore, temporary. In other words, anti-imperialism no longer served the needs of the Soviet foreign policy.[167]

EXPULSION

While Padmore insisted that he resigned from the Comintern, the Comintern maintained that it had expelled Padmore. The International Control Commission (ICC) had drafted a statement on Padmore's expulsion in February 1934. This statement was published in the June issue of the *Negro Worker* and made three accusations:

Padmore, a member of the Communist Party, despite repeated warnings did not break off his connections with the exposed provocateur Kouyatè and lived in the apartment of the provocateur Jacques. In order to deceive the Party organs, Padmore repeatedly stated that he had already broken with Jacques. Such conduct on the part of Padmore might lead to arrest as it made the work of provocateurs easier.

Padmore carried on work which undermined the class unity of the toiling Negro masses, and under the pretence of advocating the necessity for the unity of all Negroes on a racial basis, he tried to lay the path for unity with the Negro bourgeois exploiters and with their agents, the national-reformists, which could not help leading to the interests of the Negro toiling masses becoming subordinated to the exploiters.

Padmore began to work openly for the benefit of national bourgeois organisations. With this aim Padmore entered into negotiations with the national reformists on the question of saving Liberia and collecting funds to cover the expenses of Liberia. Instead of mobilising the masses for the struggle for the genuine independence of Liberia against the imperialists who enslave Liberia and against the Liberian bourgeois government which bargains with the imperialists, Padmore took his stand openly on the side of the Liberian government.[168]

The ICC took the decision to expel Padmore from the "Communist Party for contacts with a provocateur, for contacts with bourgeois organisations on the question of Liberia, [and] for an incorrect attitude to the national question (instead of class unity striving towards race unity)".[169]

The ITUCNW followed the lead of the ICC and issued a statement on Padmore's expulsion. This statement, written by Charles Woodson (Otto Huiswoud) in his capacity as secretary, echoed the sentiments expressed by the ICC, but it also added: "Because of his disruptive activities and on the basis of the above stated decisions, the ITUC of NW, decides to expell Padmore from its ranks and calls upon all members of the Executive Committee, supporters of the ITUC of NW and The Negro Worker, to break off all relationship with him, as such continued relationship will only mean giving aid and support to his anti-workingclass activities."[170]

EXAMINATION OF THE CHARGES OF THE ICC AND ITUCNW

Padmore and Kouyatè met at the fifth Conference of RILU in Moscow in 1930 and subsequently became close comrades. Kouyatè was a regular correspondent for the *Negro Worker* when it was under the editorship of Padmore, and Padmore's articles also appeared regularly in *Le Cri des Nègres*, which was edited by Kouyatè. The latter worked closely with Padmore in organizing the conference of the International of Seamen and Harbour Workers in Hamburg in May 1932.[171] Padmore supported Kouyatè in his struggles with French communists. Kouyatè was eventually expelled by the revolutionary movement of France in October 1933, a decision subsequently rubber-stamped by the ITUCNW.[172]

It was true that Padmore was told by Huiswoud to sever his association with Kouyatè, but Padmore "resented being told with whom he should associate and refused to go to Moscow to discuss the problem".[173] Valtin informs us that "Party discipline demands that you follow the Party command". He goes on to state that "loyalty to the Party, however, came before loyalty to the proletariat".[174] However, for Padmore loyalty to the liberation of black people took priority over loyalty to the party. James strongly believed that if Padmore had gone to Moscow, "he would never have returned".[175] According to Weiss, Padmore told A. Ferrat that he would only come to Moscow if they were going to discuss the liquidation of the Negro Committee and Kouyatè's expulsion. Moreover, he stressed that "he would only go with people who represented the Black working class: 'Marks' of South Africa and 'Hope' in New York".[176] According to Paul Trewhela, Albert Nzula, the first black general secretary of the Communist Party of South Africa, who was residing in Moscow, told Padmore not to come to Moscow.[177] Maurice Thorez, one of the leading figures of the French Communist Party, also told Padmore not to go to Moscow.[178] Padmore refused to go to Moscow.

In relation to the charge that Padmore was engaged in activities which weakened the class unity of blacks by advocating racial unity was evident in the proposed Negro World Unity Congress that Padmore and Kouyatè had been planning. This conference was intended to lead to the creation of a black international to direct the future of black movements throughout the world. Julien Racamond in his report on Padmore's activities in Paris, which he submitted to the ICC before Padmore's expulsion, stated that "Padmore planned to develop the ITUCNW into a Black International against the orders of the Comintern".[179] The Negro World Unity Congress was another avenue in seeking to build the black international that Padmore and Kouyatè envisioned. Hooker suggests that Padmore had started to theorize about a double revolution taking place in the colonies. The first would be a racial revolution against white imperialists and the second a class-based revolution that would be organized by the Comintern shortly after the first revolution.[180]

In relation to the Liberian question, it should be remembered that Liberia always had a special place in the heart of Padmore. This was evident in his pamphlet *American Imperialism Enslaves Liberia* and articles "Hands Off Liberia!" and "Workers, Defend Liberia".[181] Ward provides us with the details of a proposal that Padmore discussed with him "for buying out Firestone in Liberia" by raising five million dollars. During this conversation with Ward, Padmore cursed "everything that is white – capitalist, socialist, communist . . . only Negroes are good". According to Ward, Padmore stated that the "Communist International had let the Negroes down and America and Britain were both going fascist". Therefore, blacks should develop Liberia and migrate there.[182] In early 1934, Padmore wrote to Du Bois and told him that "Liberia has her faults, but since white politicians are no better than black ones, it is our duty to save the black baby from the white wolves".[183] Based on Ward's comments, it appears that Padmore had become a supporter of the Save Liberia proposal that was being promoted by William Jones, the editor of the *Baltimore Afro-America*. Jones envisioned raising capital in the United States for Liberia's development and helping unemployed African American professionals find employment in Liberia.[184] Ironically, Padmore had previously castigated Garvey's Back to Africa project and had stated that "Back to Africa was a reactionary slogan, aimed to help in saving capitalism in America".[185] If we are to believe Ward, Padmore had become extremely frustrated with the proletarian internationalism of the Comintern and was moving ideologically towards pan-Africanism.

James was convinced that Padmore's statement explaining why he broke with the Comintern suggests that "he had never been completely swept away by the Stalinist conception of Marxism" even if he was a major communist operative. Padmore told James that he lived in the Soviet Union and "saw what was going on". But he "stayed there because there was a means of doing work for the black emancipation and there was no other place that I could think of".186 Richard Wright, an author who broke with the CPUSA, argued that "the Negro even when embracing Communism or Western Democracy, is not supporting ideologies, he is seeking to use instruments (instruments owned and controlled by men of other races!) for his own ends".187 It was clear that Padmore sought to utilize the apparatus of the Comintern to assist his African brothers and sisters "in a fuller way" and to rid Africa and the Caribbean of colonialism. Cedric Robinson helps explain the behaviour of people of African descent who broke with European Marxism but remained Marxist by suggesting that "the Black Radical tradition began to emerge and overtake Marxism in the work of the black radicals".188 This was clearly evident with Padmore, although he was an important member of the Comintern and did a lot of work in promoting communist black internationalism. Even so, he felt his efforts were insufficient and more could be done to liberate black people if he were not constrained by having to concentrate his efforts on West Africa and not on the African continent and the diaspora. Padmore strongly believed that the Comintern's commitment to African independence did not match its rhetoric. He also questioned its class-over-race approach; it was glaringly obvious to him, as pointed out by many of the Africans educated in Moscow and demonstrated by the strength of Garvey's pan-Africanist philosophy, that greater emphasis should be placed on the race question in the colonies. Therefore, the liberation of black people was paramount for Padmore although the Comintern sought to emphasize the liberation of all working people from capitalist exploitation. This tension helps to explain why Padmore placed proletarian internationalism in the background in favour of the immediacy of pan-Africanism and the colonial revolution when he became frustrated with the mixed signals coming from the Comintern.

COMMUNIST ATTACKS

Helen Davis (Hermina Huiswoud), like many functionaries of the Communist Party, launched a vitriolic assault on Padmore, describing him as "a petty bourgeois anti-imperialist".[189] Similar sentiments were also expressed by Ford, the vice-presidential candidate of the CPUSA in the national elections of 1932, Padmore's predecessor at the ITUCNW and the former editor of the *International Negro Workers' Review*. Ford had written a letter of reference for Padmore when he arrived in Moscow in 1929, to George Slavin, the Negro Bureau secretary, informing him that Padmore "was a good, energetic and capable comrade".[190] He now accused Padmore of abandoning the revolutionary movement because of his "petty bourgeois background" and his "petty bourgeois nationalist activities".[191] Padmore, during his Comintern years, had also attacked many black leaders with similar accusations. Davis suggested that Padmore became impatient and was not prepared to "wait for the proletariat". She accused Padmore of not distinguishing between white rulers and white workers who were being exploited by the same rulers who exploited the inhabitants of the colonies.[192]

In the past, according to Davis, Padmore undertook the task of educating white workers, but he was no longer willing to go down this progressive path. Davis charged that Padmore "doesn't want the proletarian way ... [he wants] free colonies but not free colonial workers". She stressed that while Padmore had once been a proponent of proletarian internationalism and spoke of the class struggle, "that [had] only [been] during the transition period in the brief history of Mr. Padmore's revolutionary career". However, "he now calls on the Negroes to close ranks for the future of Africa is ours". Davis reminded her readers that Padmore had previously called Garvey an impostor but that he "now hoped to solve the problems of the 250,000,000 Negroes of the world by a financial venture of buying back Liberia".[193] Ford, in this regard, contended that Padmore's actions undermined the unity of Liberian workers in their struggle against exploitation and oppression and weakened the working-class movement under the slogan of race unity instead of class unity, thereby strengthening the hands of imperialist oppressors and their black allies.[194] He believed that Padmore's "political views and activities around the question of Liberia" were designed to further subjugate and humiliate the "downtrodden Negroes" of Liberia. Ford stressed that "instead of Liberia being seen as the last stronghold of Negro Freedom it is a vassal state of American imperialism".[195] Davis went on to say that "the supreme act which proves that Padmore had two souls; that of an anti-imperialist and that of a Negro nationalist" could be seen in his articles in the black bourgeois newspaper that "accuses the only true fighters for liberty of the oppressed peoples of the world of betraying the Negro masses". She further argued that despite Padmore's assertions that the ITUCNW and the *Negro Worker* were liquidated and that international black work was being sacrificed, the *Negro Worker* was still being published.[196] Davis was correct that the ITUCNW was still functioning and the *Negro Worker* was still being produced, though under the leadership of Huiswoud.

Padmore did not respond directly to his vilification by his communist opponents until October 1935, when he wrote an open letter to Earl Browder, the general secretary of the CPUSA. He stated that "[s]ince my resignation the American Party, the *Daily Worker* and other Party organs have been carrying on a vicious campaign of lies and slanders against me".[197] Padmore noted that the Comintern had fabricated "a number of cock and bull stories" stating that he had been expelled mainly for supporting the "bourgeoisie of Liberia in oppressing and exploiting the workers and peasants of that country". Padmore insisted that this was an outrageous untruth and he dared the Comintern to produce evidence in support of this false allegation.[198] He asked a number of questions that he hoped Browder would answer:

> "Why did not the the CI [Communist International] accuse me of this years ago, for the last article I wrote on the Liberian Question was in January, 1932, when I was still *persona grata*?"
>
> "Why has the CI never yet written an article or issued a statement criticizing me until now?"
>
> "Why did the CI refuse to discuss the liquidation of the Negro Committee and the Suppression of the *Negro Worker*, of which I was the Editor in Chief?"

"Why did the CI wait from August 1933 to April 16, 1934 – nearly 10 months after they closed down my work – to publish this frame-up story?"

"Why did it take the CI months after my resignation to discover my villainy?"[199]

Padmore opined that the "CI is politically bankrupt" because its only recourse was to fabricate lies and slurs about him and defame him, tactics which he described as "the weapon of political assassinations". This was "in order to cover up its own treachery, duplicity, rascality and perfidy in dealing with a representative of the most oppressed and exploited section of humanity".[200]

Padmore asserted that all of "this talk about championing and defending the Negro race is just a bluff". He challenged Browder to "Please tell us where and when the Communist International in the fifteen years of its existence, has ever written one article on Liberia", "Please tell us where and when your Party has ever organized a meeting or demonstration in defence of Liberia", and "Please tell us where you, as secretary of the Party, have ever written an article about Liberia."[201]

Padmore accused Browder and many other communists of "hav[ing] the vile impudence to slander" him and every black person who is seeking "to do something, right or wrong, to save Liberia from being annexed and declared a protectorate of American and European imperialist powers". Padmore denied the accusation that he gave names and addresses of black seamen to the police. He was offended that after he had created an international organization of over four thousand supporters and "made the *Negro Worker* feared by the rulers of the mighty British Empire", he was now being accused of being a spy.[202] Ford, in two articles in the *Negro Liberator*, "James Ford Answers Padmore's Charges" and "Ford Analyses Padmore as Police Agent and Spy", alleged that Padmore was "on intimate terms with well-known spies and police agents" and although he was made aware that they were spies he "refused to break with them".[203] Padmore was frustrated that having made him sacrifice his education at Howard University, the party was now accusing him of being a spy. He stressed that like all human beings, he had deficiencies but no one had ever questioned his "honesty and integrity". He ended the letter by stating that Browder must answer the charges that were being made against him because he "was going to broadcast this statement throughout the length and breadth of the black world".[204]

Browder, in response to Padmore's open letter, claimed that Padmore, who had "accepted an appointment as secretary to the Negro Trade Union Committee ... later turned against its policies". As soon as Padmore was removed, he "declared this was 'liquidation' of the Committee". Browder felt that this was "a case of delusion of grandeur", for it was only Padmore who was "liquidated" because the "Committee has continued its work and more fruitfully than under Padmore's administration".[205]

Was Browder correct that Padmore saw his removal as the end of the ITUCNW and of meaningful work among black people? Zusmanovich made the comment that Padmore did not have any "political guidelines apart from believing that he himself is the ideological leader of the Negro world". Moreover, when Padmore was told to "read Lenin's and Stalin's works", he argued that "Negroes should read his book, 'The Life and Struggles of Negro Toilers'".[206] Pennybacker suggests that "Padmore himself became the Negro Committee in the few short years of its greatest prominence".[207] Based on the above observations, it is possible that Padmore saw his removal as the end of the ITUCNW and *Negro Worker*. It is conceivable that Padmore saw the restricting of the RILU Negro Bureau in 1933 as its liquidation. The ITUCNW and the *Negro Worker* continued under the leadership of Otto Huiswoud from 1934 to 1937. However, the *Negro Worker* was forced to halt publication for a few months after Padmore resigned as editor because "serious technical difficulties, editorial shortcomings and the necessity to change our location, all contributed to the necessity of discontinuing publication for a while".[208] This break in publication might have influenced Padmore to make the assertion that the work of the ITUCNW was liquidated. However, Wilson Record argues that "while the ITUCNW was not disbanded at the time of Padmore's dismissal and while Huiswoud did function as its Executive Secretary, the former's underlying charges were basically true".[209] The Comintern toned down its anti-colonial rhetoric work during the United Front period, although it did not totally abandon it until 1937, when the organization was finally disbanded.

In Browder's opinion, the central issues around which Padmore parted company with the Comintern were his acceptance of Japanese imperialist propaganda that the Mikado was the guardian of the "darker races" and that his conquest of Korea, Formosa, Manchuria and North China (all the "darker races") was for their own good and his belief that the road to black liberation lay in a race war of these "darker races" against whites. Clearly Browder misrepresented Padmore's views because the latter wrote that "the eyes of the white world are once more focused on the black empire, in consequence of the recent commercial treaty between Ethiopia and Japan". For Padmore, this agreement had "tremendous and far-reaching importance, not only for Ethiopia but for all Black Africa", which was why European imperialists in Africa were anxiously watching this development between Japan, the most aggressive imperialist state in the world at the time, and her new African ally.[210] Padmore emphatically stated that "the Ethiopians have no illusions about the Japanese imperialists", who in their domestic and "external policies are quite as ruthless as the white imperialist nations". The Japanese ruling class, like other capitalists, were no respecters of race, colour or creed. Although it might suit their present needs to pose as the "defenders" and "champions" of the "darker races", wrote Padmore, their history had been too noticeably "written in the blood of millions of Koreans and Chinese, for us to have any doubts about their true character".[211]

Browder alleged that after Padmore resisted his removal and began to publicly attack his former associates, many seamen were arrested who had previously helped him smuggle the *Negro Worker* into Africa. Browder opined that he had no way of knowing whether Padmore was directly or indirectly responsible for the arrest of the seamen. He ended the letter by stating that it would have been better if, "instead of attacking us, you would combine forces with us in fighting for Negro rights, for Angelo Herndon and the Scottsboro boys and the defence of Ethiopia".[212]

George Padmore utilized the facilities of the Comintern to attack and undermine colonialism and imperialism while seeking to promote black internationalism. In *The Life and the Struggles of Negro Toilers* and on the pages of the *Negro Worker*, he critiqued the colonial system, provided information about conditions of black people and their struggles and offered advice as how to better their conditions. However, he severed his ties with communism when he felt that the freedom of his brothers and sisters in Africa and the Caribbean was being compromised to serve the imperatives of Russian foreign policy.

4. RADICAL PAN-AFRICAN ACTIVISM

ALEKSANDR ZUSMANOVICH, A LEADING OPERATIVE OF the Comintern, predicted that life for Padmore would stop after he left the Comintern because "he could never retrieve the sort of corporate security and sense of worth that he had known in the movement".[1] This position was supported by Jan Valtin (Richard Krebs), another Comintern operative, who made the assertion that "a true communist cannot conceive of life outside the party".[2] Indeed, the period in the immediate aftermath of Padmore's separation from the Comintern was difficult. He was ostracized, "persecuted and vilified" by some of his former comrades.[3] However, Zusmanovich's and Valtin's predictions did not come to pass because Padmore soon had a new lease on life as an important pan-Africanist. C.L.R. James informs us that "Padmore had made up his mind to continue his efforts on behalf of colonial emancipation with specific concentration on Africa".[4]

It is important to remember that during his communist career, Padmore had been critical of the ideology of pan-Africanism and the major pan-African ideologues Marcus Garvey and W.E.B. Du Bois. However, his conversion from the communist camp to pan-Africanism was not a difficult ideological transition for Padmore; as a member of the Comintern he had worked assiduously in spreading the Comintern's black internationalism through the ITUCNW, as he did as editor of the *Negro Worker*.

Even before Padmore resigned from the Comintern he was already dabbling in pan-Africanism through his involvement in planning a Negro World Unity Congress and his support for the Save Liberia project. The Comintern, when it officially expelled Padmore in 1933, accused him of advocating race unity instead of proletarian internationalism. Some of his former comrades accused him of advocating black nationalism. In her penetrating critique, "The Rise and Fall of George Padmore as Revolutionary Fighter", Helen Davis accused Padmore of having two souls: one of an anti-imperialist and one of a black nationalist.[5] As a member of the CPUSA, he was often accused of being a black chauvinist because of his sensibilities on the race question. Prior to joining the Communist Party, Padmore was instrumental in the creation of a pan-African student movement. Additionally, he felt that Edward Blyden, the great pan-Africanist, was the greatest West Indian who ever lived. Therefore, Padmore was able to easily navigate the ideological shift from communism to pan-Africanism.

The Comintern's loss became a major gain for pan-Africanism because Padmore brought all the organizational and leadership skills and journalistic and political expertise he had acquired as a member of the Comintern to the service of pan-Africanism. In the Comintern, Padmore had developed a reputation as a good organizer; he played an important role in the organization of the Hamburg Conference of Negro Workers in 1930 and the Conference of the International of Seamen and Harbour Workers in Hamburg in 1932. In addition to organizing conferences, Padmore also attended and participated in the fifth Congress of the RILU in Moscow in 1930, the Congress of the International Labour Defence held in the Soviet Union in 1932 and the International Red Aid World Congress in Moscow in November 1932. Padmore was an experienced conference organizer and participant who recognized the value of conferences as spaces for dialogue, sharing and discussing ideas and strategies, avenues of inspiration, and forging important links locally, regionally and internationally as well as for building solidarity.

Padmore took the journalistic and propagandistic skills that he developed as a communist to pan-Africanism. As Leslie James points out, "the close relationship between Padmore's political commitments and his journalism started when he became involved with the communist movement in the United States".[6] As a communist, Padmore had written and edited a small number of issues of the *Negro Champion*. He also wrote for the *Daily Worker*, *Moscow Daily News* and *Le Cri des Nègres* and edited and wrote numerous articles for the *Negro Worker*. Padmore was also a major propagandist for the Comintern, having authored the following pamphlets: *The Life and Struggles of Negro Toilers, American Imperialism Enslaves Liberia, Negro Workers and the Imperialist War – Intervention in the Soviet Union, What Is the International Trade Union of Negro Workers?* and *Forced Labour in Africa and Labour Imperialism in East Africa*. Altogether, he was adept at writing polemic and propagandistic articles and pamphlets to educate, guide and inflame anti-colonial outrage.

Additionally, Padmore drew on the numerous contacts that he had developed throughout the colonial world – more than four thousand. In a letter to Ollivierre, he boasted, "I have a loyal colonial army, which I might have to throw into battle against the white 'Reds' if they continue to be so disloyal to their allies."[7] Padmore was also knowledgeable about colonialism in Africa and the Caribbean, having lectured on the subject at the KUTV and having written extensively on the subject while he was the editor of the *Negro Worker*. Moreover, he was a sharp critic of colonialism and imperialism, and his major political objective was to "get the damn white blood suckers from the W.I. and Africa".[8] He was also acquainted with many of the emerging nationalist and trade union leaders in Africa and the Caribbean.

Padmore brought over seven years of experience as an operative in Leninist vanguard organizations. He had been a member of the CPUSA before he was a member of the ITUCNW, organizations that were influenced heavily by Lenin's vanguard party. The vanguard, according to Lenin, was the most advanced section of the industrial working class, whose task was to direct the thoughts of those who were dissatisfied with the existing socio-economic and socio-political conditions. The vanguard party was to be led by a small cadre of professional revolutionaries and was to be guided by the principle of democratic centralism. Peter Abrahams describes Padmore as the consummate Comintern man who was disciplined to the point of single-mindedness in pursuing his political objective and had little time for those who did not display the same level of commitment.[9] Padmore the professional revolutionary harshly criticized the frivolity of his colleagues. He felt that their energies should be focused solely on bringing about an African revolution. Abrahams makes the point that although "his world had changed", nevertheless Padmore's "old contacts" and political behaviour remained the same.[10]

Richard Wright made a similar observation of Padmore when he visited him in London in January 1947: Padmore was "all political talk, nothing to lift the minds or the emotions".[11] Although Padmore had broken with the Comintern, he still carried some of the vanguardist tendencies and recognized that the members of the IASB needed the kind of discipline that was associated with professional revolutionaries in order to bring about an African revolution.

Padmore's experience as a political agitator proved to be invaluable to the pan-African movement. As an activist and as the editor of the *Negro Worker*, he played an important role in helping to internationalize the Scottsboro Boys' case. In general, he helped to organize and participated in numerous rallies and demonstrations during his days with the CPUSA.

ABORTED NEGRO WORLD CONFERENCE

In November 1933, Padmore, Kouyatè, and a number of pan-African activists and intellectuals and former members of the Parti Communiste Français (including Andre Breton, Camille Saint-Jacques, Emile Faure, René Maran, Joseph Edele, Jules Alcandre, Ibrahim Sow, Rita Diallo, Medina Perez and Joan Segure) began talking about holding a black world congress in Paris in July 1935.[12] At this time Padmore was still officially a member of the Comintern, although he was already estranged from the organization, having resigned as the editor of the *Negro Worker* a few months before. Throughout 1934, Padmore and his colleagues continued to work to make this conference a reality, the principal objective of which was to examine "the moral, economic, intellectual, social and political situation of the Negro race, to unify it, to create a charter for it and to establish a universal organization destined to direct the future of the Negro movement in all countries".[13] As operatives of the Comintern, Padmore and Kouyatè had been dissatisfied with the way in which the issues affecting black people were treated within that organization, and they envisioned the creation of a "true" black international that would address all of the issues confronting black people. They hoped that this Paris gathering would result in the creation of that body.

Padmore, in the manifesto he wrote for the congress, pointed out that throughout the world, black people were "despised, humiliated, denied justice and human rights in every walk of life". He stressed that the ruling classes who oppressed them were preparing for a new war unlike anything seen before by humankind and were planning to use black people "once more as cannon fodder" to accelerate their "racial extermination".[14] Given this perceived threat, Padmore noted that African workers, students and intellectuals had decided to organize a conference "of the Negro peoples of the world for the purpose of establishing unity in our ranks and adopting a platform of struggle for the Africans and people of African descent the world over".[15] In the tradition of his pan-Africanist forebears, he recognized the value of a united front, appealing for unity and solidarity among West Indians, African Americans and Africans.[16]

In order to drum up support for the Negro World Congress, Padmore wrote to Du Bois, the patron of the 1919, 1921, 1923 and 1927 pan-African congresses, requesting assistance. In his letter, he reported that French blacks had recently held a conference under the leadership of Kouyatè, the expelled communist and the editor of *La Race Nègre*, where many of the problems facing blacks were discussed, most importantly the current economic crisis of capitalism, the attendant social crisis facing the world and the fascist danger that threatened racial extermination. In Padmore's judgement, the discussion at this gathering "was the most serious political discussion" he had ever heard among black people. He remarked that it was at this meeting that the idea first surfaced to "convene a Negro World Unity Congress, for the purpose of hammering out a common programme of action around which world unity among blacks can be achieved". Padmore pointed out that black students in Europe were demanding action in light of the challenges confronting black people. He asked Du Bois for assistance in helping "us in trying to create a basis for unity among Negroes of Africa, America, the West Indies and other lands".[17] It is important to note that Padmore, who had been critical of Du Bois and pan-Africanism, was now seeking to build a more harmonious relationship with him.

Padmore was extremely concerned with the rise of fascism throughout Europe and the attendant danger it posed to Africans and people of African descent. In 1933, while still an operative of the Comintern and living in Hamburg, he had been a victim of fascism when he was roused from his sleep, imprisoned for two weeks and deported from Germany.[18] He had editorialized in the *Negro Worker* that the majority of blacks in Europe, United States and the colonies had not recognized that "fascism is the greatest danger which confronts not only the white workers, but is the most hostile movement against the Negro race". In Padmore's opinion, the "most glaring manifestation" of anti-black sentiment was to be seen in Germany "where the fascists carried on the most intense protest against Negroes, Jews and so-called non-Nordics", and he observed that since Hitler had become the chancellor of Germany, "Nazi agitation has taken the form of open physical violence against all coloured peoples".[19]

Padmore was not surprised by racist attacks on blacks because the fascist mouthpiece *Nationalsozialistiche Monatshefte* had carried racist comments about black people:[20]

> The leading newspaper in Berlin had demanded the expulsion and arrest of Mrs Ada Wright during her tour of Germany. Captain Goering ordered his men to round up all blacks and deport them from Germany. The Nazis were demanding the return of Cameroon, Togoland, Tanganyika and other African colonies to Germany. Negroes and Jews faced fascist terrorism daily. Negro musicians and theatrical artists would not be permitted in Germany. Negro students and intellectuals were to be excluded from all German institutions of learning.[21]

The aim of the Nazi government was to create a pure German Aryan state that did not include Jews or blacks, and Padmore warned that the current system "of terror and bloodshed against the German working class, Jews and Negroes" should act as a warning to blacks in the United Kingdom, the United States and throughout the world.[22]

The Negro World Congress did not materialize for two major reasons: Padmore was unable to procure the finances to make the conference a reality, and Kouyatè, the other mover behind the initiative, became seriously ill and spent an extended period of time in hospital in the spring of 1934. In 1935, Padmore moved to London and nothing more was heard about a Negro world congress.

INVASION OF ETHIOPIA

The Italian invasion of Ethiopia in October 1935 had a major impact on Africans worldwide. Ethiopia was the only truly independent African territory, given that Liberia's independence was compromised by US economic imperialism. In 1896, Ethiopia had defeated the Italians at the famous battle of Adowa and halted the march of European colonial domination in Africa. For Padmore, this victory was of great significance, and "Ethiopia's prestige went up overnight". Menelik was the first black ruler in modern times to defeat a European nation, and this victory "became the subject of discussion in every chancellery of Europe". Moreover, all the leading nations of Europe sought to win the approval "of the Conquering Lion of Judah". Britain, France and Russia sent ambassadors to Ethiopia, and even the Italians "came trying to ingratiate themselves into the favour of their conqueror".[23] France and Ethiopia signed the Franco-Ethiopian treaty of 20 March 1897, and Britain and Ethiopia signed the Anglo-Ethiopian agreement of 14 May 1897.[24] In a similar vein, Joseph Harris notes that "Ethiopia's defeat of Italy in 1896 enhanced the fascination the African Nation historically held for people of African descent".[25] This position is also shared by S.K.B. Asante, who argued that "[a]fter the victory of Adowa in 1896, Ethiopia acquired a special importance in the eyes of Africans as the only surviving independent African state".[26] For many Africans and people of African descent, Ethiopia was regarded as a symbol of black liberation.[27]

In May 1935, Padmore, writing in the *Crisis* from Paris, warned that war in Africa seemed inevitable. On 5 December 1934 the Italians and the Ethiopians clashed at Wal Wal, a town in southeastern Ethiopia. It was reported that about 110 Ethiopians and over 30 Italians were killed. The Italians demanded compensation for this incident and sought to use it as a pretext for Italian expansionism into Ethiopia. The Italians' muscular rhetoric and aggressive actions suggested that war with Ethiopia was inevitable. Padmore felt that if his worst fears were realized then it was the responsibility of every black person "to render the maximum moral and material support to the Ethiopian people in their struggle against Italian fascism".[28] He envisioned the NAACP or some other black group arranging a conference of all black groups for the purpose of organizing common action on behalf of Ethiopians. He strongly believed that pan-African solidarity could "achieve tremendous results and demonstrate to the peoples of Africa that their descendants in the New World have not forgotten their ties of blood and race with them". Padmore stressed that the Ethiopians' battles were "a part of the struggles of the black race the world over for national freedom, economic, political, social and racial emancipation".[29]

In London, Padmore worked as a journalist, writing for newspapers in Britain, the United States, East and West Africa, South Africa, and the West Indies. Many of these newspapers "paid irregularly" or did not "pay at all", but Padmore continued to supply them with articles.[30] While Padmore concentrated his writings on Africa, he also wrote about developments in the United States and the West Indies. In this way, "independent little papers and magazines in the colonies received a non-European perspective of what was happening in the world".[31]

Around this time the Ethiopian struggle began to take centre stage among pan-Africanists living in London. Padmore joined the International African Friends of Abyssinia/Ethiopia, whose main purpose was "to arouse the sympathy and support of the British public for the victims of fascist aggression" and "to assist by all means in their power in the maintenance of the territorial integrity and political independence of Abyssinia".[32] The leading members of this organization were C.L.R. James, Dr Peter Milliard, T. Albert Marryshow, Jomo Kenyatta, Amy Ashwood Garvey, Sam Manning, Mohammed Said and Ras Makonnen. Although Padmore was not a founding member, he quickly began to play a leading role in the organization, a development that was inevitable given his international standing, reputation and knowledge about issues affecting Africans. James, the chairman, noted that "any organization dealing with African affairs saw George Padmore as Chairman as a right".[33] Padmore was an active member of the International African Friends of Abyssinia/Ethiopia, holding meetings in Hyde Park, addressing labour organizations, semi-revolutionary groups, trade union conferences and groups of citizens who wanted to hear about a particular colonial question. He also maintained communications with his contacts abroad.[34]

Padmore observed that the Ethiopian crisis had generated "a tremendous feeling of racial solidarity among blacks" and that this unity transcended all colonial barriers. He was at a loss for words that adequately captured the feeling of kinship that existed among black people globally, which he compared to that of Jews, theorizing that it was the product "of centuries of oppression and persecution". He stated that the Italo-Ethiopian conflict "acted like dynamite in arousing and consolidating racial solidarity among Africans and peoples of African descent, as never before". He further noticed that blacks throughout the world had rallied to the defence of Ethiopia as though they were themselves subjects of Emperor Haile Selassie.[35] Asante advanced a similar view to that of Padmore, that is, the protest against the Italian invasion of Ethiopia "was Pan-African in sentiment, scope and activity".[36]

ETHIOPIA'S BETRAYAL BY THE LEAGUE OF NATIONS

Padmore argued that never in the "history of predatory Imperialism" had there been an example "of such cynicism and treachery as the betrayal of Abyssinia by Great Britain and France", the two leading imperialist countries that were supposed to be the main guardians of "Collective Security" in the League of Nations. For Padmore, this behaviour was to be viewed against the background of machinations by France and Britain against Ethiopia that had begun in the latter part of the nineteenth century. The major European nations, since the "new imperialism" offensive of the nineteenth century, had imperialistic designs on Ethiopia and though the Treaty of 1906 between France, Britain and Italy was meant to ensure the autonomy of Ethiopia, it did not mask the imperialistic intentions of these countries in regard to Ethiopia. Italy's invasion of Ethiopia in October 1935, Padmore claimed, was "merely a culmination of half a century of such plotting", epitomizing the darkest episode in "the history of European colonial expansion in Africa".[37]

Emperor Haile Selassie invoked the Italo-Ethiopia Treaty of 1928 on 8 December 1934, requesting that the two countries meet to determine who had been responsible for the Wal Wal incident. The Italians snubbed this invitation, forcing Ethiopia to take the matter to the League of Nations. In

January 1935, Ethiopia invoked article 11 of the Covenant of the League of Nations, demanding that the league take "every measure effectually to safeguard peace".[38] Padmore accused British diplomats of paying lip service to article 16, which clearly stated that the League of Nations would "undertake immediately to subject [the delinquent state] to the severance of all trade or financial relations, the prohibition of all intercourse between their nationals and the nationals of the covenant-breaking State, and the prevention of all financial, commercial or personal intercourse between the nationals of the covenant-breaking State and the nationals of any other State, whether a Member of the League or not".[39]

Under article 16, member states were supposed to take economic sanctions against an aggressor state as a first step before using military sanctions. Moreover, the members of the league were supposed to support the state that was the victim of the attacks.[40] However, the League of Nations refused to take any immediate action against Italy.

Padmore charged that the British, on the one hand, pretended that they were advocates of "peace and justice", while on the other, they were conducting "negotiations with Italy" at every stage of the disagreement to ascertain whether they could "share in the spoils". During the summer of 1935, Minister for the League of Nations Anthony Eden visited Rome with a British plan to settle the dispute. The British proposed a "territorial exchange through which Italy would receive a portion of Ethiopia in return for an outlet to the sea for the Ethiopians". Mussolini rejected the British offer and told Eden that "if Italy had to resort to war to accomplish her goals, she would wipe the name of Ethiopia from the map".[41] Padmore made the strong assertion that Britain never intended to protect Ethiopia, and when it failed to get what it wanted, it deserted not only Ethiopia but the League of Nations and collective security. The British lacked the foresight to see that when Ethiopia fell, the harmony "of Europe would go down with it".[42]

Padmore contended that the slow-paced tactics pursued by the democratic powers assisted Italy's fight to conquer Ethiopia and that after seven months of bloodshed and brutality, the League of Nations was powerless to settle this dispute. In fact, it was "unable to stem the tide of Italian imperialistic greed". The league continually established "committees of twos, of thirteens, of eighteens, *ad infinitum*". Padmore summed up his frustration in these words: "seven months of bombs, of poison gases, of forbidden instruments of warfare and the League of Nations remained throughout inert, impotent and drowsy".[43]

Padmore maintained that at every stage of aggression against Ethiopia, it was "tricked, deceived and led to the slaughter" by the league and "peace-loving" Great Britain and France.[44] It was widely rumoured that at the 1935 Stresa Conference between Italy, France and Britain, guarantees "had been given to Mussolini by the French that Italy would have a free hand in Ethiopia so far as the French were concerned". The British were aware of these assurances but said nothing with regard to them, "thus giving passive assent".[45] P. Laval, the French foreign minister, admitted that he had used the phrase a "free hand without any qualifications, so that it might be interpreted either in a political or an economic sense".[46] Verich posits that in the earlier meeting between Laval and Italy on 7 January 1935, the French assured Mussolini that they would not stand in Italy's way in establishing Italian economic influence over Ethiopia.[47]

Padmore did not limit his attack to Great Britain and France, but also attacked the Soviet Union, the only progressive state within the League of Nations, for its duplicity. He charged that the Soviet Union did nothing to support Ethiopia. Instead "she supplied oats, coal and petroleum" to the Italians throughout the war.[48] Although the Soviet Union opposed the arms embargo on Ethiopia, implemented economic sanctions on Italy and appealed for more economic bans on Italy, it continued to export oil to Italy, though it did stop exporting iron ore, manganese and chromium.[49] The position taken by the Soviet Union vindicated Padmore's position that the Soviet Union's national interests had taken precedence over its internationalism. James argued that if the Soviet Union had called "for a boycott against all war-material to Italy or any other country which interfered in Abyssinian affairs", it would have been in a strong position as the axis of the "whole anti-imperialist struggle". Moreover, the "mass feeling that had been aroused all over the world would have been directed into a single channel under the direction of the Third International".[50]

Padmore contrasted the Soviet Union's response to the Ethiopian saga with its response to the Spanish Civil War. Russia sent tanks, aeroplanes and other arms to Spain and allowed Russian workers to collect funds for medical supplies. In 1936, the Soviet Union provided Spanish communists with 106 tanks, 60 armoured cars, 136 aeroplanes, more than 60,000 rifles, 174 field guns, an unspecified amount of ammunition and about fifteen hundred military specialists and volunteers.[51] In contrast, it did not send "one rouble" or "one ton of wheat" to Ethiopia.[52]

Padmore excoriated the "labour movement of Western Europe" for not giving Ethiopia any material support. He made the assertion that they could have done more than just express "pious words of sympathy" and maintained that the influential leaders of the "Second and Third Internationals and their national sections" did nothing to concretely assist Ethiopia. In Padmore's cynical view, these great defenders who championed the rights of "colonial peoples and subject races did not provide one gas mask, one ambulance outfit, much less financial assistance to help these Abyssinians fight the battle". He posited that "bourgeois humanitarians did more in a practical way to help the Abyssinians than any of the national sections of both Internationals".[53] In October 1935, communist parties in South Africa, Egypt, Tunis, Palestine, Syria, Iraq and Italy signed a joint declaration in support of Ethiopia.[54] In May 1936, the International Conference of Negroes and Arabs was held in France under the auspices of the League against Imperialism. Several organizations participated in the forum: the League against Imperialism, the French Communist Party, the Italian Communist Party, the International Trade Union Committee for Negro Workers, the League of Coloured Peoples, the National Negro Congress, the African Church Mission, the Association of Haitian Writers, the Ligue de défense de la race nègre, the Étoile nord-africaine, and the Union nationale malagache. The conference condemned fascist aggression, and demanded that the League of Nations refuse to recognize any annexation of Ethiopian territory and stressed that sanctions should be maintained against Italy.[55] During the Spanish Civil War, the Communist International was able to recruit thirty-five thousand volunteers from fifty countries and colonies into the international brigades that were an integral part of the Spanish Republican Army.[56] In Padmore's opinion, Ethiopian fighters with their "primitive weapons, fighting against overwhelming odds to throw back Fascist-imperialist barbarism from the shores of Africa" would be long remembered when "many so-called 'revolutionary internationalists' who betrayed them [would] be forgotten".[57] The church was not spared Padmore's criticism. He charged that *L'Osservatore Romano*, the official organ of the Vatican, openly endorsed this imperialist war of conquest.[58] This perspective was similar to that of F.A. Ridley, who claimed that the papacy supported the Italian conquest of Ethiopia "in spite of its wanton aggressive character and flagrant barbarities against unarmed civilians, which shocked the conscience of the civilized world, including the non-Catholic religious opinion". According to Ridley, when Addis Ababa fell it was "celebrated at the Pope's order by thanksgiving services and the ringing of bells in all the churches of Italy".[59] Padmore contended that this was not "the first time that Europeans masked their predatory designs against colonial peoples" by using religion. The Christian church had been one of the main instruments of western imperialism when the Europeans colonized Africa, pilfering its land while announcing that it was "carrying the blessings of Christianity and civilization to the Africans". Padmore asserted that the rationale behind the silence of the pope and the archbishop of Canterbury in not condemning Mussolini was because they were also guilty of using the name of Christ in the service of capitalism.[60] The silence of Pope Pius in not condemning the atrocities being carried out against Ethiopians convinced Padmore and many pan-Africanists that the Catholic Church and Mussolini were acting in unison against Ethiopia.[61]

For Padmore, the Italo-Ethiopian conflict was an eye-opener in many respects. It served to reveal to the black people of the world who was friend and who was foe. It exposed the duplicity of the European statesmen, and it revealed the contradictions and weaknesses of the European imperialist economies in a clearer light than the diplomats in Geneva had anticipated when the Ethiopian emperor made his first appeal to the league in January 1935.[62]

THE INTERNATIONAL AFRICAN SERVICE BUREAU

In March 1937, Padmore and some former members of the International African Friends of Abyssinia/Ethiopia established the IASB. The other leading members were Ras Makonnen, Wallace-Johnson, Chris Jones, James and Jomo Kenyatta, many of them Marxists or former Marxists. The IASB "was formed to assist by all means in our power the uncoordinated struggle of Africans and people of African descent against the oppression from which they suffer in every country".[63]

It is important to note that the IASB restricted its active membership to Africans and persons of African descent and its associate membership to European and other races. This was not done because of any racial discrimination. The IASB repudiated the idea of "substituting a black racial arrogance for a white", as this was the "policy of reactionaries and the enemies of human progress".[64] Padmore added that the IASB was "opposed to racial exclusiveness".[65] It did, however, take the position that it was not going to have European leadership, although it was prepared to work with any group to fight against their common enemy.[66] The members of the IASB believed that African emancipation could not be achieved in isolation, and they were prepared to work with all political movements that were genuinely working against the forces of imperialism and fascism in the world at this time: the Spanish revolution, China's fight against Japan, India's struggle for independence and the struggles of workers against fascism.[67]

The IASB published two short-lived magazines, *Africa and the World* and the *African Sentinel*, edited by Wallace-Johnson. But the *International African Opinion*, with its motto of "Educate, co-operate, emancipate: Neutral in nothing affecting the African peoples" and edited by C.L.R. James, was the most successful publication of the IASB. The *International African Opinion* saw itself as "the mouthpiece of the black workers and peasants and those intellectuals" working on behalf of blacks. The paper proclaimed that it would be "no literary journal or giver of advice from the mountain-tops". Instead it would be a journal of action. It called upon "our black brothers to look upon the *International Opinion* as their own, to see with us that it is through their co-operation that we can make it effective". Moreover, the editor pleaded with its subscribers to understand that the journal belonged to them and they should "write to us, stating their problems, their victories and their defeats, their plain spoken criticisms and their approval". It was only on that basis that the

International African Opinion could become "a living weapon in the struggle, a reflection of the everyday demands of the masses as they fight their way to the larger goal".[68]

The IASB quickly became one of the leading anti-imperialist and pan-Africanist groups in London under the leadership of Padmore. He viewed the IASB as a platform to continue the anti-imperialist work he had carried out as a member of the Comintern and to advocate pan-Africanism as the ideology that would save Africa. The Italian invasion of Ethiopia served to radicalize many Africans and people of African descent who were prepared to do everything in their power to defeat imperialism. Padmore regarded the IASB as the vanguard of pan-African activities in London and, like Lenin, thought it was not sufficient to "call ourselves the 'vanguard', the advanced contingent; we must act in such a way that all the other contingents recognise and are obliged to admit that we are marching in the vanguard".[69]

Padmore's experience of agitation proved invaluable in this effort. He wrote articles in numerous newspapers that kept "every situation [in the Caribbean and Africa] alive".[70] Leslie James contends that Padmore wrote in order to communicate to "a mass audience the common position of black peoples and the structural reason for this situation, thus nurturing resistance".[71] Padmore, in his articles, sought to fan the flames of protest and turn every act of atrocity into widespread indignation. He did this in "Cocoa War on the Gold Coast", "Fascism in the West Indies", "Truth about Cocoa Slaves", "Labour Unrest in Jamaica", "British Empire Is the Worst Racket Yet Invented by Man", "Police Swoop on Workers' Leaders in the Colonies", "Fascism Invades West Africa", "We Gave Them Copper, They Gave Us Lead!", "To Defeat Nazism We Must Free the Colonies", "No Atlantic Charter for the Colonies", "How Colonies Are Ruled" and "Democracy Runs Amok in the Colonies".

Many of Padmore's articles appeared in the *New Leader*, the journal of the ILP, under the byline "The Negro Socialist Leader". The ILP abandoned communism when the Soviet Union joined the League of Nations in September 1934. Padmore, who during his Comintern days had been critical of social democratic parties, now described the ILP as "the only British political party which consistently opposed colonialism". He worked so closely with the ILP that he was described as one of the leading intellectuals of the party in the late 1930s and early 1940s.[72] Makonnen, the leading black nationalist in the IASB, was uncomfortable with Padmore's relationship with the ILP and told Padmore "it was almost as treasonable as working for the British Communist Party".[73] Makonnen felt that Padmore's close affiliation with the ILP could compromise the self-reliant approach of the IASB. Padmore, in his defence, argued that he wrote in the *New Leader* because it provided good publicity.[74] From his experience in editing the *Negro Worker* as well as writing for other newspapers, Padmore recognized the value of reaching a wider audience to educate readers, and the *New Leader* allowed Padmore to communicate with an audience that he might not otherwise have been able to reach. Carol Polsgrove reminds us that Padmore, by writing for the *New Leader*, was able to "draw on another organization's resources – a common strategy for social movements – and speak to a sympathetic audience that already existed rather than hav[ing] to mobilize their audience from scratch".[75] During World War II, Padmore wrote for *Left* and the newspaper *Controversy*, which carried many IASB notices.[76]

C.L.R. James credits Padmore with turning the IASB into a genuine political force. He tells us that nobody held as many meetings as Padmore, who would counsel "don't let anything happen" without convening a meeting: "When three or four incidents take place, the press is full of it and when you do nothing about it . . . people will say that these people have no interest."[77] Therefore as soon as an incident took place, Padmore would call a meeting and pass a resolution. The next day Padmore or one of the members of the IASB would visit the colonial office or write a letter to that office informing them that the IASB had held a meeting the previous night and "passed resolutions and we would like you to have a copy".[78] They also sought to convince members of the ILP who sat in Parliament to take positions that were sympathetic to the views of the IASB.

James, in his assessment of the work of the IASB, noted that it was a success. Padmore spent many hours speaking to people from Africa and from throughout the world. His wide-ranging experience and knowledge "drew them like a magnet".[79] Dudley Thompson informs us that Padmore "could give details of the party's struggle in Cambodia, or the duties of church elders in Barbados or compare agrarian problems in Jamaica and Tanganyika".[80] His conversations would produce "an article, a resolution, a manoeuvre with the Colonial Office, an approach to a Labour Member of Parliament, an avenue for some propaganda in the British press".[81] Many African politicians – Wallace-Johnson, Kenyatta, Nkrumah, Azikiwe, Joe Appiah, Musazi, Mayanja and Sudanese leaders – came to Padmore "for advice on tactics and strategies to utilize in their various anti-colonial struggles". James observed that Padmore provided "invaluable assistance" and "direct inspiration in this regard".[82] He added that these politicians depended on Padmore for briefings on the general political situation and the political attitudes of parties and personnel to colonial problems. Moreover, Padmore would provide information on which colonial official to meet with and boasted to his friend Ollivierre that "they all hang around daddy, or is it Uncle George".[83]

Padmore argued that the IASB, by holding lectures and discussions, soon caught the attention of a band of brilliant young black intellectuals in Britain, many of whom held Marxist views, although they never joined the Communist Party of Great Britain. Padmore described them as despising "the opportunism of the British Communists", who, throughout the Popular Front period (1934–39), viewed "Africans as backward unsophisticated tribesmen". He was of the opinion that British communists minimized the African desire for "immediate self-government", and only paid "lip-service to Indian independence". Many intellectuals turned away from these communist charlatans and "oriented themselves to Pan-Africanism as an independent political expression of Negro aspiration for complete national independence from white domination – Capitalist or Communist".[84]

For Padmore the anti-fascist Popular Front period, which coincided with the formative years of IASB and the duration of the International African Friends of Abyssinia/Ethiopia, was one of the most exciting and productive in the history of pan-Africanism. At this juncture, pan-Africanists had to confront "the ideological challenge from the communists" and "the racist doctrines of the fascists", while championing the agenda of pan-Africanism – "the fundamental right of black men to be free and independent". A number of black intellectuals began to study European political theories and systems as a way to enrich the ideology of pan-Africanism. Padmore posited that by utilizing this approach, young pan-Africanists were able to build upon the work of early pan-Africanists and "formulate a programme of dynamic nationalism, which combined African traditional forms of organization with Western political party methods".[85]

PAN-AFRICAN FEDERATION

In 1944, the IASB proposed that the various pan-African organizations in Manchester should come together and form a broad "Pan-African united front movement", to be known as the Pan-African Federation (PAF).[86] This proposal was accepted by the following pan-African organizations: the IASB, Negro Welfare Centre, Negro Association, Coloured Workers' Association, United Committee of Coloured and Colonial Peoples' Association, African Union, Association of Students of African Descent, Kikuyu Central Association, African Progressive Association, Sierra Leone Section, African Youth League and Friends of African Freedom Society. According to Padmore, the objectives of the PAF were in line with the broad principles proclaimed at the earlier pan-African congresses, namely, to promote the well-being and unity of African peoples and peoples of African descent throughout the world, to demand self-determination and independence of African peoples and other subject races from the domination of powers claiming sovereignty and trusteeship over them, to secure equality of civil rights for African peoples and the total abolition of all forms of racial discrimination, and to strive for cooperation between African peoples and others who share their aspirations.[87]

The PAF sought to establish links with black organizations in various colonial territories and to bring them into direct fraternal contact with each other to "speak with one voice on all matters affecting the economic, political, educational and moral well-being of the black peoples throughout the world".[88] Although the IASB was part of the PAF, it still saw itself as the vanguard within the organization, and Padmore continued to be the dominant ideologue within the PAF.

The PAF published a number of pamphlets dealing with specific colonial problems, authored by its members: *The West Indies Today*; *Kenya, Land of Conflict; African Empires and Civilizations; The Negro in the Caribbean; The Voice of the New Negro; The American Negro Problem; The Native Problem in South Africa; The Voice of Coloured Labour; Hands Off the Protectorates* and *White Man's Duty*. It is noteworthy that Padmore, the experienced pamphleteer, wrote *Hands Off the Protectorates*, co-authored *White Man's Duty* and edited *The Voice of Coloured Labour*. The members of the PAF "through writing and publishing together" helped to reinforce "their common belief that they could bring into being a new, independent Africa".[89] Their pamphlets sought to preserve the research of members of the PAF in a single document instead of being scattered in various newspapers. These pamphlets provided a body of information for anyone interested in developments affecting black people worldwide.

According to Peter Abrahams, "George Padmore, Chairman of the International Africa Service Bureau, threw out the idea of convening another Pan-African Congress."[90] Padmore and the PAF stole the initiative from Amy Jacques Garvey, the widow of Marcus Garvey, Harold Moody of the League of Coloured Peoples and Du Bois, who were also discussing the possibility of organizing a pan-African event after World War II. Du Bois confessed that he received letters from Garvey and Moody requesting his cooperation in "looking toward a post-war conference to consider the demands of Negroes", to take place in "London as soon as practical after the end of the war".[91] Du Bois had last planned a major pan-African congress in 1927.

Padmore and the PAF issued the call for the conference in February 1945, at the same time that the World Federation of Trade Unions held its preliminary meeting in London. Representatives from Nigeria, the Gold Coast, Sierra Leone, Gambia, Jamaica, Trinidad, Barbados, British Guiana and "other colonial lands" attended this historic gathering. The call was made at this opportune moment to solicit the cooperation and participation of federation delegates when they would return later in the year for the full meeting of the World Federation of Trade Unions. It is important to remember that Padmore was formerly the executive director of the ITUCNW and was still a trade unionist at heart. He was cognizant of the fact that although trade unions had only recently been legally recognized in many territories, they had a large membership, and many of the trade unions were connected to the emerging political parties in the various colonies. By targeting trade unionists, Padmore was trying to secure the broadest possible representation for the conference. Past pan-African congresses had been attended by bourgeois reformers and black intellectuals who lacked any organic connection to the mass movements in their respective territories. Additionally, there was insufficient representation at these conferences from the African continent.

PLANNING FOR THE FIFTH PAN-AFRICAN CONGRESS: CORRESPONDENCE WITH DU BOIS

The congress call was carried in the *Chicago Defender*, where Du Bois read about plans to hold the fifth PAC in Paris. He promptly wrote a letter to Padmore seeking additional information about the proposed conference, triggering an interesting discussion between the established leader of pan-Africanism and the emerging trailblazer. Du Bois suggested to Padmore that a pan-African congress should be held in Africa. In the past, the congresses had been held in Britain, France, Portugal and Belgium. In 1929, Du Bois wanted to hold the congress on African soil, but the French government opposed the idea. Also, the onset of the Great Depression prevented the congress from becoming a reality.

Du Bois inquired about the date, which organizations had participated in drafting the conference manifesto and how the planning had unfolded.[92] In response, Padmore informed Du Bois that he was glad to hear that progress was being made in connection with the PAC being planned by Du Bois. He told Du Bois that his proposal was not an "attempt to monopolize or to by-pass the work of others engaged in a similar undertaking" and revealed that the manifesto evolved out of concrete proposals discussed during the visit of the colonial delegates to the World Trade Union Conference in London. Desmond Buckle had written the document, and it was "discussed, amended and endorsed by the coordinating committee – by the International African Service Bureau, Negro Association and Negro Welfare Association".[93] Padmore informed Du Bois that the date was strategically chosen to coincide with the formal launch of the new Trade Union International, when a large group of representatives from colonies would be in Europe. He concurred with Du Bois that Africa would be the best place to hold the congress because none of the previous pan-African congresses had been held on African soil, but he felt that the colonial powers would prohibit such a meeting. Padmore thought that it might be possible to have a conference in Liberia, because America "is not a colonial power in Africa", and it, therefore, might be possible for the NAACP or some other group to obtain "facilities for us to meet in Monrovia".[94]

Padmore, the veteran conference organizer, informed Du Bois that to have a successful conference, "the concrete procedure would be for your group in America to recognize the principle of democratic decentralization" and set up a coordinating committee in New York that would organize the US and West Indian delegations. He suggested that the organizing committee in London could give the coordinating committee in New York contact information of Caribbean organizations to help them prepare draft resolutions. Padmore wrote that the coordinating committee in New York would broaden the existing "Coordinating Committee by co-opting other organizations" that were not part of the organization and transform it into the Pan-African Convening Committee of Great Britain. The committee in London would send the draft documents to all the African organizations for amendments and observations, after which the two coordinating committees could decide upon the best time and place to have this conference. He informed Du Bois that there were no relevant organizations in Britain because there were no organized communities, but the organizing committee had contact and influence with organizations in the British colonies. Padmore told Du Bois that "the African masses are wide awake and are not blindly looking to doctors and lawyers to tell them what to do". This was manifested in the composition of the trade union delegates to the preliminary conference of World Federation of Trade Unions, who Padmore believed "came from the masses and have deep roots in the masses".[95]

In another letter, Du Bois notified Padmore that they were still planning the congress and had been advised that the minister of the colonies of France would be "willing and pleased to have such a congress in Paris". Du Bois suggested to Padmore that, based on his involvement with previous pan-African congresses, they hardly needed any "preliminary machinery" and they needed to let the assembly "organize its own machinery after the convocation". Du Bois warned Padmore that the planning should be very "catholic and cooperative and avoid trying to force the people too far or to get any particular set of ideas adopted too quickly". He felt that this could result in divisions before the congress even took place, given that Harold Moody and the West African Students' Union were conservative and wary about trade unionism and communism.[96] In response, Padmore told Du Bois that "our provisional committee welcomes the view you have expressed, that no attempt should be made to impose any fixed ideological pattern upon the Conference". However, Padmore felt there would be common agreement about the basic objectives "the conference desire[d] to arrive at" and was of the view that there was "complete unity of purpose and outlook among the colonial peoples of the British Empire". Padmore also noted that the initial expression of political awareness for those living under colonial rule took on the appearance of "national liberation and self-determination". He pointed out that this position was shared by conservatives and radicals even though they might be at variance over the pace of reform and the political method of arriving at their goal. Padmore added that the progressive elements emphasized self-determination and separation from the British Empire, while the more conservative elements wanted dominion status within the empire.[97]

In Padmore's opinion, the ideological disputes of communism, anti-communism, Trotskyism and the other ideological tendencies that were present in the United States did not exist in Britain. He explained that African Americans were "part and parcel of the American body politic", and they found it problematic to insulate themselves from the political tendencies that were present in American society. Conversely, blacks from the British colonies lived outside of Britain and those who lived in Britain comprised "an alien minority". Consequently, when blacks came to Britain, they tended to link up with other organizations that were calling for self-determination for their colony. Padmore acknowledged that while some of them subscribed to political philosophies like socialism, communism or anarchism, these positions were more in the nature of idiosyncrasies than practical politics.[98] He contended that "even those who described themselves as Communists are really nationalists" because they recognize that their countries must be liberated before "they can practise their communism". Padmore mentioned that while he had strong Marxist views, "which Dr Moody does not support", it would be dishonest to say that Dr Moody was "hostile to Socialism" because he did not endorse Marxism as Padmore did. It is noteworthy that although Padmore had severed his connections with the Comintern over a decade ago, he still identified as a Marxist. He maintained that notwithstanding their individual views, there was no division between himself and Moody as regards "self-government for Africa". Padmore apprised Du Bois of the ease with which the PAF was formed because "when it comes to imperialism" black people were united. He admitted that while they "have their petty squabbles", they had never had any deep-seated quarrels to bring about the kind of division predicted by Du Bois.[99]

Padmore reminded Du Bois that the organizing committee was familiar "with the modus operandi of running conferences". He reported that the committee was in agreement with his suggestion that they should have only a few pre-arranged plans and allow the conference to evolve. However, there had to be a "minimum amount" of organization, otherwise there would be anarchy. Padmore further explained that the duties of the provisional committee were to establish contacts with organizations in Britain and overseas, issue invitations and look after the logistics of the conference, budgeting, entertainment, securing the venue and so on. After the delegates arrived, the provisional committee would become a standing orders committee, to register credentials and elect reporters for the various subjects to be discussed. When the conference commenced, the entire organization would be in the hands of the delegates. Padmore told Du Bois that they would not present "any resolutions cut and dried for the delegates to approve or reject". Instead, they would have reports from the different "parts of the world which are to come under review". The information from these reports and the attendant discussions would be used by the subcommittee tasked with drafting resolutions.[100]

Padmore also agreed with Du Bois that the conference should be a preliminary congress and they should hold a larger congress "next year, especially as a new government has come into being in Britain since we started planning the forthcoming Conference". He told Du Bois that since the World Trade Union Conference was slated to take place between

25 September and 9 October, the PAC would be held between 9 and 15 October to enable the "Colonial delegates to get from France to England" to attend the meeting.[101]

In another piece of correspondence, Du Bois instructed Padmore to avoid the appearance of making the congress largely a British meeting: "they must not neglect the interests and opinions of the French, Belgians, Portuguese and Spanish Africans as well as Africans of West Indian and American descent".[102] Padmore replied that they were expecting delegates from every territory in British West, South and East Africa and French blacks. He informed Du Bois that they had not overlooked the French, Belgian, Portuguese and Spanish portions of Africa because the young Africans who "form the vanguard" of pan-Africanism think "in terms of Africa as a whole", transcending the haphazard boundaries that Europeans had created in Africa. Padmore admitted that the challenge they faced was one of logistics. They had contacts throughout Africa but the difficulty lay in getting them out. He pointed out that his executive would like Du Bois to know that if all the congress wanted was attendees from all of Africa, then that goal would be met because there were Africans from every part of the world residing in Britain. Padmore stressed that all the representatives attending the congress had to have mandates from mass-based organizations and would not speak for themselves but rather "for the masses of people", not for "the middle class strata and professionals in the Colonies" but for "workers' organizations, the cooperative societies, peasants' associations, labour parties and national liberation organizations".[103]

FIFTH PAN-AFRICAN CONGRESS

Planning for the fifth PAC began in 1944. From the time the decision was taken to have the fifth PAC, "Padmore, the master planner, was in his element".[104] Padmore's contacts throughout the British Empire were asked to assist in publicizing the congress.[105] Kwame Nkrumah, who shared secretarial duties with Padmore on the organizational committee, revealed that they "worked night and day in George's flat" to dispatch "hundreds of letters to the various organizations throughout Africa and the West

Indies explaining the aims of the congress and the political tactics that should be adopted to achieve liberation in the colonies".[106]

The fifth PAC took place in Manchester, 13–21 October 1945. With over two hundred delegates from political, social and trade union organizations in Africa, the West Indies, Britain and America, it "was the most representatives yet assembled by Africans and persons of African descent to plan and work for the liquidation of Imperialism".[107] This congress was preceded by two Subject Peoples Conferences in London; one on 10 June 1945 and the other in October 1945. Padmore and many of the leading personalities of the PAF were active participants at these conferences, where the delegates attacked imperialism, called for independence and discussed the struggle for liberation in Indo-China, India, Malaysia and other areas of Asia. African-Asian unity was continually stressed throughout the deliberations.[108] The Nigerian general strike also helped radicalize many Africans and blacks resident in Great Britain. The strike started on 21 June 1945 and lasted fifty-two days. Padmore told Ollivierre that he was responsible for the action taken by the PAF in seeking to assist the workers in a concrete way. The PAF dispatched cables to "all Colonial and American organizations appealing for support on behalf of these strikers". Replies came "from all over the world and over £300 was collected at meetings in London, Manchester and Liverpool. . . . In all of it I am the Elder statesman behind the scene."[109] Chief A. Soyemi Coker of the Trade Union Congress of Nigeria informed the delegates at the congress that "the pan-African Federation was the first organization to come to our aid during the general strike; the PAF gave moral and financial support beyond our expectations".[110]

Thus, the congress took place at a time when militant anti-imperialism was pervasive in Asia and Africa. This aggressive anti-imperialism was evident throughout the conference and was seen in the language of the Challenge to the Colonial Powers, one of the main resolutions to emerge out of this gathering, where the delegates were clear that Africans "may have to appeal to force in the effort to achieve Freedom, even if force destroys them and the world".[111] The statement boldly declared "we are determined to be free" and "we demand for Black Africa autonomy and independence".[112] The statement ended by adding that "we will fight in every way we can for freedom, democracy and social betterment".[113] According to Padmore, the delegates "returned home to put their hands to freedom's plough and furrow the ground for the seeds of liberty to grow".[114]

In the Declaration to the Colonial Workers, Farmers and Intellectuals, the other important document produced by the congress, the issue of independence also took centre stage: "the delegates of the fifth pan-African Congress believe in the right of all peoples to govern themselves". The statement added that "we affirm the right of all Colonial peoples to control their destiny ... all colonies must be free from foreign imperialist control, whether political or economic ... [and] the peoples of the Colonies must have the right to elect their own governments, without restrictions from foreign peoples".[115] In Padmore's assessment, pan-Africanism had arrived at "a new stage of Positive Action", having evolved from a protest movement intent on improving the conditions of Africans globally to one demanding independence with a plan in place to fight if their demands were not realized. However, the success of this strategy hinged on the extent to which the Africans were organized; organization was the "key to freedom".[116]

One distinguishing feature in Padmore's appraisal of the congress "was its plebeian character" when compared with past pan-African congresses. Representatives came from "the political parties, trade unions, farmer movements and 'nationalistically minded' students". He also detected a militancy that had not been evident before. Padmore attributed this development to the congress's organic link with popular movements in the colonies, a departure from the earlier congresses, which had been dominated by a "small intellectual elite and bourgeois reformists". Padmore contended that the congress displayed "a mass movement intimately identified with the underprivileged sections of the coloured colonial populations". In his view, this link between progressive middle-class intellectuals and ordinary people was crystallized in a series of resolutions resulting from detailed discussions of the many aspects of the African problem.[117]

Padmore must be given much credit for the success of the fifth PAC. He was intimately involved in the planning from conception to execution. Timing the call to coincide with the World Federation of Trade Unions' ensured that unlike previous congresses, pan-Africanism was rooted in the masses and in mass-based institutions. One cannot downplay the role of his network of contacts in promoting the congress. His skills as a conference organizer cannot be overstated; whether wittingly or unwittingly, the conference position closely coincided with Padmore's pan-Africanist and anti-imperialist outlook.

Padmore was at the centre of radical pan-Africanism in Britain from the mid-thirties up to the fifth PAC in 1945. He was able to bring his journalistic and propagandistic writing skills as well as his organizational skills and revolutionary discipline to the pan-African movement. The IASB and the PAF were two important entities that assisted Padmore in pushing a more radical brand of pan-Africanism. The fifth PAC was a culmination of the work done by Padmore and pan-Africanists in London. This conference benefited from Padmore's organizational skills as well as his intellectual leadership of the pan-African movement. The invasion of Ethiopia and World War II provided the environment that contributed towards the radicalization of pan-Africanism.

5. RADICAL ANTI-IMPERIALIST CRITIQUES

GEORGE PADMORE, FROM HIS UNDERGRADUATE DAYS AT Fisk and Howard universities, developed a reputation as a strident critic of imperialism and colonialism. As a member of the CPUSA and a functionary of the Comintern, he continued to be one of the most trenchant critics of colonialism and imperialism as shown in his work *The Life and Struggles of Negro Toilers* and the numerous articles he wrote in the *Negro Worker* and other publications. After Padmore broke with the Comintern, he remained unrelenting in his criticism of colonialism in general and British colonialism in particular, as seen in many of the books he wrote, especially *How Britain Rules Africa*, *Africa and World Peace* and *Africa: Britain's Third Empire*, as well as his many newspaper articles. F.A. Ridley, one of the leading members of the ILP, who was familiar with Padmore's writings, stated that "if there is a more dynamic critic of imperialism in the British Empire" than Padmore, "I do not know his whereabouts".[1]

It is an open secret that Padmore's position on imperialism was heavily influenced by Lenin, but it was also inspired by J.A. Hobson, who wrote *Imperialism: A Study*, and Parker Moon, the author of *Imperialism and World Politics*. Even though Padmore was no longer a member of the Comintern, he still identified himself as a Marxist and continued to employ Marxist-Leninist analysis, extending Lenin's model of imperial plunder by focusing it mainly on Africa: Africa, in the eyes of European imperialists, was a source of raw materials for manufactured goods, a space in which to invest surplus finance capital for the exploitation of mineral resources and the attendant infrastructure to exploit these resources, and an outlet for European settlers to secure employment and land.[2] For Padmore, Africans were doubly exploited as a class and as a race. They were exploited more viciously than the working class in Europe because of their colonial status, because trade unions were prohibited, or where they existed, were, weak and ineffective.[3]

Padmore, in his evaluation of the impact of imperialism on Africa, was dismayed by the devastation that it had inflicted on Africa. According to Padmore, "the African masses are poor, ignorant and diseased" because "they are victims of a cruel social system of imperialism" that exploits them and cares little for their well-being.[4] He described colonialism as "a socially backward system" that stunted the economic development of Africa. Therefore, Africa would always be underdeveloped as long as it was viewed as "estates of the Crown to be exploited for the benefit of Europeans".[5] For Padmore, the system of imperialism did not bring any tangible benefits to Africans because the exploitation of resources and labour was inherent to imperialism. In *How Britain Rules Africa*, he attempted to show "every conceivable crime" that was associated with imperialism: taxation without representation, oppression, exploitation, racial ignorance and arrogance, atrocities and genocide. In his opinion, the most outrageous of these offences was the brutal "methods used by the white settlers" in appropriating the best land from Africans and then compelling them to work for the settlers. He was perturbed that Europeans showed no remorse for the crimes they committed against Africans and hoped that bringing the crimes of imperialism to the attention of the British public would outrage the working class into demanding an end to this vicious system.[6]

THE MANDATORY SYSTEM

With the rise of fascism in Germany and Italy during the 1930s, the question of whether they should have colonies became a subject that was widely discussed throughout Britain and Europe. Hitler and Mussolini were arguing that colonies "were essential to Italy, Germany and Japan in order that their manufacturers may be supplied with raw materials and their peoples with food".[7] During a meeting with the British foreign secretary in 1935, Hitler conveyed his wish for the restoration of former German colonies.[8] For Mussolini, "the historic objectives of Italy had two names – Asia and Africa".[9] For Padmore, nations that possessed colonies had two advantages over those that did not: they could link up their colonies with their own currency systems and in this way obtain the raw materials produced in the colonies without needing to find the currency to pay for such products and they could sell their manufactured goods to their colonial subjects at a high rate of profit.[10]

To stave off the seeming inevitable war in Europe, some liberals and socialists in Britain proposed extending the mandatory system to "all of the African territories which are at present administered as Crown colonies or protectorates in tropical Africa".[11] The mandatory system was established under article 22 of the covenant of the League of Nations on 28 June 1919. This system was formulated to address the disposal of the German and Turkish colonial territories following World War I. It was felt that the colonial subjects of these former empires "were not able to stand by themselves under the strenuous conditions of the modern world" and their care was "entrusted to advanced nations who, by reason of their resources, their experience or their geographical position can best undertake this responsibility".[12] Mandates were divided into three classes. Class A mandates were territories that had reached such advanced development that they could function as independent nations but needed some administrative advice in the interim. Class B mandates were less advanced than class A mandates and were subject to more supervision and were given definite guarantees for the welfare of their inhabitants. Class C mandates, characterized by their small size and remoteness from metropolises, were assigned to neighbouring mandatory powers and governed as integral portions of their own empires, subject to safeguards for the inhabitants.[13]

The idea of extending the mandatory was to allow Italy and Germany to gain access to the raw materials they desired and avert the prospect of war. Sir Arthur Salter, a former director of the League of Nations and professor of political theory at Oxford, was one of the leading proponents of the extension of the mandate system.[14] The British Labour Party called for an international conference on "access to raw materials and to markets".[15]

In September 1935, the Trade Union Congress passed a resolution that was adopted by the Labour Party Conference: "We call upon the British Government to urge the League of Nations to summon a World Economic Conference and to place upon its agenda the international control of the sources of supply of raw materials, with the application of opportunity to all nations in the underdeveloped regions of the earth."[16]

In October 1935 the National Peace Council held the Peace and the Colonial Problem conference, at which the issue of colonial revision to meet the demands of the dissatisfied imperialist powers was discussed.[17] Padmore was critical of the position taken by progressives who seemed to believe that Africa belonged to the white race and could be traded from one European nation to another as circumstances demanded. He felt that it was necessary to educate those who were calling for the extension of the mandatory system about the imperialistic nature of the system, its undemocratic nature and how Africans were being exploited under it.

For Padmore, the mandatory system was a disguised form of imperialist annexation.[18] Leonard Woolf, a political theorist, argued that the mandatory system was the "opposite of imperialism".[19] Lord Hailey was of a different opinion: he "condemned [this system] as a subterfuge by which certain of the Allies obtained control of some of the areas they coveted, while pretending non-aggrandizement".[20] Britain and France, the two leading imperialist powers, were able to increase the size of their colonial empires after World War I because of the mandatory system. Padmore noted that of the 971,377 square miles of former German and Turkish territories, the British and French were in possession of 671,867 square miles of them. Britain acquired the Turkish territories of Iraq, Transjordan and Palestine, while France got Syria and Lebanon. Of the former German territories, Britain got Tanganyika, British Cameroon and British Togoland and France got French Togoland and French Cameroon.[21] Although the mandates were not technically colonies, they were considered integral to the greater colonial empire. Padmore maintained that in acquiring these territories, Britain and France were able to convince the world that they had not seized these countries as "spoils of war" but were holding them in trust for the local populations, who were "unfit to govern themselves".[22]

Padmore posited that it was the commonly held view that the mandatory system was based on the humanitarian principle of trusteeship. Mandatory powers were supposed to discard their imperialistic propensities in the spirit of Christianity and promote "the material well-being and social progress of the inhabitants of the territories subject to the present mandate".[23] The first two paragraphs of article 22 of the Covenant of the League of Nations made this abundantly clear.[24] Padmore emphasized that the idea of trusteeship was, however, nothing new and had been articulated in the Berlin Act of 1885, when Europeans divided Africa into European territories. At this infamous gathering, European imperialists announced "in the name of almighty God" that they would set themselves the "task of furthering the material and moral well-being of the native populations".[25] Padmore noted that these lofty objectives were never achieved. Instead, atrocities were carried out in the Congo by the Belgians, Germans implemented a regime of floggings, the French instituted forced labour and the Portuguese employed a slavery-like system in Angola.[26] Indeed, the material and moral well-being of Africans was retarded rather than developed.

The concept of trusteeship was also embodied in the Brussels Conference Act of 1890, after representatives from Europe, the United States and Persia and the sultan of Zanzibar met and were "equally actuated by the firm intention of putting an end to the crimes and devastations engendered by the traffic in African slaves, of efficiently protecting the aboriginal population of Africa, and of securing for that vast continent the benefits of peace and civilization".[27] Padmore took aim at this agreement: "What peace, what civilization have they brought to the Africans? Is it the peace that makes their land a desert, the civilization that turns them into hewers of wood and drawers of water for their predatory masters?" He dismissed talk about trusteeship and protecting the interests of blacks as nonsense because the actions of the Europeans did not suggest that they were interested in the well-being of Africans.[28] Padmore warned his readers not to be duped by pronouncements "of trusteeship and mandates" because they are "devices to mask imperialistic exploitation" of colonized people and to hoodwink the European masses about the actual conditions in the colonies.[29]

Padmore observed that Africans in mandated territories had no say in public affairs and were denied the most basic of human rights. In Tanganyika and South West Africa they were subjected to pass laws, residential restriction ordinances and master and servant acts. Under the repressive master and servant acts, Africans could be imprisoned for six months for failing to begin work after signing a contract with a white employer, neglect of duty, refusal to work or carry out a master's orders, drunkenness at work, insulting an employer, his wife or daughter, supplying false information, using the master's property without permission and absence from work without leave.[30]

For Padmore, the most damning charge that could be brought against the mandatory system was "the ruthless military methods" that had been employed against the mandate's inhabitants. In his opinion, the most outrageous action taken against any mandated people was the bombing of the Bondelzwarts of South West Africa by the South African government.[31] In 1922 the Bondelzwarts protested a number of colonial measures: the non-restoration of their captain Jacobus Christian, the continuing white penetration of their land and the imposition of a graded dog tax that severely limited their ability to keep packs of dogs for game hunting.[32] The South African government, the mandatory power responsible for South West Africa, responded to the protest by bombing the Bondelzwarts, killing over one hundred men and some of their flocks.[33] Although this matter was discussed at the Permanent Mandates Commission of the League of Nations, the League of Nations did not reprimand the South African government or propose compensation for the families of those who were killed. It only acknowledged that the "dog tax and other measures taken by the South Africa government were unduly severe". Padmore was dissatisfied with the league's refusal to recommend compensation or to condemn the South African government and declared that whether mandated or non-mandated, "the colonial peoples are brutally exploited and oppressed by the Great Powers", who believe that those peoples "have no rights which they are bound to respect".[34]

In Padmore's assessment, there was no distinction "between conditions prevailing under mandates and those in non-mandated territories".[35] Under a mandate government, the people of such territories could not bring their complaints directly to the League of Nations but had to address their petitions to the Mandates Commission. The commission comprised nine members appointed by the Council of the League of Nations to examine the annual reports presented by representatives of the mandatory powers and ensure that the stipulations of the mandates were being followed. This body was only advisory in nature and had "no right to send representatives into the mandated territories to investigate into the grievances of the natives".[36] Padmore described the Mandates Commission as a "mutual admiration society which meets at Geneva from time to time to hear reports, formally accepts whatever the representatives of the ruling State says, and departs in peace".[37]

Padmore argued that the actions of the mandatory powers clearly demonstrated that the mandates were an essential part of the imperialist system, a fact that advocates of the mandates could not obscure. He excoriated socialists, pacifists and liberals in Britain for disseminating the false impression that the extension of the mandatory system was the only solution to preventing imperialist conflicts and warfare. Padmore hoped that the working people of Britain would reject this "utopic" project and "demand the complete independence of the colonial peoples", which he strongly believed would ensure world peace.[38]

UNITED NATIONS TRUSTEESHIP: THE "NEW IMPERIALISM"

During World War II, Padmore became even more critical of imperialism and continually called for the independence of colonies in Africa, Asia and the Caribbean. In the immediate aftermath of World War II, Padmore observed that European statesmen were once again faced with the problem of finding some way to maintain their imperialist system under a new guise. The League of Nations had been replaced by the United Nations in October 1945. The UN introduced the system of trusteeship for the former mandates. Padmore contended that the mandate system had served its intended purpose, and it was now necessary for the new imperialism to change form, though not substance. Hence the proposal of trusteeship as a replacement for the discredited mandates. For Padmore, the trusteeship system was an extension of the mandate system, altered and reformed to "accommodate the conflicting ideologies of the Great Powers".[39] This position was also shared by W.R. Crocker, who contended that trusteeships carried "on the old League Mandate idea" and that all that was different was the "administrative provisions for examining more closely, including visiting the Trust territories".[40]

The UN Charter stipulated that member states that had assumed responsibility for territories "whose people have not yet attained a full measure of self-government" would "recognize the principle that the interests of the inhabitants are paramount".[41] They would also accept as "a sacred trust the obligation to promote the well-being of the inhabitants to the utmost". To this end, they were to ensure "the political, economic, social and educational advancement of the inhabitants, their just treatment and their protection against abuses".[42] This language was similar to the language used for the mandates. However, the trust power would continue to exercise sovereignty. Padmore insisted that while there were minor administrative differences for trusteeships, there was no fundamental change since the arrangement remained inherently imperialistic.[43] He felt that the former mandates should have been given their independence instead of being placed under a trusteeship system.

CROWN COLONIES/DIRECT RULE

Padmore was strongly opposed to the presence of crown colonies/direct rule in Africa because they maintained imperialist domination and exploitation. This form of government was practised in West Africa, northern Rhodesia, Nyasaland, Tanganyika and Uganda. Unlike the crown colony system in place in the Caribbean, crown colony governments in West Africa combined some elements of indirect rule with the administration of the central government. Under this form of government, the governor had immense power: he was the president or Speaker of the legislative council, and able to appoint members of the legislative executive from among the white people in charge of the various departments of the civil service. The legislative council was made up of officials, nominated unofficials and elected unofficial members. The officials, recruited from the heads of departments in the civil service, were obligated to vote in support of the governor.⁴⁴ The governor also selected the unofficial members to represent special interest groups within the colony. Since the unofficial members held office at the discretion of the governor, they would logically "support official policy which invariably work[ed] in their economic and social interests".⁴⁵

Padmore described the legislative council under the crown colony system as "nothing but a debating chamber", with the real instrument of government being the executive council, which formulated all draft legislation that was subsequently brought before the legislature for formal discussion and assent. The role of the legislative council was solely advisory, limited to advising the governor, who was not obligated to consult it, and there was no collective responsibility.⁴⁶

The governor was the sole "authority responsible to and representative of the King". Padmore made the point that a governor symbolized "a sort of constitutional trinity – King's Representative, President of the Executive/sort of Prime Minister/Speaker of the Legislative Council" with "the power to veto any Bill passed by the Assembly". Most colonial governors, therefore, enjoyed wide and even dictatorial powers.⁴⁷ While governors had immense powers and those sections of the middle class that met the property qualifications could participate in the electoral process, the majority of people were excluded from this form of government. For Padmore, crown colony government was "as totalitarian as any fascist state with the Governor as an absolute dictator".⁴⁸

INDIRECT RULE

Indirect rule was the system of governing Africans through their own chiefs and political institutions under the supervision of European bureaucrats.⁴⁹ This form of government was used in sections of Nigeria, the Gold Coast, Sierra Leone, east central Africa, Uganda and Tanganyika. For Padmore, indirect rule was an inexpensive system of governing large areas that would otherwise necessitate a large bureaucracy, like areas where crown colony/direct rule government was in place. The arch-imperialist Lord Lugard was forced to institute this system in northern Nigeria because few white men could be induced to settle there; the British government was still deeply involved in the Boer War and was in no position to send reinforcements to establish military occupation of Nigeria, and the treasury was against spending money on setting up an elaborate British administration.[50] Padmore argued that indirect rule was the result of a historic accident, justified in Lugard's book *The Dual Mandate in British Tropical Africa*. The explanation given by Lugard and his supporters that this system was "an unavoidable philosophical system" was seen by Padmore as ingenious.[51] However, indirect rule was lauded as a "new philosophy of colonial government and many books were being written extolling the virtues that this form of government had conferred upon Africans".[52] It was also trumpeted as an "example of British genius" in not disrupting the indigenous institutions while guiding the Africans on the path to "responsible government".

Padmore was not swayed by this line of reasoning and attacked the so-called attributes of this form of imperialist administration. He posited that before the arrival of the British, "the chiefs derived their authority" from the populace.[53] They had specified power that was firmly regulated by elders and councillors according to local law and traditions. The British, through legislative enactments, had given the chiefs comprehensive authority that resulted in many of them becoming autocratic and concerned not with carrying out the will of the people, but with satisfying their European colonizers.[54] In the pre-colonial Gold Coast, Padmore claimed, the Fanti had developed an effective method of control over their leaders: chiefs were "crowned" presidents, rather than absolute monarchs, "elected" or installed from among certain of the ruling families by recognized procedures and could be removed if their conduct conflicted with the general will.[55]

Under indirect rule, chiefs were no longer subject to the democratic will of their people, and native authorities or administrations derived their power directly from the colonial government and became an integral part of the machinery of government.[56] The main tasks of chiefs as colonial administrators were to maintain law and order, administer justice, administer certain branches of local government, collect taxes and supply forced labour.[57] In many cases, chiefs had been converted into "agents of the occupying power". They had become government servants, many appointed by the governor without consulting the people over whom they ruled. Padmore claimed that "in their anxiety" to expand the system of indirect rule into the south-eastern province of Nigeria, a place where the British could not locate chiefs, they "disregarded the ancient democratic traditions of the people and resorted to the creation of their own lackeys, known as Warrant Chiefs".[58] This also occurred in northern Ghana and in eastern Nigeria. A large number of warrant chiefs were chosen because of services rendered to the colonial government, and according to Padmore, "these puppet rulers having no tradition of responsibility, soon fell into corruption and were neither obeyed nor trusted by the people".[59]

Padmore observed that indirect rule was spreading as rapidly in Africa as fascism was sweeping through Europe.[60] Throughout the 1920s and early 1930s, fascism was growing at an alarming pace throughout Europe. Fascist regimes held control of Italy, Germany, Portugal, Austria, Hungary and Romania, and fascist parties witnessed considerable growth in many other European countries. During the 1930s, throughout British Africa, indirect rule was the gospel of colonial rule and came to be its primary form of expression.[61] The system of indirect rule was extended by the British in equatorial Africa and then emulated by the French after World War I and the Belgians in the 1930s.[62] Padmore insisted that indirect rule, like fascism, was dictatorial and authoritarian, as the only obligation of African populations was "to obey authority".[63] Chiefs had enormous power and were only answerable to the "white official stationed in his state as adviser". Padmore added that "no oriental despot ever had greater power than these black tyrants".[64] Mahmood Mamdani similarly notes that "the authority of the Chief thus fused in a single person all moments of power: judicial, legislative, executive and administrative".[65]

The advocates of indirect rule also advanced the argument that it educated Africans in self-government. However, Padmore raised a salient question: "How can a people learn to rule themselves under such an autocracy backed up by British bayonets?"[66] He asserted that "this is a vast deception" because "people who are denied education and the most elementary democratic rights and civil liberties are in no position to develop self-government".[67] He strongly believed that indirect rule was being utilized by the colonial office to decelerate nascent African nationalism and to postpone the establishment of "Western democratic institutions".[68] For Padmore, indirect rule hindered the "economic and cultural development of the masses".[69] It was not merely "a farce" but a danger to the harmony and contentment of the masses of the people.[70] Padmore argued that to claim, as British imperialists did, that they had introduced political democracy to the Gold Coast was absurd. On the contrary, they had slowed-down the "development of an indigenous system of government that was fundamentally democratic and which would certainly have evolved to meet the social and economic needs of the twentieth century".[71]

Padmore maintained that there was no place for educated Africans under indirect rule and described it "as a form of government of illiterates, by illiterates, for illiterates". He recognized that with the spread of education and the growth of economic development and industrialization taking place in many African territories, "it is doubtful whether the effete and decadent chiefs could long maintain their traditional hold upon the people without the continued support of the British Power".[72] Margery Perham, a historian who wrote extensively on Lord Lugard, the father of indirect rule, acknowledged that "[m]ost educated Africans, especially in West Africa and the Sudan, criticize and strongly condemn Indirect Rule. They say that Indirect Rule gives power to uneducated Chiefs and elders instead of the educated."[73] The majority of nationalist leaders came from the newly created intelligentsia who were educated in British universities.[74]

Padmore contended that by eliminating the authority enjoyed by the "reactionary tribal rulers", it would be possible to use the existing structure of native administration and transform it into real organs of democratic government. He felt that doing this would progressively involve the populace in public affairs and return power to the people. Padmore noted that this constitutional break was the "only means of bridging the difference in outlook between the discredited tribal and feudal aristocracy and the young intellectuals – the torch bearers of Pan-Africanism".[75]

COLONIAL FASCISM

Many people in Britain were concerned with the rise of fascism throughout Europe and Germany's advance into Poland. Padmore, in turn, was concerned that while Europeans were outraged by the actions of fascists in Europe, they did not display this indignation over similar or worse developments in colonies. For Padmore, "Crown Colony government, Indirect Rule and Native Administration meant one thing – Colonial Fascism."[76] In *How Britain Rules Africa*, Padmore included a subsection entitled "Colonial Fascism". In *Africa: Britain's Third Empire*, chapter one is entitled "Colonial Fascism in South Africa". However, Padmore neglected to give a concise definition of what he meant by colonial fascism.

In extrapolating from Padmore's writings on colonial fascism, one can conclude that this formulation implied the rule of a white minority over a black majority in the interest of the colonial power, where force, terror and repression were used to maintain political and economic power and to ensure the exploitation of the resources of the territory and the people. In the territories where colonial fascism existed, the government was dictatorial and denied the majority of citizens basic human rights such as the right to join a trade union, the right to join or form a political party, the right to vote and the freedom of assembly. Racist legislation, land alienation, racial discrimination, racism, violence, repression, aggressive nationalism and the desire for territorial expansion were essential characteristics of colonial fascism.

It was generally accepted that the roots of fascism could be traced back to World War I and the crisis of capitalism in the late 1920s and the early 1930s. However, Padmore located the origins of twentieth-century fascism in Europe in a much earlier period: the imperialist project of the late nineteenth century in Africa. He maintained that the fascist mindset was evident at the Berlin Conference of 1885, when Otto von Bismarck, the German chancellor, conspired with other European imperialists to carve up Africa into European territories. In the quest for a piece of the continent, all the "European powers used identical methods to those now being employed by the Fascist cutthroats in Europe".[77] Padmore opined that despite the horror of Poland, Europeans committed similar or worse atrocities in Africa: the Belgians in the Congo, the French in equatorial Africa, the Portuguese in Angola, the Spaniards in Morocco, the Italians in Libya and Abyssinia and the Germans in South West Africa.[78]

Frantz Fanon, a revolutionary theorist, reminds us that the European colonial project was "marked by violence" during the conquest and the system of colonial rule was maintained "by dint of a great array of bayonets and cannon".[79] Like Padmore, Hannah Arendt traced the roots of totalitarianism that engulfed much of Europe during the 1930s to the new imperialism of the late nineteenth and early twentieth centuries. She recognized that the genocidal impulses of Europeans were justified on racist terms, whether "the Boers' extermination of Hottentot tribes, the wild murdering by Carl Peters in German Southeast Africa, [or] the decimation of the Congo population – from 20 million to 14 million to 8 million people".[80] Mamdami argues that the mass slaughter of the Herero in South West Africa by the Germans was "the first genocide of the twentieth century".[81] It was estimated that under the German policy of annihilation in response to the Herero uprising of 1904, 80 per cent of the Herero had been killed by 1907, and over 50 per cent of the Nama people.[82] Mamdami contends that the links between the actions of German colonizers and the Holocaust went beyond the building of concentration camps and the execution of an annihilation policy.[83] Eugen Fischer, a German geneticist who later became chancellor of the University of Berlin, initiated his medical experiments on race among the Herero.[84] A number of Fischer's "associates and other scientists who were involved in the colonial effort would surface as racialization proponents and activists during the Nazi period".[85]

Padmore contended that the whites in Poland were going through the same suffering that Africans had experienced for centuries. He reminded his readers that Africans in the German colony of Tanganyika were flogged for the least offence and entire tribes chained and forced to work on plantations. In German East Africa, women were held as hostages to compel their husbands to work. Therefore, while the Germans had lost their colonies, they had not lost the colonial methods of savagery that they applied with equal ferocity against their own citizens – communists, socialists, pacifists, democrats and Jews.[86]

SOUTH AFRICA

South Africa represented the best example of colonial fascism for Padmore. It was arguably the most racist country in the world; racism had been present in South Africa from the beginning of white settlement in South Africa in 1652. According to Padmore, "the theory of racial superiority of the Whites over the non-European races" permeated all aspects of life, and legislation was established on the grounds of race.[87] Nigel Worden points out although racism existed in other colonies in Africa, Asia and the Caribbean and in the United States, racism in South Africa developed "into a systematic and legalized discrimination shaping the economic and political structure of the whole country in a more pervasive way than elsewhere".[88] Padmore argued that blacks in South Africa were "subjected to worse forms of racial discrimination and persecution than the Jews in fascist Germany".[89]

The South African government passed a number of racist pieces of legislation. The Mines and Works Act (1911) enforced racial discrimination in mines and on railroads. The Natives Land Act (1913) forced the majority of the black population to live on 7 per cent of the total land area of South Africa. This act was amended by the Native Trust and Land Act (1936), which increased the land available to blacks to 13.5 per cent. The Native (Urban Areas) Act (1923) imposed residential segregation in towns.[90] Padmore contended that the Native Land Act was "the most inhuman piece of legislation ever conceived by white men in the history of European colonization"[91] and the "economic foundation stone upon which the superstructure of South Africa's segregation policy has been built".[92] It should be noted that the most fertile land was allocated to whites, and much of the land given to Africans was not suitable for cultivation or pastoralism. Padmore was of the view that the Native Trust and Land Act "accentuated the policy of racial discrimination, making obligatory the employment of European instead of African overseers and foremen".[93] Apartheid was legally codified and instituted in South Africa in the late 1940s and early 1950s.

Blacks in South Africa were not allowed to sit in the same trains or buses with whites and were barred from attending the same churches and schools and frequenting the same hotels and restaurants as whites. Pass laws were introduced into South Africa around 1852. Africans were required to carry a pass with them in order to be able to travel unimpeded. Failure to produce the pass when required by the authorities was a criminal offence. Padmore contended that the pass laws weighed heaviest on the black population, who were required to have twelve different passes: six-day special pass, monthly pass, identification pass, day special pass, night special pass, location visitor's pass, lodger's permit, poll tax receipt, trek pass, travelling pass, daily labourer's pass and exemption pass.[94] Stanley Payne asserts that "the Afrikaner society of South Africa may have registered the greatest degree of popular support for something approaching European-type fascism during the middle and late 1930s".[95] In South Africa the theory of the racial superiority of whites encompassed every sphere of society, with legislation determined on the basis of colour. Africans were "completely dis-enfranchised and economically they have been reduced to the status of helots".[96] The Native Representation Act of 1936 disenfranchised blacks from Cape Province, who had had a right to vote since 1854, while blacks in the other parts of South Africa who had never had the franchise were also prohibited from voting.[97]

Padmore insisted that "Hitler has nothing new to teach South African politicians in race baiting". Indeed, after reading the pamphlet *Racial Problems in South Africa* (published by Friends House, London) he was convinced that Hitler's anti-Semitic laws had been "borrowed lock, stock and barrel from the statute book of South Africa".[98] He also put forward the argument that black people in South Africa were "more terrorized, exploited and oppressed than in any other country in the world". Although blacks in the United States faced similar discriminatory practices under the Jim Crow system, their general economic and social conditions were not as bad as those of black South Africans as they had "theoretically been granted full citizenship rights under the 14th and 15th Amendments to the American Constitution". However, in South Africa a "racial *minority* lords it autocratically over a *majority* without the slightest regard for the human rights of the non-European".[99]

Padmore pointed out that European colonizers in South Africa, Kenya, Rhodesia and other settler territories had used tactics similar to the Nazis' in order to relegate black people to the status of an inferior people. To justify their actions, the British branded Africans as racially inferior, barbaric and incapable of self-government, which was the same language used by Nazis to describe Jews, Poles, Czechs and other Slavic people in Eastern Europe.[100] Africans were robbed of their best lands to provide *Lebensraum* for the English *Herrenvolk* and were confined to special areas called reserves. In urban centres, Africans lived in ghettoes, just like Poles and Jews in Eastern Europe. And like these particular Europeans, Africans were disenfranchised, barred from all skilled occupations, denied the right to education and forced to carry identification badges.[101]

KENYA

Padmore contended that with the exclusion of South Africa, Kenya had the vilest colonial government of any country in Africa. He strongly believed that the "conditions under which blacks lived in Kenya can without exaggeration be described as colonial fascism". He arrived at this position because of the level of repression and racial discrimination taking place in the colony: trade unions had been banned, there was an absence of social legislation, the Kikuyu Central Association had been declared illegal in 1940, and the Native Authority Ordinance made it illegal for more than five people to assemble without the permission of the authorities. Padmore contended that Africans had as little freedom in Kenya as Jews had in Germany.[102] Africans were disenfranchised and had no representative on the legislative council. Instead, a missionary was appointed by the governor to represent them. Africans were terrorized by repressive racist legislation: the Native Authority Ordinance, the Native Registration Ordinance, township residents' permits, the Squatters Registration Ordinance, Masters and Servants Act, and the Native Permit and Land Ordinance Act.

In 1921 every adult African male under the Native Registration Ordinance was required to carry a labour passport called a *kipande*, which contained his name, fingerprints, employer's name and his wages. The main purpose of this ordinance was to control African travel outside of the reserves. Any African who tried to flee from a European plantation could be detained and returned to his employer, much as how the runaway slaves in the Caribbean or North America were returned to their masters.[103] Padmore was critical of how African workers were punished under the Masters and Servants Ordinance. In many cases, planters who resided far away from the administrative centres inflicted the floggings. Africans were also fined or imprisoned for "breach of contract", which Padmore described as fascist law.[104] The Crown Lands Ordinance of 1915 established reserves; whites were assigned the most fertile land and Africans were placed on reserves, which were often on infertile land. A small population of twenty-nine thousand Europeans controlled 12,750 square miles of land, while five millionAfricans were forced to live on 43,000 square miles.[105] Padmore argued that Kenyans had no legal right to land, whether in or outside a reserve, as laid down in the Crown Lands Ordinance of 1915 as well as the amended ordinance of 1926.[106] The land question became the central issue that concerned Kenyans for many years. Padmore noted that Kenyans had as little freedom as Jews in Germany, since they were not allowed to vote and they had no African representative on the legislative council.[107]

Padmore contended that while the economic problem of Kenyans was the most fundamental issue confronting the mass of the people, there was also the problem of racism, which no serious student of African affairs could disregard. According to Padmore, there was "a definite fascist mentality among European settlers in Kenya".[108] Many of them had come from South Africa in the early twentieth century and hoped to fashion a society like the one they had left in South Africa. This fascist mindset was aptly summed up by Captain W. Wickins, who stated that whites in Kenya "are members of the dominant white race", and see themselves as "superior, socially, economically and mentally to all Blacks".[109] Padmore raised the salient question: "What difference is there between the racial philosophy of the British in East Africa and the Nazis in Germany?"[110] In Padmore's opinion, apart from South Africa and the protectorates, Kenya was the most poorly administered colony in Africa if the welfare of its African inhabitants was used as the benchmark.[111] To further demonstrate the plight of Kenyans, Padmore quoted Dr Norman Leys, a white colonial civil servant who spent many years living in Kenya: "When the historian of the future looks for examples of the worst result of the capitalist system of society, where avarice allied with racial pride and domination showed least signs of shame, where the common people were most despised and poorest, where the law was least regarded and loyalty least possible, he will point to South Africa and Kenya."[112]

COLONIAL FASCISM IN WEST AFRICA

While conditions in West Africa were not the same as in the settler colonies of South Africa, Kenya and Rhodesia, Padmore was concerned about the level of repression there. This was evident when a political crisis developed in Sierra Leone in 1939 that had implications for colonial policy throughout British West Africa. In January 1939, workers at the War Department Defence Works and the Mabella Coaling Company went on strike. Around this time some gunners in the West Africa Frontier Force stationed in Murray Town refused to parade. The *African Standard*, edited by Wallace-Johnson, contributed to the industrial and political ferment with its articles. Colonial authorities responded to this crisis by introducing legislation to quash "anti-colonial opposition and contain the labour movement".[113] Sir Douglas Jardine, the governor, introduced four ordinances to the legislative council with the object of hindering all efforts "of the masses to organize for any improvement" in their social, economic and political condition. For Padmore, these bills were fascist and targeted any "literate or politically conscious leadership which could guide the workers to action".[114]

The few rights that Sierra Leoneans enjoyed were being stolen from them under a variety of emergency war regulations, including the Emergency Powers Act.[115] The first victim of this "policy of official terrorism" was Wallace-Johnson, organizer of the West African Youth League and secretary of the Sierra Leone Trade Union Congress. He was arrested and charged in 1939 for libel, detained under the emergency Colonial Defence Regulations, and imprisoned on Sherbro Island in Sierra Leone until 1944. As a militant trade unionist, Wallace-Johnson was deemed dangerous, and he was incarcerated lest he stir up trouble during the war. For Padmore, the case of Wallace-Johnson illustrated how Africans who dared to demand justice and fair play for their people during World War II would be treated. Padmore and Wallace-Johnson were long-time comrades, having met at the International Conference of Negro Workers in Hamburg in 1930. They worked together when Padmore was the executive secretary of the ITUCNW and editor of the *Negro Worker*. Wallace-Johnson had assisted Padmore with selecting West African recruits for training in the Soviet Union and wrote articles for the *Negro Worker* when Padmore was the editor. Wallace-Johnson was also a founding member and the first general secretary of the IASB, which was chaired by Padmore. According to the Deportation Ordinance that had been enacted the previous May, the governor had the right to order the arrest and deportation of any inhabitant whom he considered undesirable. In the eyes of the bureaucrats, trade union organizers were most undesirable, and the war had given the authorities the occasion to use their dictatorial powers to the maximum.[116]

Padmore felt that African Americans had a moral duty to stand behind black "workers and peasants in their struggle to ward off the tightening up of the democratic imperialist yoke".[117] He believed they should encourage their organizations to pass resolutions against the way Africans were being treated and submit copies to the secretary of state for colonies and the governor of Sierra Leone. Padmore reminded his readers of the outstanding contribution made by Wallace-Johnson and many Africans in highlighting the injustices of the Scottsboro boys' case and the Angelo Herndon struggle. In 1931, nine African American youths in Scottsboro, Alabama were charged with raping two young women. Eight of them were sentenced to death by a jury of all white men. The attempt to free the Scottsboro boys, as they came to be known, became a cause célèbre, and an international campaign was launched on their behalf. Padmore as the executive secretary of the ITUCNW and the editor of *Negro Worker*, played an important part in internationalizing this struggle. Wallace-Johnson played a significant role in helping to popularize the struggle in Nigeria and the Gold Coast. Leo Spitzer and LaRay Denzer confirm that "[t]he collection of funds for the Scottsboro boys appeal took up much of Wallace-Johnson's time at the beginning of his work in the Gold Coast".[118] The Angelo Herndon case was another cause célèbre, but it did not have the same international scope as the Scottsboro boys affair did. Angelo Herndon, a young communist, led a demonstration in

Atlanta, in 1932. He was subsequently charged with attempting to incite insurrection against the state of Georgia. Under the Insurrection Code that was enacted in 1866 and amended in 1871, any person who circulated insurrectionary materials could be sentenced from five to twenty years and any person convicted of attempting insurrection or inducing others to do so could be put to death.[119] Herndon was sentenced to eighteen to twenty years in prison. However, after waging a legal battle for about five years, along with local and international agitation on the matter, he was released in 1937.[120] Padmore felt that given the fact that Africans rallied to the struggles of African Americans in the above struggles, this was the opportune moment for African Americans to show their solidarity with their brothers and sisters in Africa.[121]

"COLONIAL FASCISM" IN TRINIDAD

Padmore posited that the government in Trinidad and Tobago was "inaugurating a policy which savours of Colonial Fascism", but this was a milder form of colonial fascism than that which existed in South Africa and Kenya. In the wake of the 1937 labour rebellion in Trinidad, "a wave of terror and intimidation was sweeping the island". This was evident in a proposed new sedition bill, the prohibition of public meetings, threats to newspaper editors, British troops landing on the island and imprisonment of twenty trade union leaders. Padmore believed that if the repressive policies in Trinidad and Tobago were not challenged immediately, workers would be deprived of their most basic civil rights.[122]

SELF-DETERMINATION

Padmore was a passionate advocate of self-determination for Africa and the Caribbean colonies. He was a major critic of the mandatory system, crown colony/direct rule and indirect rule. Lenin's position on self-determination had a profound impact on Padmore's conception of self-determination. According to Lenin, "the right of nations to self-determination implies exclusively the right to independence in the political sense, the right to free political separation from the oppressor nation".[123] Padmore argued that self-determination was a fundamental right of all peoples, regardless of their stage of social development, and all colonial peoples "have an inalienable right to freedom".[124]

Like many commentators throughout the colonized world, Padmore was disappointed with the interpretation that Britain applied to clause 3 of the Atlantic Charter of August 1941 issued after a meeting between President Franklin Roosevelt of the United States and Prime Minister Winston Churchill of Britain: "they respect the right of all peoples to choose the form of government under which they will live; and they wish to see sovereign rights and self-government restored to those who have been forcibly deprived of them".[125] Padmore felt that the Atlantic Charter should apply to all colonial peoples and not be limited to the European states that were under Nazi rule, as explained by Churchill's government.

This clause proved to be an embarrassment to Britain when African and Asian nationalists and trade union leaders who were in the vanguard fighting for independence pointed out that it did not apply to the colonies.[126] However, Churchill made it clear that he had "not become the King's First Minister, in order to preside over the liquidation of the British Empire".[127]

After critically examining the Atlantic Charter, Padmore concluded that to colonized peoples within the British Empire, the Atlantic Charter meant only that the regime of exploitation and colonial fascism under which they existed would continue after the war and that the system of imperialism would continue indefinitely.[128] He held the view that clause 3 of the Atlantic Charter should be applied to all peoples, regardless of the stage of their social development. Moreover, the economic structure of any colony should directly benefit its people, under their direction and control.[129]

Padmore advanced the argument that the West Indies had reached the stage in its political development where "[d]emocratic institutions based upon universal adult suffrage, including fully representative institutions" and responsible government should be established. The islands should be federated to form the United West Indies. The federal government would take responsibility "for governmental services applicable to all the territories concerned".[130] Padmore contended that "every progressive individual realizes the advantages of the political federation of national and geographic units as the best way of promoting the economic and social well being of the people".[131] It was no secret that Padmore was a keen supporter of a West Indies federation, as seen in his endorsement for this project, beginning in the late 1920s. At the summary of resolutions passed by the British Guiana and West Indies Labour Congress in 1938, "a draft Bill embodying a constitution for the creation and governance of a Federated West Indies was agreed".[132] Arthur Lewis indicated that political federation was an important issue in the West Indies; the demand for it was based on West Indian national aspirations and economies.[133] Padmore indicted the colonial office for continuing to disregard the demand for a West Indian federation. In his view, West Indians had more in common with each other than the peoples of Europe did. They belonged, in the main, to the same ethnic stock – African. They spoke the same language, they professed the same religion (Christianity) and they had the same cultural outlook.[134]

However, Padmore overlooked the fact that Trinidad and Tobago and British Guiana had sizeable East Indian populations who were Muslim or Hindu. Therefore, while the West Indies might not be as heterogeneous as the peoples of Europe, there were still major differences among the people.

Padmore argued that the natural resources of all the various territories should be nationalized so as to provide the foundation for carrying out the desired social transformations in the Caribbean.[135] The West Indian Labour Congress, held in November 1938 in British Guiana, supported the nationalization of the sugar industry and suggested to the royal commission that legislation be enacted in several West Indian colonies providing for the purchase by government of large-scale sugar estates for redistribution among workers at a reasonable cost, the prohibition of ownership by a single individual, firm or company, directly or indirectly, of a sugar plantation of more than fifty acres, the ownership by the government alone of all sugar factories, the establishment of a single government purchasing agency in each colony for sugar and that this agency should be the sole exporter of sugar.[136]

In relation to West Africa, Padmore noted that "political institutions should be democratized as speedily as possible". The principle of self-government should be based on elected assemblies in place of indirect rule.

Sierra Leone, Gambia, the Gold Coast and Nigeria should be federated along the model suggested for the West Indies.[137]

Padmore, in *How Russia Transformed Her Colonial Empire*, examined how Lenin and the Soviets dealt with the different nations that were part of the czarist Russian empire as a template for the British to follow during and after World War II. Padmore was critical of socialist intellectuals and liberals in Britain who passed judgement on which colonies were ready for self-government and refused to give it to those they deemed not ready. He contended that in the final analysis they were no better than Hitler because this was the same approach taken by Hitler, who "singled out the Sudeten Germans and other sections of the Aryan peoples for self-determination and denied it to non-Aryan peoples, such as the Czechs, Poles and Jews, whom he regards as unworthy".[138] For Padmore, the support of colonized peoples in the fight to defeat fascism and imperialism could only be won by the repudiation of colonial domination. He was clear that freedom was indivisible. Moreover, he contended that the existence of just one colony would justify a struggle against imperialism and the basis of modern wars would continue.[139]

Padmore made the point that the liberation of the Russian working class could not be disconnected "from the agrarian revolution and the national liberation movement". However, such an alliance between advanced peoples in colonies had never been entertained by the British labour movement, which consistently "looked upon the colonial empire" as a necessary adjunct to the developed metropolis in which it operated. Padmore observed that a new school of "Fabian reformers" was disseminating the erroneous belief that all colonized peoples of the empire needed were "bigger and better Colonial Development and Welfare schemes". It was ironic that these proposals were to be carried out by the same colonial administrators who had kept the indigenous peoples in their place for centuries while "British capitalists, traders, settlers and industrialists had exploited their lands and labour".[140] Padmore reminded his readers that Lenin and his followers had repudiated such socialists as "chauvinists" because they did not advocate the right of all nations to self-determination.[141]

Padmore contended that the sagacity of Lenin's obstinate defence of the right of self-determination for the subject nations of the Russian empire was observed in the zealous support "of the former colonial peoples of Russia in defence of the Soviet system". Lenin and the Bolsheviks gave Finland her independence in 1917; they gave Estonia, Latvia, Lithuania and Poland independence in 1918. For Padmore, the granting of independence "had a tremendous political and psychological effect". It inspired confidence in the Bolsheviks and was instrumental in rallying millions of subject peoples of the czarist empire to the side of the Soviet government at the most critical period of the struggle against the counter-revolutionary and interventionist armies.[142] He contrasted this development "with the apathy, disinterestedness and open hostility of large sections of the coloured subject races of Malaya, Burma, the Dutch East Indies, India, Africa, and elsewhere" to the British after many years of colonial rule.[143] In 1942, when the Japanese imperial forces invaded Indonesia, some of the nationalists welcomed the arrival of the Japanese with the creation of independence committees. In Burma and Singapore, the populace did not aggressively resist the invaders. It was only the Philippines that, Padmore observed, showed valiant resistance to the Japanese invaders, and he credited this development to the fact that they had been promised independence in 1946.[144]

Padmore asserted that before the colonies were "subjected to imperialist domination they had existed as independent political or social units". Moreover, they had attained different levels of development, owing to "the law of the uneven development of capitalism". However, imperialism "arrested the growth of the productive forces" and cultivated a sense of exasperation.[145] Padmore reminded his audience that "no nation can be free if it subjugates other nations". Therefore, the task of socialists from colonizing nations was to fight all forms of national oppression and defend the right of self-determination.[146]

Padmore was an uncompromising critic of colonialism and imperialism and he attacked the mandatory system, trusteeship and crown colony/direct rule government. He clearly demonstrated that colonial rule was dictatorial, racist, undemocratic, repressive and exploitative and recognized that the roots of European fascism were deeply embedded in the European colonial project. While many were outraged by the rise of fascism in Europe, they were not equally offended by the colonial fascism that was manifested in the settler colonies in Africa. Padmore felt that the fight against fascism in Europe had to be connected to the fight against fascism in the colonies and that one could not be separated from the other. This led him to advocate for self-determination for all colonized peoples as soon as possible. Self-determination, Padmore believed, was a God-given right, which all nations were entitled to regardless of their economic and political development.

6. PAN-AFRICAN THEORIZING

GEORGE PADMORE'S MOST EXTENSIVE THEORIZING ON PAN-AFRICANISM appeared in his work *Pan-Africanism or Communism*. His main motivation for writing this book was "to record the rise and growth of the contemporary Negro political movements: Pan-Africanism and Garveyism or Black Zionism".[1] This work was an important contribution to pan-African thought. C.L.R. James tells us that Padmore called the book *Pan-Africanism or Communism* because he was convinced that "the revolution is going to take place in Africa" and "unless the Africans themselves produce their own leaders the Communists are going to take it over and then God help them". By "the Communists" Padmore meant "those people" in the Soviet Union with whom he was formerly associated.[2] The needed revolution for Padmore was not the socialist revolution that Marx envisioned in advanced capitalist countries, but the struggle for national liberation in Africa. He held the view that the struggle for national liberation was a "manifestation of the class struggle in its acutest form, since the colonial masses are the oppressed of the oppressed".[3]

The reception of his book was mixed: on the one hand, it was widely accepted by many pan-Africanists, black nationalists and African nationalists. On the other, it was heavily criticized by Marxists and pan-Africanists. Oscar Kambana, a young law student in London, wrote to Padmore in 1957 and told him that he placed *Pan-Africanism or Communism* on the same level as "the achievement of Dr Kwame Nkrumah in bringing his country to independence".[4] The achievement of independence by Ghana was a significant accomplishment for that colony, the people of Africa and especially sub-Saharan Africa, the people of the Caribbean, African Americans and all people oppressed by colonial rule. Thus, to place Padmore's *Pan-Africanism or Communism* on a comparable level suggested the high esteem in which he held this book. Azinna Nwafor, a Harvard political scientist who wrote the introduction to the 1971 edition of *Pan-Africanism or Communism*, felt that the book "shares the distinction common to most great works of historical writing, as with Thucydides, Machiavelli and Trotsky's *History of the Russian Revolution*, in being the creation of a participant as historian".[5] The historian Imanuel Geiss described *Pan-Africanism or Communism* as "a somewhat abortive construct: it neither succeeded in giving a history of Pan-Africanism nor in supplying a theoretical framework". He acknowledged that the book was written with Padmore's "unusual verve and intellectual courage and will always retain its significance" and credited the book with causing him to "take up African history and the study of Pan-Africanism".[6]

Walter Rodney, a Guyanese Marxist pan-African historian writing about two decades later, was critical of Padmore's main argument and suggested that Padmore created a false antithesis between pan-Africanism and communism.[7] Rodney's line of attack was followed by the pan-African scholar Horace Campbell, who argued that Padmore in his book made a sharp distinction between pan-Africanism and communism. Campbell felt that this theoretical division was significant on the ground, as divisions between Marxists and pan-Africanists plagued the African liberation movement throughout the 1950s and 1960s.[8] The best example of this division was the split within the African National Congress of South Africa that led to the formation of the Pan-Africanist Congress of South Africa in 1959. The black nationalist section of the African National Congress felt that the party was being dominated and hijacked by communists. Many South Africans had been profoundly influenced by George Padmore's *Pan-Africanism or Communism* because the book "seemed to speak to their own difficulties with the South African Communist Party and to offer a way forward that skirted vulgar anti-communism".[9] Paul Trewhela informs us that Padmore was held in high esteem by members of the Pan-Africanist Congress, who viewed him as the leading theorist of pan-Africanism and the father of African emancipation.[10] Echoes of the tension between communism and black nationalism were also heard among the liberation movements in Angola. It was also evident in pan-African circles outside of Africa between black nationalists and revolutionary black nationalists, or black Marxists. It must be stated for the record that Padmore was opposed to divisions within the anti-colonial movement. He stressed that "a split within an anti-imperialist movement is always regrettable before the attainment of self-government". However, he was clear that "Communists cannot be allowed to squander the peoples' sacrifices and jeopardize the limited opportunities grudgingly conceded them to plant their feet firmly on the constitutional road to independence, just to conform to some myopic pseudo-Marxist doctrinaire that bears little relation to the immediate needs of the masses at their level of political development".[11]

The anti-communist paranoia of the period led to the expulsion of some of the leading communists from the Convention People's Party in 1953. As one of Kwame Nkrumah's key advisers, Padmore supported the dismissal of communists on the grounds that it was essential "to protect the party and Government from Communist infiltration as well as to avoid a constitutional crisis as in British Guiana".[12] Nkrumah even sought to defend the non employment of communists in the civil service.[13] In Jamaica, the People's National Party also purged the party of its Marxist wing, in 1952.[14] These expulsions served to rob the Convention People's Party and the People's National Party of some of the leading working-class organizers and ultimately weakened the parties.

It is important to note that the hostility between pan-Africanism and communism had been going on long before Padmore wrote his book. It had started in the early 1920s when communists attacked Garvey and his UNIA and Du Bois and pan-Africanism. This hostility was sanctioned by the sixth Congress of the Comintern in 1928. As a member of the Comintern, Padmore was one of the leading critics of Garveyism and pan-Africanism. Paradoxically, Padmore was now attacking communism as a pan-Africanist. Colin Legum correctly points out that the only thing new about the confrontation between communism and pan-Africanism was that it was now playing itself out on African soil.[15]

TENSION BETWEEN COMMUNISM AND AFRICAN NATIONALISM

Padmore observed that following World War II, the media and some political groups in Europe and North America credited communism for inspiring African nationalism. He was offended at this "hypocrisy", which was a component of Cold War propaganda devised to damage the reputation of African nationalists and isolate "the sympathy and support of anti-colonial elements within Labour and progressive organizations".[16] In a similar vein to Padmore, Arthur Lewis and other scholars observed that Africans who fought against colonial rule and demanded their independence were branded as communists. The communist label was deliberately utilized "to discredit all social discontent and resistance to colonial rule".[17]

Padmore argued that none of the African independence movements at this post–World War II juncture were influenced by communism; African nationalism had a history that had begun nearly a century before the Soviet Union became a world power.[18] Padmore forcefully maintained that Africans did not need communism to inspire them; their position as colonial subjects had "infused their determination to be free" and they wished to realize independence under the banner of pan-Africanism.[19] Richard Wright reminds us that Padmore's comments on African nationalism should not be taken lightly, because he was the leading expert on the nationalist offensive that manifested itself in sub-Saharan Africa during the 1950s. He stressed that Padmore knew the movements intimately – their leaders, aims and ideologies – and had for more than twenty-five years helped to shape those movements in all of their complexity. Padmore was the ideological father of many nationalist movements in black Africa, having been the mentor of scores of African nationalists who now held or would soon hold power.[20]

One must remember that Padmore was once an important member of the Comintern, and for many years after his departure, he refused to write anything negative about his time in the Soviet Union. He felt that it could be "used as evidence against them [the Soviet Union] by people whom he had fought all of his life and for whom he had the greatest contempt".[21] In *Africa and World Peace* he opined that "the Soviet Union is the only great Power whose foreign policy is motivated by a genuine desire for peace and not merely political expediency".[22] However, he became more critical of Stalinism after the start of World War II. C.L.R. James, who broke with Stalinists in the early 1930s and with Trotskyites at the end of the 1940s, wrote that up to 1939 Padmore was working in the traditional Marxist mode, which he had learnt from the Stalinists, but "by 1945, he had broken new ground".[23] Between 1930 and 1945, some Marxist revolutionaries saw African emancipation as being reliant upon the collapse of imperialist powers in Europe. They felt that the war would bring about revolutionary upheavals by the metropolitan working class, which would lead to the downfall of "the imperialist state". The failure of this revolutionary upheaval to materialize caused Padmore to reassess his strategy as it became ever more apparent that the liberation of Africans from colonial rule depended on Africans.[24]

It is clear from his involvement with the ILP (even though he never formally joined the party) that Padmore was moving ideologically into the social democratic camp and away from Marxism-Leninism. In October 1939, when the Soviet Union invaded Finland, Padmore wrote "Hands Off the Soviet Union", in which he commented that working class movements in capitalist countries should evaluate their position on the Soviet Union. He felt that the invasion was a major blow against international socialism. This attack against Finland was widely condemned because it was felt that Finland posed no threat to the Soviet Union. Padmore pointed out a number of errors made by Stalin, namely attempting to build socialism in the Soviet Union at the expense of the world revolution and suppressing "the revolutionary policies of the Comintern in order to present a respectable front to their potential allies". Nevertheless, he argued that the Soviet Union was a workers' state and was therefore in a different category from capitalist-imperialist nations. However, this should not "blind us to the many economic and social inequalities and the absence of any really genuine proletarian democracy in Russia". He acknowledged that Stalin was wrong, "but only socialists and true internationalists have the right to say that Stalin is wrong, for we are consistent in our attitude".[25]

In *How Russia Transformed Her Colonial Empire*, Padmore noted that the "Soviet government has within twenty-five years achieved more than any great power has accomplished in centuries". And while he admitted that it had committed grave errors forced upon it by historical circumstances, he cautioned that in passing judgement one "must remember not only the heights to which the Soviet Union has risen but also the depths from which it emerged". Padmore felt that Stalin should be praised because he had adhered to the fundamental principles laid down by Lenin on the right of self-determination for the Soviet Union. While critical of Stalin and the Communist Party of Great Britain, Padmore acknowledged that notwithstanding "all the short comings in the Soviet Union, it is fundamentally a Workers State".[26] It was the first nation "in which the working class and peasants ... achieved power and abolished the system of private property which permits a handful of capitalists and landlords, financiers and Stock Exchange speculators to exploit the vast majority of people".[27] It was for the above reasons that Padmore felt that the Soviet Union should be defended. Developments within the Soviet Union made it virtually impossible for Padmore not to be critical of Stalin's policies, for example, the dissolution of the Comintern in 1943, which convinced Britain and the United States that the communist parties in the third International would not seek to utilize the moment to overthrow capitalism in the West.[28]

Padmore's engagement with the IASB and the PAF fuelled his anti-communist crusade, especially against the CPGB. Arthur Lewis described Padmore as "a dynamo of anti-communist activity". He added that "if any colonial politician showed the slightest sign of partiality towards communism, George would wrestle with his soul until his brain was completely washed".[29] Furthermore, pan-Africanists in the IASB were not only "united for the cause of political freedom for the colonies" but by their "common repudiation of Stalinist policies in the colonies".[30] The PAF, of which Padmore was one of the leading lights, did not want to support communism because doing so would allow it to strengthen its position in the colonies and so it warned African students in London to keep away from communists.

The rejection of Stalinism by the PAF was vividly manifested when Kwame Nkrumah was accused of double-dealing with pan-Africanism and communism and was placed on trial by the Central Committee of the

PAF. During the hearing, Ras Makonnen, the main prosecutor, made it clear to Nkrumah that "our anti-colonial movement must be unfettered". Moreover, he believed that if the colonial authorities found out that Nkrumah had "affiliations to the communist movement", they would use this information "to damn the movements towards freedom from colonialism".[31] This was also why Padmore sought to steer Africans away from having any dealings with the Communist Party of Great Britain. His opposition to African involvement with communism was more a question of tactics than an ideological disagreement.

Padmore recognized that the struggle for self-government was "a skilful game of manoeuvring". Therefore, African nationalists could not afford to give colonial powers the slightest excuse to intervene in the African territories, as occurred in British Guiana.[32] In October 1953 the British government sent troops into British Guiana to remove Cheddi Jagan and the People's Progressive Party from government after one hundred and thirty-three days in office, on the grounds that the party was establishing a communist government.[33] Padmore argued that instead of "indulging in revolutionary romanticism", Jagan should have made the most of the limited power available to him, to demonstrate to the people his party's ability to govern. Then he would have been able to "mobilize the widest popular support for a more advanced constitution". Padmore believed that had Jagan followed this path he would have been able to achieve self-government like the Ghanaians. Instead, "Jagan and his amateur band of revolutionaries played right into the hands of the local reactionaries and foreign imperialists".[34] The Guianese had no power over foreign policy, national defence or internal security. Padmore's criticism of Jagan and the People's Progressive Party was extremely harsh and indicated that Padmore's anti-communism was affecting his ability to objectively assess what had transpired. The party held office for a very short time and espoused moderate, rather than revolutionary, policies. Its manifesto called for a free and independent Guyana and the building of a just society in which the industries of the country would be socially managed for the common good.[35] Moreover, it sought to bring all schools under the supervision of the government and local education committees, to bring in universal adult suffrage, to revise the fees of government medical officers in order to make medical care available for the poor and bring about social security and worker's compensation.³⁶

Padmore observed that in the immediate post–World War II period, Africans and Asians were particularly resentful of the arrogance of European communists in believing they alone possessed the skills and expertise necessary to pilot the development of colonized peoples. He posited that Africans were capable of governing themselves and "developing a philosophy and ideology suited to their own special circumstances and needs".³⁷ Padmore reminded his readers that one of the first responses of "a politically awakened self-respecting coloured leader is the desire to be mentally free from the dictation of Europeans regardless of their ideology". He observed that most Africans regarded communism as a foreign ideology that came from Europe, a continent that had exploited Africa for centuries.³⁸ During the Cold War, the majority of African leaders parroted the idea that scientific socialism was a foreign ideology. However, as Campbell points out, this was a "baseless argument" designed to be the "façade of ideological confusion".³⁹ Padmore saw that many communists in the colonies gave the impression that they were more concerned with endorsing the "foreign policies of the Soviet Union than in advancing the national liberation of their own dependent countries". He stressed that this was the main reason for the tension between communists and nationalists even when they agreed on a plan of "national reconstruction and economic development". Padmore contrasted this position with that of Russian communists, whom he classified as the most patriotic and nationalistic people in the world. He insisted that communists in the colonies should learn to love their countries with the same passion as Russians loved the Soviet Union, and if not, they ought to be treated with disdain by their compatriots.⁴⁰

Padmore held the view that Africans were eager to receive guidance and assistance from the West if it was offered "in a spirit of true friendship".⁴¹ As a lifelong anti-imperialist who had written eloquently and extensively on the exploitative nature of imperialism, this change of heart – that it was possible to have a relationship based on true friendship with European imperialists – was astounding. Henry Winston argues that all of this "talk about true equality between imperialist oppressor and the oppressed is no less a fantasy than the idea of equality between slave and master on the plantation".⁴² However, Padmore insisted that Africans wanted to chart their own path under their own leadership and warned that if they were thwarted they might turn to communism as the only means of achieving their independence. He believed, therefore, that the future shape of Africa "will, in this context, be in large measure determined by the attitudes of the Western nations".⁴³ Padmore noted that the only force capable of containing communism in Asia and Africa was dynamic nationalism based on a socialist programme of industrialization and the cooperative method of agricultural production. In a letter to Richard Wright, Padmore expressed his fears of what might happen in Africa after the colonial powers were forced out. He felt that "[i]f the boys fail to provide a dynamic ideology of a distinctive African character, even cooperating with elements of Communistic ideology and practice, the Kremlin will rush into the vacuum left by colonialism".⁴⁴ Padmore failed to see that the former colonial powers would still have an economic presence in the country after a colony achieved its independence. A new form of colonialism would entrench itself in Africa after the retreat of the colonial powers.

The example of Kwame Nkrumah in Ghana convinced Padmore that "only popularly elected leaders can harness the emotions and loyalties" of the people and direct their enthusiasm "along the path of peaceful economic and social reconstruction". He felt that no foreign ruler, however compassionate, could accomplish this and firmly believed that political independence would be insignificant unless it was accompanied by an ample measure of economic self-reliance and by the correct amount of autonomy from external capital.⁴⁵ In seeking to use the West's fear of communism as a form of leverage, he suggested that the colonial powers should remove the grievances of the "backward peoples", which communists everywhere sought to exploit for their own ends, and should be prepared to fix a date for the complete transfer of power and give technical and administrative assistance to the emerging colonial nations during the transition from internal self-government to complete self-determination.⁴⁶ Azinna Nwafor correctly pointed out that there was nothing original about this prescription because this was the approach favoured by "the colonizing powers in the decolonizing process of the winds of change".⁴⁷ Padmore admitted that the pace of granting independence would be determined by how much pressure was placed on colonial authorities because it was only when mass protest "assumed an explosive character that the imperialists grudgingly make any substantial concessions".[48]

Padmore opined that "doctrinaire Marxism" espoused by British communists "has no particular appeal for colonial nationalists".[49] In fact, he believed that Africans only listened to communists "when they feel betrayed and frustrated" and when they had lost all faith in the assurances of the "Western so-called Christians" who continued to exploit Africans. Padmore was also critical of British communists who parroted the assertion that "only the proletarian vanguard can liberate Africa" although the evidence suggested otherwise, as was seen in India, Pakistan, Ceylon, Burma, the Gold Coast and Sudan. Padmore, who had abandoned his belief in the viability of proletarian internationalism to liberate Africa when he broke with the Comintern in 1934, countered this position by pointing out that in China, Chinese peasants did the liberating.[50] He strongly believed that only the African working class and peasants, and not the international proletariat, would be able to liberate Africa from European colonial rule.

NON-ALIGNMENT

According to Padmore, "Pan-Africanism endorses the conception of an Asian-African front against colonialism." The fifth PAC proposed a resolution authored by Padmore pledging solidarity with the Indian struggle for national freedom and social emancipation. The congress also pledged solidarity with the struggling peoples of Indonesia and Vietnam in the fight for national and economic emancipation from Dutch and French imperialism, respectively. The Bandung Conference held in Indonesia in 1955, which brought together the independent territories of Africa and Asia, sought to highlight the "similarity of purpose and unity of action amongst oppressed peoples to address their common problems and to take an active role in changing the existing world order". A.W. Singham and Shirley Hune make the point that "Bandung informed the world that the newly independent states of Asia and Africa, though small or medium-sized and developing, were determined not to allow the major powers to decide the future of humankind".⁵¹ At this conference, the idea of non-alignment was developed.

Padmore pointed out that the anti-colonial struggles of Asian territories were a substantial inspiration for pan-Africanism and that it favoured the Gandhian "doctrine of non-violence" as a method of obtaining independence and racial fairness. The struggle for self-determination in India and Burma motivated the anti-colonial movement in Africa. Many African nationalists sought to emulate the non-violent direct-action strategy that Gandhi and the Indian independence movement used to liberate Indians from the grip of British colonialism. The fifth PAC had advocated the utilization of positive, non-violent, direct mass action as the way to overthrow colonial rule. This strategy was successfully applied in Ghana, which Padmore viewed as the first victory for pan-Africanism.⁵² C.L.R. James credited Padmore and Kwame Nkrumah with working out this theory and programme of action for the emancipation of Africa.⁵³ For Nkrumah, the weapons of positive non-violent action were legitimate political agitation, newspaper and educational campaigns and, as a last resort, the constitutional application of strikes, boycotts and non-cooperation based on the principle of absolute non violence.⁵⁴

For Padmore, pan-Africanism "reject[ed] the unbridled system of monopoly capitalism of the West" and the "political and cultural totalitarianism of the East". It firmly "identifie[d] itself with the neutral camp".⁵⁵ Peter Willetts describes non-alignment as a policy of new states that were still searching for their identity and says that it rejected the claim that the Cold War was for everybody.⁵⁶ Clearly Padmore wanted a non-aligned form of pan-Africanism that was independent of the Cold War politics of the West and of the East. The Marxist historian Manning Marable argues that although Padmore claimed to represent a non-aligned position in the Cold War, his interpretation of Marxism-Leninism placed him within the ideological camp of Western imperialism.⁵⁷ In contrast, Nwafor argues that "we find in Padmore the intellectual forerunner of the theories of 'non-alignment' and positive 'neutrality'" which the newly independent countries of "Africa and Asia universally adopted in their foreign policy declarations and in their involvement in world affairs".⁵⁸ In light of Cold War politics, Jack Woodis, a Marxist-Leninist, questioned whether it was possible for Africa to remain non-aligned in a world of two dominant blocs.[59] Ali Mazrui, however, thought that the ultimate goal of non-alignment was to reconcile Africa's weakness with a certain degree of diplomatic freedom. He added that pan-Africanism and non-alignment implied anti-factionalism, and non-alignment joined pan-Africanism "in being a declaration of war against the forces of division in Africa and the world at large".[60]

CONTINENTAL PAN-AFRICANISM

Padmore argued that the idea of pan-Africanism extended beyond the limited boundaries of the nation state. Moreover, "its perspective embraces the federation of regional self-governing countries and their ultimate amalgamation into a United States of Africa".[61] According to Padmore, African countries would have to embark on the following stages in order to achieve the unification of the African continent: first, the struggle for national independence, second, social revolution and third, regional unity as the forerunner of a United States of Africa. However, until independence was achieved, the energy of the people could not be mobilized for the attainment of the second and third stages, which were even more difficult to achieve than the first.[62] Padmore envisioned that in this nation "all men regardless of tribe, race, colour or creed shall be free and equal". He asserted that "this is our vision of the Africa of Tomorrow – the goal of Pan-Africanism".[63]

In *White Man's Duty*, Padmore had called for the federation of Sierra Leone, Gambia, the Gold Coast and Nigeria. However, his pan-African project had further evolved to encompass all of Africa. Padmore's continental pan-African project was built on the ideas of his early black nationalist mentors Edward Blyden and Blyden's disciple Casely Hayford, but it represented a major departure from a regional West African federation by advocating continental unification. This development represented a major innovation – and contradiction – in the conception of pan-Africanism. Historically, pan-Africanism/black nationalism was based on racial solidarity of black people. The enslavement of Africans, the ideology of racism and the oppression and exploitation of black people on racial grounds gave rise to racial solidarity and unity in the struggle of all black people. When Padmore called for the federation of the British colonies in West Africa, the underlying philosophy of this project was black nationalism/pan-Africanism. Extending pan-Africanism to the unification of the African continent meant that his conception of pan-Africanism was defined racially as well as continentally. It was clear to Padmore that there was a growing feeling among some sections of politically aware Africans throughout the continent that their destiny was interconnected and that what transpired in one region of Africa would affect Africans living in other regions.[64] The revolutionary theorist Frantz Fanon, not unlike Padmore, also identified a strong emotional attachment to the notion of African unity during the anti-colonial struggle.[65] Although African colonies had diverse histories, cultures and languages, their similar "experience of Western domination, common sufferings, interests and problems, provided a solid basis for unity among the various African peoples and had become a powerful force".[66] Of note is that Padmore's conception of the unification of Africa was also influenced by Lenin's socialist federation in the Soviet Union. Lenin argued that the objective of socialism was not only "to bring nations closer to each other, but also to merge them".[67]

Padmore firmly believed that nations whose political life was based on a socialist economy preferred unity in the common interest of all.[68] In Padmore's articulation of continental pan-Africanism, the African continent became the nucleus of pan-Africanism, but he was silent on the relationship of global pan-Africanism with his continental pan-African project. Historically, pan-Africanism has always been internationalist in its orientation. Therefore, his pan-African project was reductionist, as it was continental and not international. As a member of the Comintern, he had worked assiduously to build a black international, and after he left that organization he still sought to build that black international with the Negro World Congress and the fifth PAC, which he organized. It was clear that Padmore wanted "Ghana to lead a Pan-African movement" to bring about the unification of the African continent.[69]

To further the objective of promoting a United States of Africa and pan-Africanism on the continent, Kwame Nkrumah held two conferences in Ghana, the Conference of Independent African States (April 1958) and the All African People's Conference (December 1958).⁷⁰ Padmore's wife Dorothy Pizer tells us that "these conferences were the legitimate heirs on African soil" of the fifth PAC held in Manchester. She adds that it was not accidental that Nkrumah and Padmore, who had worked as joint "secretaries for the Fifth Pan-African Congress, should have been associated in bringing these two conferences together, one as Prime Minister ... of Ghana, the other as his Advisor on African Affairs".⁷¹ On 12 November 1957, the Ministry of Information and Broadcasting in Ghana announced that George Padmore, the West Indian exponent of pan-Africanism, had been appointed Special Advisor on African Affairs to the prime minister. A report emanating from the parliamentary secretary, Ministry of Defence and External Affairs, stated that Padmore was being "brought to Ghana specifically to organize the Congress of Independent African States and to deal with any of its later developments".⁷² His appointment as special advisor was resented by some Ghanaians who felt that a "West Indian could hardly have anything to teach an African about Africa".⁷³ However, according to James, when Padmore was appointed as Nkrumah's advisor, he had more knowledge of African political movements and personal contacts and relations than any person living in Ghana.⁷⁴ In the previous twenty-five years, Padmore had cultivated a network of contacts with trade unionists, nationalist leaders, political parties and journalists across the African continent. Dr Jantuah, the acting high commissioner for Ghana in London, stated that George Padmore had been given that post not as a reward for past services but because he was the best man for the job.⁷⁵

In spite of Jantuah's assertion, Padmore was put into this position as compensation for the past service that he had rendered to Nkrumah. Padmore was Nkrumah's political mentor, and they had a history that went back to when Nkrumah was residing in the United States and an avid reader of Padmore's articles. In his autobiography, Nkrumah confessed his admiration for Padmore's anti-colonial writing. He told James of his desire to meet Padmore when he migrated to England, and James wrote a letter introducing Nkrumah to Padmore. Moreover, Padmore and Nkrumah worked closely as joint organizing secretaries for the fifth PAC. Padmore functioned as Nkrumah's personal advisor and propagandist in London in the late 1940s and early 1950s, where he wrote articles such as

"Bloodless Revolution in the Gold Coast", "Pan-Africanism and Ghana" and "The Press Campaign against Ghana". He also wrote the book *The Gold Coast Revolution*, which "sought to trace the evolution of Gold Coast nationalism from the foundation of the Ashanti Confederacy to the emergence of the CPP [Convention People's Party] and after".[76] The articles and books were favourable to Nkrumah and the Convention People's Party. Indeed, one reviewer of *The Gold Coast Revolution* argued that the language Padmore "use[d] to describe the political opponents of the CPP can be described as uncouth; his opinion of Nkrumah borders on religious veneration – no adjective is good enough to describe the absolute infallibility of Nkrumah".[77] Notwithstanding the fact that Padmore was Nkrumah's advisor and propagandist, he was still eminently qualified for the post. According to Nkrumah, "Padmore's understanding and appreciation of African affairs and problems was unique", since for over twenty years he had immersed himself in the anti-colonial struggles taking place on the African continent.[78]

Padmore worked tirelessly to ensure the success of the Conference of Independent African States and the All African People's Conference in Ghana. St Clair Drake makes the point that Padmore's book *Pan-Africanism or Communism* constituted the ideological foundation for Nkrumah and Padmore in developing the philosophy that lay beneath these conferences.[79] However, June Milne, Nkrumah's biographer, claims that Nkrumah politically parted company with Padmore because of the anti-communist views expressed in *Pan-Africanism or Communism* that implied that the two ideologies were incompatible. She claims that Padmore and others like him were primarily concerned with black nationalism and adds that "it was the issue of racism, a concept which Nkrumah detested, which lay at the root of some of the political rifts which occurred between Nkrumah and several of his African American friends".[80]

Padmore was critical of the racism that had infected the communist parties of Great Britain and the United States and disparaged Stalinism in the Soviet Union for changing its strategies and tactics to suit its own self-interest, and so it is difficult to conclude that Padmore was racist. Indeed, his pan-Africanism went beyond black nationalism to include all Africans on the continent. The South African writer Peter Abrahams, who worked with him in the IASB and the PAF, tells us that "Padmore seemed incapable of judging people in racial terms". He adds that "his enemies were the people who served capitalism, imperialism, fascism, colonialism", while "his allies were the progressive forces, whether he agreed with them on all points or not".[81]

Given the role that Padmore played in organizing the conferences and his influence on the resolutions passed, it is hard to imagine that there was a parting of ways between Nkrumah and Padmore. Padmore and Ako Adjei, Ghana's minister of external affairs, visited Sudan, Liberia, Ethiopia, Libya, Egypt, Morocco and Tunisia to publicize the Conference of Independent States. According to Dorothy Padmore, "the tour provided personal affirmation for Padmore since all the African heads of state knew of his work and had his books on their shelves".[82] He also travelled to the above countries as part of a delegation led by Nkrumah as a follow-up to the conference.[83] In addition, Padmore continued to be Nkrumah's advisor and was the chief ideologue of the National African Socialist Students' Organization. According to W. Scott Thompson, "[o]nly Nkrumah had a greater hand than Padmore in shaping Ghana's foreign policy during the first two years of its independence".[84]

The All African People's Conference was "closer to and nearer to his heart than the Independent African States Conference".[85] As early as 1954, Padmore had informed Du Bois that Nkrumah was keen on convening a sixth pan-African congress in Ghana as soon as independence was formally declared.[86] The All African People's Conference was that pan-African congress. W. Scott Thompson asserts that "Nkrumah insisted – in spite of Padmore's objections – on changing the name from Pan-African to All African to make it clear that Ghana and Nkrumah had begun a new tradition".[87] In the discussions that led up to the fifth PAC, Padmore had agreed with Du Bois that a pan-African congress should be held on African soil, and this provided Padmore with the opportunity to realize his desire. He was more comfortable in the company of the conference delegates, who represented nationalist political parties and trade unions, than with state managers, political elites and bureaucrats who had attended the first Conference of Independent States earlier in the year. The main objective of the conference was to encourage nationalist political groups inside Africa in their anti-colonial activity as a means to advance "continental unity and a socialist transformation".[88] The aspirations were near and dear to Padmore's heart, as for many years he had advocated self-determination for the African territories and was now on a crusade to bring about the organic unification of the African continent based on pan-African socialism. Over two hundred delegates from sixty-two political parties and trade unions attended the conference. As he had for the fifth PAC, Padmore played a major role in organizing the conference and influencing the resolutions passed. He authored the call for the conference:

> This Conference Will Formulate and Proclaim the Philosophy Of Pan-Africanism As The Ideology Of The African Non Violent Revolution.
>
> Henceforth Our Slogan Shall Be: Peoples Of Africa Unite!
>
> You Have Nothing to Lose But Your Chains!!
>
> You Have A Continent To Regain!!
>
> You Have Freedom And Dignity To Attain!!
>
> Hands Off Africa!!
>
> Africa Must Be Free!!!![89]

Padmore was responsible for designing the backdrop of the conference room, which featured a large black man breaking the chains of slavery and colonialism. This image was used by the ANLC on its letterhead, pamphlets and flyers, and it was the picture that Padmore had carried on the *Negro Worker* when he was its editor and on the original cover of *The Life and Struggles of Negro Toilers*. It is also important to note that Padmore was instrumental in the resolutions that were passed, and his ideas on pan-Africanism as articulated in *Pan-Africanism or Communism* are evident in these resolutions. As a specialist in organizing conferences, Padmore was adept at shaping a conference in line with a particular position. The Resolution on Frontiers, Boundaries and Federations closely mirrored Padmore's position on African unification, affirming that it

> (a) endorses pan-Africanism and the desire for unity among African peoples;
> (b) declares that its ultimate objective is the evolution of a Commonwealth of African states;

(c) calls upon the independent States of Africa to lead the peoples of Africa towards the attainment of this objective;
(d) expresses the hope that the day will dawn when the first loyalty of African States will be to an African Commonwealth.⁹⁰

To institutionalize the objectives of the conference, the Pan-African Secretariat, with Padmore as director, was created

(a) to promote understanding and unity among peoples of Africa;
(b) to accelerate the liberation of Africa from Imperialism and Colonialism;
(c) to mobilize world opinion against the denial of political rights and fundamental rights to Africans; and
(d) to develop the feeling of one community among the peoples of Africa with the object of the emergence of a United States of Africa.⁹¹

Unfortunately, the secretariat was not fully operational until 1960, after the second All African People's Conference in Tunisia.

Ras Makonnen, an important organizer of the conference, was of the view that the All African People's Conference signified the end of the old pan-Africanism of five thousand miles away and the beginning of a new iteration of it in Africa itself.⁹² Makonnen was correct that the conference signalled the beginning of continental pan-Africanism as the main branch of pan-Africanism, but it did not mean the demise of global/racial pan-Africanism. St Clair Drake argues that continental pan-Africanism was "heralded by Padmore's book *Pan-Africanism or Communism* and that took on actual political content at the First Conference of Independent African States in April 1958".⁹³ Similarly, Immanuel Wallerstein, in his assessment of the conferences, noted that this was the "first time in history that Pan-Africanism was defined continentally to include the Arab north as well as the Negro people". Moreover, "the continental unity of Africa now became a central theme of Pan-Africanism".⁹⁴ From the observations of the above commentators it is clear that Padmore's work had a definitive impact on the conferences and the conception of pan-Africanism at this juncture.

As Nkrumah's advisor on African affairs and the leading theoretician of pan-Africanism, Padmore joined the Ghanaian delegation when

Nkrumah and Sekou Touré formed the Ghana-Guinea union in November 1958. Leslie James argues that Padmore was the foremost "influence behind the scenes in the Ghana-Guinea Union". In the course of the negotiations, Padmore "encouraged a strong Ghanaian demonstration of financial support for Guinea, arguing that a common currency should be a top priority".[95] This union was the first attempt at African unification between two newly independent colonies. It was no doubt intended to be the nucleus for a larger union and ultimately, the unification of the African continent, based on Padmore's model. Padmore was also part of the delegation when Nkrumah and presidents Tubman and Touré met in July 1959 to discuss the Community of Independent African States. Padmore was optimistic, perhaps overly optimistic, that there would be a United States of Africa in his lifetime, even though his model suggested that the organic unification of the continent was a long-term project. In an interview with an unnamed correspondent in March 1959, he stated that "in 1960, the Nigerians will join and form that union like that of the United States of America, which grew from 13 states to 49".[96] It appears that Padmore had abandoned social revolution as one of the prerequisites for the unification project. Unfortunately, he died a few months later and his dream has not yet been realized.

PAN-AFRICANISM OR COMMUNISM

Padmore's pan-Africanism acknowledged the usefulness of historical materialism because it provided a useful analysis of the exploitation and oppression of Africa and its people. However, pan-Africanism was not in line with the "pretentious claims of doctrinaire Communism, that it alone has the solution to all the complex racial, tribal and socio-economic problems facing Africa". He further posited that pan-Africanism rejected communist intolerance of those who did not subscribe to its ever-changing party line, even to the point of liquidating them as "enemies of the people".[97]

Between 1923 and 1943, there were five major changes in the Comintern's strategy that affected communist parties across the world. From 1923 to 1928, the Comintern advocated a strategy of a "united front from above": communist parties were encouraged to work with social-democratic parties for joint action in defence of the working class. Between 1928 and 1934, the Comintern shifted its approach to a "united front from below": social democratic parties were attacked for protecting capitalism and viewed as the greatest enemy within the labour movement. Communist trade unions were viewed as the only impartial and trustworthy advocate of the working class. During the years 1935–39, the Comintern promoted the "popular front", and communist parties were instructed to build an all-encompassing, anti-fascist popular movement that entailed working with all people and groups who accepted an anti-fascism programme. As part of the popular front, communist exclusivity in relation to other parties and to "pre-revolutionary governments" was abandoned. The task of a popular-front government was not the destruction of capitalism but the purging of fascism from capitalism and the economic basis that gave rise to fascism.

Next, the Comintern claimed that it had been betrayed by its allies in the united and popular fronts, thus making it impossible to continue with this tactic. The new approach taken by the Comintern from 1939 to 1941 called for the creation of "united and popular fronts from below". These were characterized by fierce attacks on social democracy and a "virtual silence against fascism". This line was abandoned between 1941 and 1943 after Germany invaded the Soviet Union in June 1941. The popular front from above was then repackaged and reintroduced as a broad anti-fascist grouping of all opponents of Hitler's Germany and the other Axis powers. Its main task was defeating fascism.[98] These strategic zigzags "meant that non-Communist movements for black civil rights or self-determination were viewed as implacable foes during left turns and as potential allies when the party moved in the opposite direction".[99]

During the late 1930s, the Soviet Union held a series of show "trials" during which most of Stalin's opponents were tried and eliminated. This was also a period of widespread terror when thousands of people were arrested and killed. Stalin's regime was widely condemned for this.[100] Padmore offered a veiled critique of Stalin's terror by claiming that the dictatorship of the proletariat had degenerated into the dictatorship of Stalin, characterized by violence and repression. He stressed that "democracy and brotherhood cannot be built on intolerance and violence".[101]

At this time, Padmore described himself as a socialist and a democrat, suggesting that he had broken with a fundamental tenant of Leninism, the dictatorship of the proletariat. According to Padmore's reading of Marxism-Leninism, it would not be necessary to adopt wholesale what happened in the Soviet Union and apply it to Africa without adapting it to local conditions. However, while Padmore touted the democratic line, he simultaneously "encouraged Nkrumah in his resolve to consolidate power and move towards the creation of a one-party socialist state".[102] Marable charges that Padmore's polemic against communism was not intended for the African proletariat as much as the US government and corporate interests, which might underwrite many of Ghana's state expenses after independence.[103]

Padmore noted that in their struggles to achieve independence, the new leaders of pan-Africanism had to build "upon the ideological foundations laid by Dr Du Bois, the father of Pan-Africanism". However, he acknowledged that the problems confronting these leaders were much more diverse and complicated than those that affected the "founders of the Sierra Leone and Liberian settlements". He further challenged young pan-African leaders to develop "new political means and organizational techniques adapted to African traditions and circumstances". They would have to develop a social philosophy that would incorporate and elevate peoples, making possible a conversion from unsophisticated "tribal forms of society to modern industrialized states".[104] Padmore advised nationalist leaders in Africa to speedily settle their disagreements and tribal disputes, which was necessary to deprive the imperial powers of any excuse to withhold power from popularly elected governments. He observed that once a colonial people achieved independence, they would know how to defend it against destabilizing groups within their territories who might seek to make them "pawns in the power politics of the Cold War".[105]

Padmore felt that the coming struggle for Africa would be between the ideologies of "Pan-Africanism and Communism". In a letter to Nkrumah in 1955, Padmore said: "Brother, they are going to be in a fix, as to what to do with Pan-Africanism. It exposes the role of the Communists on the one hand and that the imperialists will like, but on the other they will hate the ideas of Pan-Africanism-Black Nationalism plus Socialism."[106]

The British Foreign Office did not view pan-Africanism as a revolutionary ideology that the colonialists should fear: "Pan-Africanism, in itself, is not necessarily a force that we need to regard with suspicion and fear. On the contrary, if we can avoid alienating it and guide it on lines generally sympathetic to the free world, it may well prove in the longer term a strong, indigenous barrier to the penetration of Africa by the Soviet Union."[107] It was clear that the British were not fearful of pan-Africanism because it lacked a militant anti-imperialist working-class orientation. Nwafor argued that neither pan-Africanism nor communism offered a revolutionary alternative to the liberation of the African continent, adding that the question of "African nationalism or communism", which had been a major preoccupation of Cold War–era international relations, appeared to be "a red herring to divert attention from the real needs of the colonized peoples of Africa and elsewhere".[108] The fundamental issue was "whether the African territories and people are to acquire and enjoy genuine independence, complete sovereignty over their own resources, economy, culture and their military dispositions".[109]

For Padmore, "Communism exploits misery, poverty, ignorance and want". Therefore, to effectively stave off communism, "the wants and the material needs of the common people, food, clothing, and shelter" must be satisfied. He felt that "any honest, incorruptible government" seeking to carry out the above task "provided the best guarantee against Communism" and further posited that "Pan-Africanism sets out to fulfil the socio-economic mission of Communism under a libertarian political system".[110] Padmore was convinced that Africans had no need to fear the communist bogeyman if their "political leaders remain true to the ideals and principles of Pan-Africanism", explaining that since the end of World War II and the emergence of political parties and trade unions in the colonies, communists had been able to infiltrate the "ranks of African and West Indian students".[111] A large section of these "students come from artisan families and peasant communities" and were therefore more receptive to "communist propaganda" than those associated with the chieftain class and the professional and middle-class families. However, Padmore dismissed this development as just a part of youthful independent curiosity. From his observation, most students discarded their Marxism as soon as they returned home and went back "to what they have always been at heart, bourgeois nationalists". He further elucidated that "it is largely a case of being revolutionary at twenty, moderate at thirty, conservative at forty and reactionary at fifty".[112]

Daniel Guérin reminded Padmore that, based on his comments, there was a "class struggle and the communists were on the good side, the side of the poor but you seem to be delighted when you say that they will resort to being bourgeois nationalist and reactionaries at fifty".[113] Hakim Adi posits that student interest in Marxism did not mean that they were disciplined revolutionaries, and they often held to an interpretation of Marxism not favoured by the Communist Party of Great Britain. As the colonies moved towards self-government and career prospects opened up, many returning communist students became as bourgeois in Lagos as they had been proletarian in London.[114] Padmore sought to downplay the significance of the class struggle in Africa and did not speak to it in *Pan-Africanism or Communism*. When he wrote *The Life and Struggles of Negro Toilers*, Padmore argued that African people were oppressed as a class and as a race. Shortly before Padmore broke with the Comintern, he advocated a racial revolution aimed at white imperialists, followed by a class-based revolution. Padmore was also clear that all of the delegates who attended the fifth PAC should have mandates from mass-based organizations to speak on behalf of their worker and peasant organizations. Therefore, his silence on the class struggle was deafening; in a book dedicated to the "youth of Africa – the torchbearers of Pan-Africanism" this was a major omission. He argued that "Communism ... is no immediate threat to African national unity", in spite of the preventative actions of West African governments, ranging from prohibiting communist literature to restricting travel to communist countries to excluding communists from employment in the civil service.[115]

TRIBALISM

For Padmore, tribalism was "a present menace".[116] It was a threat to the liberation and unification of the continent and was being exploited by "unscrupulous politicians" to spread division among the "politically backward" segments of the populace and weaken the "forces working for national integration".[117] He contended that the only force that could oppose tribalism effectively was "Pan-Africanism which advocates the formation of democratically-based nation-wide political parties on a non-tribal, non-regional membership".[118] Kiven Tunteng is critical of Padmore's position on the tribal question and posits that Padmore failed to "distinguish between tribalism as an important feature in the organization of African society and its exploitation for personal advantages". Moreover, "if Padmore meant that loyalties hitherto directed to traditional authorities should be channelled to the new entities, then he was not entirely clear on this point".[119] Tunteng further explains that an overwhelming majority of African people belong to tribal units, which are akin to an extended family.[120]

In looking at the devastating impact of tribalism on the anti-colonial struggle, Padmore believed that only the trade union movement could offer the "ideological allegiance" that could reduce tribalism and ensure workers' "adhesion and loyalty to their own class". He felt that this task could not be left to intellectuals and professionals who exploited the illiteracy of the people and their tribal prejudices.[121] Padmore noted that European colonizers did not create tribalism. However, they were responsible for keeping it alive by holding back the industrialization of their colonies. He believed that industrialization could unshackle Africans "from their conservative traditions and prejudices and open up wider vistas".[122]

Tribalism was one of the main issues discussed at the All African People's Conference in 1958, and delegates acknowledged that it plagued the nationalist and liberation struggles taking place on the continent. This was expressed in a resolution that "strongly oppose[d] the imperialist tactics of utilizing tribalism and religious separatism to perpetuate their colonial policies in Africa". The conference also affirmed that tribalism and religious separatism were destructive practices that constituted a serious obstacle to the realization of African unity, the political evolution of Africa and the rapid liberation of Africa.[123]

Padmore felt that "the traditional African way of life need[ed] a cataclysm to free it from its own decay". He believed that the recently liberated younger generation of Africans who were exposed to Western political thought and technology could "bring about the necessary regeneration".[124] Imanuel Geiss, a scholar of pan-Africanism, holds the view that only a few pan-African leaders adequately understood African social forms and customs and that one of the things they wanted to preserve was an African version of a semi-nomadic and semi-agrarian tribal society. He maintains that "these forms had to disappear as progress was made towards modernization and industrialization, just as they disappeared in Europe". Geiss describes Padmore as one of the more sensible leaders on this issue.[125] However, Bruce Berman, Dickson Eyoh and Will Kymlicka in *Ethnicity and Democracy in Africa* are of the view that

> contemporary ethnic communities and identities in Africa did not and will not fade away with the inevitable advance of global modernity, but rather represent critical aspects of the particular African experience of modernity itself. They are the outcomes of continuous and continuing processes of social construction emanating from the encounters of indigenous societies with the political economy and culture of the West, as well as the deliberate manipulations of diverse political actors.[126]

REPARATIONS OR NEO-COLONIALISM?

Padmore, in looking at the whole question of aid to Africa, stated that if the United States was worried about communism gaining a foothold in Africa, it should stop endorsing the discredited system of colonialism by reinforcing European rule in Africa and instead implement "a Marshall Aid programme for Africa", similar to the programme used to rebuild the war-torn economies of Western Europe after World War II.[127] It should be noted that the Marshall Plan was used to promote and buttress capitalism in Western Europe and prevent the spread of socialism. Padmore felt that European countries that benefited from colonialism should seek to rebuild the African economies that had been underdeveloped by colonialism, pointing out that millions of Africans were taken from the Guinea Coast during the transatlantic slave trade and their labour used to lay the foundations of the wealth of the republic. Therefore, there could not "be a finer way of making restitution for past wrongs inflicted upon Africa than for the US Congress to construct the Volta River project in the Gold

Coast".[128] Unfortunately, Padmore's call for reparations was limited, as they were not extended to all colonial powers that had benefited from their involvement in the transatlantic slave trade. Many of his critics did not recognize that his call for reparation represented a progressive development in the struggle for the dignity of Africans.

The Volta River project was considered to be the foremost developmental project in Ghana in the post–World War II period. In the project, a dam and a hydroelectric power station were to be constructed on the Volta River that would provide enough electricity to exploit the bauxite deposits of Mpraeso and Yenahin. It was also envisaged that the hydroelectric station would make power available for electric railways, mines and secondary industries as well as for public and domestic purposes. However, this project was expected to cost about £230 million. Padmore opined that such "a free national gift" without any strings attached "would achieve more than all the propaganda in the world to cement the bonds of eternal friendship between a grateful African people and a generous American nation". He pointed out that this gesture would not be a novel one, since Russia had already offered such aid to Egypt, Sudan, India and Burma.[129] As early as 1952 Padmore wrote to the economist Arthur Lewis expressing his apprehension about how British investment in the Volta River project would allow Britain to perpetuate its power in Ghana after independence.[130]

Henry Winston, the leader of the CPUSA, one of Padmore's fiercest critics, was critical of Padmore's request for aid from the United States. He felt that this was a clear indication that Padmore had acquiesced to imperialism and that "his willingness to accept support from Western imperialism provided 'it [wa]s offered in the spirit of true equality' . . . between imperialist oppressor and the oppressed [wa]s no less a fantasy than the idea of equality between slave and master on the plantation".[131] Moreover, Winston was of the view that Padmore's intention in calling for US "Marshall Aid" to Africa was not motivated by the struggle to oust imperialism. Rather, it would allow colonialism to remain in Africa and he helped it persist "by implying that it had already gone and was no longer a threat".[132] In a similar vein, Marable makes the point that with Padmore's call for an African version of the Marshall Plan, he had completely severed any residual ties he might have to Marxism.[133] However, Padmore still claimed that he was a Marxist and favoured pan-African socialism as the economic model for African countries to follow, and his conception of a Marshall Plan for Africa was not designed to promote capitalism but to assist the development of the continent. Wallerstein posits that before 1960 the United States had the reputation of being minimally anti-colonialist and sympathetic to African aspirations, but after 1960, the United States began to play a role as large as and often far larger than that of the former colonial powers.[134] A.M. Babu notes that "America's alleged anti-colonial record, especially Roosevelt's firm stance against Britain during India's struggle for independence, was sufficient grounds to justify the hope that Americans could be won over".[135]

PAN-AFRICAN SOCIALISM

In the late 1950s Padmore wrote "A Guide to Pan-African Socialism", a pioneering work on the creative application of socialism in Africa as the ideological handmaiden of pan-Africanism. According to William Friedland and Carl Rosberg, Padmore's article contains one of the earliest statements on African socialism. They also assert that Padmore's contribution was exceedingly significant for, probably more than any other figure, he helped to shape African socialism.[136] David Apter makes the point that Padmore's article helped to form some of the key ideas of African socialists in Ghana and elsewhere. He adds that Padmore's work addressed both the racial factor and the ideological which find expression in pan-Africanism, with the African freedom fighters and the African trade unions and farmers' associations.[137]

"A Guide to Pan-African Socialism" indirectly addresses the charge levelled by Daniel Guérin, a friend of Padmore, who wrote a biting critique of *Pan-Africanism or Communism* and Padmore's conception of pan-Africanism in this work, namely, that "Pan-Africanism without economic content is hollow".[138] "A Guide to Pan-African Socialism" is evidence that Padmore was grappling with the economics of pan-Africanism and believed that the economic arm of the pan-African political project should be socialist. He insisted that it was important for Africans "to understand the workings and objectives" of Marxism so that "we may be able to adopt and blend it to our own economic and social needs without accepting it wholesale as dogma". He maintained that the Russian Revolution offered an example for Africans because of its accomplishments but cautioned that "they must not apply the information [about it] uncritically". Padmore warned that Africans should not allow Western misinformation to prejudice their thinking about the successes of the Russians and opined that while they might reject the Soviet Union's political system, "we cannot ignore their scientific and technological contributions if we are to emerge from our present stagnation and backwardness".[139]

Padmore argued that the error that many so-called Marxists had made was to turn Marxism into a dogma instead of using Marxism "as an intellectual instrument for understanding the evolution of human society and a guide to chart the course of future social development". He noted that the Chinese communist leader Mao Tse Tung had warned the Chinese people "against becoming slaves of Marxist dogmatism".[140] According to Padmore, the goal of socialism was to raise the standard of living so that the majority of the people could "enjoy the benefits of the abundance which machine techniques and modern science have made possible".[141] He sought to clarify misconceptions about socialism by pointing out that socialism did not mean merely taking from the rich to redistribute to the poor because a "mere re-division of the present available wealth in the hands of a few individuals will not satisfy to any appreciable extent the gap that now exists between the haves and have nots". For Padmore, the primary aim of socialism was "the scientific planning of production and distribution, through the common ownership of the basic means of production and services". This system would insure that all "people regardless of race, colour, creed, or social origin will be able to enjoy exactly what they want to fill their needs". However, like Marx, he acknowledged that this stage would not be reached until socialism evolved into full-fledged communism.[142]

Padmore pointed out that pan-Africanism should not follow blindly the socialistic lines of approach that were used either in the Soviet Union or in Eastern Europe, where conditions were entirely different from those in Africa. To support this position, he stressed that Lenin and the Bolsheviks "did not blindly follow Marxism in creating the instruments best suited to Russian conditions". As with Lenin and the Russians, he felt that the African approach to socialism had to be based on a policy of adaptation and adoption, while keeping in mind their goal of a peaceful advancement of African socialism. This would be achieved in various aspects:

> *Politically*, African Socialism shall strive to promote and safeguard popular democracy based upon universal adult suffrage (one individual one vote, regardless of race, colour, creed, or sex), fundamental human rights, social justice, and the rule of law.
>
> *Economically*, African Socialism shall seek to promote and safeguard the people's well-being through the common ownership and control of the essential means of production and distribution and ultimately the abolition of power to live by rent, interest, and profit.
>
> *Socially*, African Socialism shall seek to promote and safeguard full employment by the state and performance by all citizens of work of social value according to their ability, while all citizens will share in the common resources of the nation according to their needs.[143]

For Padmore, socialism was more than an economic system. It was a social agreement where "the people hold in common the means of production and share according to their needs in the fruits of their collective labour, that is, the goods and services which they together fashion from the productive means". He averred that unlike individualistic capitalism, socialism stressed the maximum collaboration "between all the members of the society, because it is this cooperation alone which will bring that abundance which will make the good life available for all".[144] Padmore held the view that economic reconstruction in Africa in general, and in Ghana in particular, had to start with the land because of the nature of its "communal ownership and production and its element of cooperative self-help". This, he argued, "is the foundation stone on which we must build the new socialist pattern of society".[145]

He believed that the agricultural sector had to be given a higher profile and the condition of the farmer transformed from one of subsistence to "one which would produce a surplus of wealth", to supply the accretion of money "necessary to pay for the importation of the machinery and technical know-how required for the industrial sector". In Padmore's view, agriculture in Ghana should be diversified from the over-reliance on cocoa production to food production, to alleviate the importation of foodstuff, which constituted a drain on foreign exchange. He envisioned that the village should be the focal point of the surrounding farming community and should provide the social and cultural amenities that would bring urban life to the countryside and prevent drift away from the land.[146]

Padmore made the point that the aim of the economic programme had to be to reposition the economy "from a trading economy to an industrial economy". He felt that as long as African businessmen continued to think only about selling other people's goods they would not change the imperialist pattern of their economy. The only way they would embark on the socialist road to "self-sufficiency and prosperity" was if they were able to transform the present economic structure from trade to manufacturing. He stressed that it was imperative to have both economic and technical planning and posited that a whole new educational system was needed with "an African perspective [that would] provide the human instruments for carrying through socialist planning". This educational system should seek to produce a different kind of citizen, one who would be knowledgeable about their history and socialist future and who "needed to live in cooperation with his neighbours and to give unselfish service to his country".[147]

Padmore insisted that a government had to use all the powers at its disposal to accelerate the process of industrialization. This initiative would call "for bold planning on all fronts of our national life and the complete reorganization of the basic foundations of our society". Ideas, outlook and social habits of the people would have to be readjusted, and the "spirit of self-help and cooperation will have to be encouraged and bribery and corruption harshly punished". He called for long terms of imprisonment and the confiscation of properties for anyone guilty of stealing state funds or property.[148]

Padmore contended that Ghana, "the first independent African nation to embark upon a programme of economic planning", had to make a conscious effort to evolve new forms of socialist techniques applicable to the African environment and cognizant of Africa's history, which could serve as a guide to other African countries when they attained independence.

According to Padmore, it was vitally important to have dedicated socialists responsible for socialist planning. Only through that "approach will we be able to achieve our socialist objectives and make socialism a reality for the people of Ghana and an example for the rest of Africa".[149]

George Padmore's theorization of pan-Africanism was an important contribution to pan-African political thought. For him the ultimate aim of pan-Africanism was to see the creation of a United States of Africa with pan-African socialism as its economic basis. Pan-Africanism was the ideological alternative to communism and tribalism, a non-aligned philosophy suited to the prevailing Cold War context and, for Padmore, a philosophy to make Africa politically, economically and ideologically independent of Europe.

CONCLUSION

IN A STUDY OF PADMORE'S SOCIAL AND POLITICAL THOUGHT, the obvious question is, What was Padmore's contribution to the advancement of Marxist thought and the development of pan-African thought? Although Padmore was at one time a major functionary within the Communist International, he did not make any significant contribution to the development of Marxist-Leninist thought. During his career as a communist, Padmore was an engaged Marxist intellectual who did not have the luxury or the inclination to engage in the kind of theorizing that would have led to an enrichment of Marxist thought. The atmosphere and activities that he was involved in, whether as a Comintern courier, the executive secretary of the ITUCNW, the editor of the *Negro Worker* or as a journalist and political agitator, were not conducive to and left little time for the production of deep Marxist theorization or reflection.

Padmore was more of a revolutionary pragmatist and a polemist than a revolutionary theoretician. He once told a friend that he was not interested in intellectual theorizing; his primary interest was getting the parasitic colonial powers who were exploiting the resources and people out of the Caribbean and Africa. Padmore became a Marxist because he felt that communism would be a useful ideology to liberate his brothers and sisters in Africa. Therefore, from the beginning of his engagement with Marxism, he viewed it pragmatically as a tool to realize his objective and not for the sake of the ideology or to fulfil an intellectual need.

Some of the pamphlets written by Padmore when he was in the Comintern (*What Is the International Trade Union Committee of Negro Workers?*, *Negro Workers and the Imperialist War: Intervention in the Soviet Union*, *American Imperialism Enslaves Liberia* and *The Life and*

Struggles of Negro Toilers) can be classified as agitational or propagandistic and devoid of any deep theoretical or conceptual reworking of Marxist-Leninist thought. The primary purpose of these writings was to propagate the virtues of socialism within the Soviet Union, examine the conditions of black workers, critique the system of imperialism and colonialism, attack non-communist black leaders, attack socialists and call on blacks to defend the Soviet Union. In *The Life and Struggles of Negro Toilers*, his best-known work from his time in the Comintern, Padmore attacked the civilizing mission of colonialism and pointed out how colonialism was savaging Africans and people of African descent globally. He also examined the conditions of black workers internationally in light of the crisis of capitalism and the capacity of these workers to overthrow it. This work was also an important text in forging a black international and promoting black internationalism rather than advancing Marxist thought.

As the editor of the *Negro Worker*, Padmore's pragmatism was also evident as he sought to fashion this paper into a popular journal. He was clear that he did not want a theoretical journal to discuss abstract topics but one that would examine and analyse the everyday problems of black workers and connect them with the international struggles and problems of other workers. In his journalistic offerings in the *Negro Worker*, Padmore wrote on the same topics and themes as he did in his pamphlets. From these articles, it is evident that Padmore contributed little to Marxist theorization even while he made an important contribution to black radical thought.

After Padmore left the Comintern, he continued to use a Marxist-Leninist framework of historical and dialectical materialism to analyse the system of imperialism and colonialism in Africa in general and British West Africa in particular. This was best illustrated in his major anti-colonial writings, *How Britain Rules Africa*, *Africa and World Peace* and *How Russia Transformed Her Colonial Empire*. However, in these works, Padmore examined the impact of European imperialism on Africa and contributed, not to the enrichment of Marxist-Leninist thought, but significantly to anti-colonial thought. Padmore was critical of all forms of colonial rule in Africa and suggested that all territories under colonial domination should be given their independence regardless of their level of economic development.

In his writings, he was relentless in attacking colonial rule in all its administrative forms, whether the mandatory system, crown colony/direct rule government, or indirect rule. These colonial political systems facilitated the exploitation and oppression of African workers, and despite slight administrative differences, labour conditions and the level of repression in various colonies were basically the same. For Padmore, the mandatory system, crown colony/direct rule government and indirect rule were all forms of colonial fascism.

The development of the concept of colonial fascism was one area of radical anti-colonial thought in which Padmore made a significant contribution. He identified a link between fascism and colonialism and rooted fascism in the European colonization of Africa in the late nineteenth century. Europeans, in the scramble for a piece of the African continent, committed atrocities of all kinds, even genocide, that foreshadowed European fascism in the 1930s. Racism was the handmaiden of the European colonizing project; colonizers believed in their God-given right to rule over Africans, whom they considered racially inferior, barbaric and incapable of ruling themselves. Padmore pointed out that the atrocities committed by the Germans against the Jews in the 1930s paled in comparison to those the Europeans had committed against Africans for centuries. He observed that the settler colonies of South Africa, Kenya and Rhodesia provided the clearest manifestation of colonial fascism in Africa.

Padmore felt that South Africa presented the best example of colonial fascism, where blacks were more terrorized, exploited and oppressed than in any other place in the world. The majority black population was ruled by a white minority who had no regard for the human rights of the black population. Padmore felt that as Hitler's fascist policies were causing consternation throughout Europe, that same fascism in the colonies should be equally condemned. However, blacks had endured this kind of treatment for many years without any outrage from Europeans. Colonial fascism was also evident in the settler colonies of Kenya and Rhodesia, where Africans were placed in reserves, disenfranchised, barred from all skilled occupations, denied the right to an education and forced to carry identification badges.

Padmore, an engaged pan-African intellectual, made a significant contribution to the development of pan-African thought. Unlike during his tenure in the Comintern, in later years he had more time for reflection and theorization. It should be noted that he was a communist for about seven years but was actively involved in pan-Africanism for over two decades. For him pan-Africanism was more than a protest movement of people of African descent in the diaspora. Pan-Africanism was a non-aligned philosophy that was relevant to the Cold War context of the 1950s because it rejected the unrestrained "system of monopoly capitalism" of the United States and Western Europe and "the political and cultural totalitarianism" of the Soviet Union and Eastern Europe. This non-aligned position was stressed at the Bandung Conference of 1955. For Padmore, pan-Africanism endorsed the conception of an Asian-African front against racist apartheid ideology.

Padmore saw pan-Africanism as an ideological alternative to communism. He felt that it provided Africans with the necessary philosophy and ideology to govern themselves and that any politically astute, self-respecting African leader would make every effort to be politically and ideologically independent from Europe. For him, historical materialism was a useful framework for analysing African society, but pan-Africanists refused to accept the idea that communism was the answer to all of Africa's problems. In Padmore's view, communism thrived where there was "misery, poverty, ignorance and want". Therefore, African political leadership had to satisfy the wants and the material needs of the people in order to prevent communism from taking root.

Padmore's idea of pan-Africanism extended beyond the restricted boundaries of the nation state, to the amalgamation of regional self-governing territories leading to the unification of a United States of Africa, the ultimate goal of his pan-African project. In his model, the first step was the achievement of national independence, the second step was to bring about social revolution and the third step was regional unity as the precursor to a United States of Africa. Padmore's United States of Africa was inclusive of all the territories in Africa, though he recognized that its realization would require enormous effort.

Padmore made a major contribution to pan-African socialist thought with his work "A Guide to Pan-African Socialism", a pioneering work on the theorization of socialism in Africa. He felt that pan-African socialism should not be a carbon copy of Marxism-Leninism and had to be based on existing conditions in Africa. He rejected the dictatorship of the proletariat and favoured a democratic form of socialism that would promote and safeguard popular democracy based on universal adult suffrage, fundamental human rights, social justice and the rule of the law. His pan-African socialist model sought to promote and safeguard the people's well-being through common ownership and control of the essential means of production and distribution. He was of the view that land should be the foundation on which Africans built a new socialist pattern of society. Economic reconstruction in Africa had to begin with land because of its communal ownership, and the nature of production and its elements of co-operative self-help.

POLITICAL ORGANIZATION/POLITICAL PRAXIS

It is important to remember that Padmore was both an engaged Marxist and a pan-Africanist. Therefore, it is necessary not only to examine his political thought but to look at his political organization, or political praxis. He was influenced heavily by the Leninist method of political organization. During the seven years he was a communist, he worked in highly centralized vanguard organizations, whether it was in the CPUSA or its auxiliary, the ANLC. This method of organization was also evident in the ITUCNW.

On leaving the Comintern, he sought to bring some of this Leninist political organization to the pan-African formations in which he was a dominant figure. This was evident in the IASB and the PAF. He felt that pan-Africanists in these organizations were the most advanced sections of the race whose task was to bring to the attention of the public the atrocities of colonialism. His dedication came about because he was a trained professional revolutionary who was committed to freeing Africa and the Caribbean from the grip of colonialism. Therefore, all of his activities had a political dimension – some means of advancing the struggle against colonialism and imperialism – and he was annoyed at others who did not display the same level of commitment in the battle against colonialism. Given the enormity of the task, Padmore recognized that it was imperative that pan-Africanists in the IASB and the PAF should have the requisite discipline and be focused on the task of bringing about an African revolution.

One must note that pan-African organizations were not as rigid or doctrinaire as Marxist organizations. This is evidenced in that Padmore wrote for and worked with other pan-African groups, socialist groups like the ILP, progressive trade unionists, the left wing of the British Labour Party and Asian organizations. It must be remembered that he worked closely with the ILP and wrote for its publications the *New Leader*, *Left* and *Controversy*. Padmore was an internationalist who was prepared to work with anyone or any progressive organization to defeat colonialism. He participated in two Subject Peoples conferences, comprising Africans and Asians, was a member of the Centre against Imperialism, and spoke to labour organizations, trade union conferences or any group that wanted to know about the colonial situation, thereby forging an alliance with anyone who was sympathetic to the colonial question or any group that was fighting against colonialism and imperialism. The sole exception was communists because of the acrimony between them and Padmore.

Like Lenin, Padmore recognized the value of political journalism and viewed the press as a necessary organizational tool for knowledge production, agitational work and propaganda. He saw newspapers as a tool that exposed readers to the ills of capitalism and colonialism and inspired them to challenge and oppose these systems. He felt that a revolutionary newspaper was imperative in building a revolutionary movement.

When Padmore was made the editor of the *Negro Worker*, he sought to fashion it into a popular journal that discussed and analysed the daily struggles of black workers and connected those struggles with those of workers internationally. The newspaper under his editorship contributed towards raising consciousness among black workers. It provided information, advice and guidance about black oppression and international black struggles, and it allowed Padmore to communicate with his constituency of "Negro toilers" and to increase his community of readers. He utilized the *Negro Worker* to attack colonialism, provide propaganda for the Soviet Union and to help build an international movement of black workers.

During this period, he also wrote articles for *Le Cri des Nègres, La Race Nègre* and the *Moscow Daily News*, exposing the ills of colonialism and attacking capitalism.

After Padmore left the Comintern, he no longer had the luxury of a newspaper like the *Negro Worker* to disseminate his ideas. However, he was mindful that he needed to connect with his former followers and build a new following. Padmore wrote for many newspapers and periodicals: *Crisis, Chicago Defender, Pittsburgh Courier, New Leader, Controversy, Forward, International African Opinion, Tribune, Survey, Socialist Leader, Phylon, United Asia* and several newspapers in Africa and the Caribbean. By writing for these publications, he was able to reach new readers as he attacked colonialism in Africa and the Caribbean. He wrote many articles on the negative impact of colonialism on Africa and made it a habit to stress the need for independence for the African territories. Padmore also wrote extensively on the Caribbean, looking at colonial rule and the disturbances that rocked the Caribbean in the 1930s; he consistently called for self-determination for the Caribbean territories. He also wrote numerous articles attacking the British Empire, fascism, imperialism, colonialism and indirect rule, seeking to fan every spark of popular anti-colonial and labour outrage into an inferno.

In a similar vein, while in the Comintern, he wrote a number of pamphlets: *What Is the International Trade Union Committee of Negro Workers?, The Life and Struggles of Negro Toilers, Negro Workers and the Imperialist War, Forced Labour in Africa, American Imperialism Enslaves Liberia* and *Labour Imperialism and East Africa*. After leaving the Comintern, he wrote two pamphlets, *Hands Off the Protectorates* and *The White Man's Duty* (co-authored with Nancy Cunard) and edited the *Voice of Coloured Labour* and *Colonial and Coloured Unity: A Programme of Action – History of the Pan-African Congress*. Some of the pamphlets he wrote were extensions of newspaper articles, but they did not have the immediacy of a newspaper article that could address an issue as soon as it arose. Nevertheless, his pamphlets also kept many of these issues in the limelight and served as a useful point of reference. The major reason he wrote and edited pamphlets was to provoke the interest, sympathy and understanding of colonial workers for the plight of colonized Africans and people of African descent. He also hoped to win over sympathizers and allies to the struggle to end colonialism and capitalist exploitation.

Padmore also wrote *How Britain Rules Africa*; *Africa and World Peace*; *How Russia Transformed Her Colonial Empire*; *Africa: Britain's Third Empire*; *The Gold Coast Revolution*; and *Pan-Africanism or Communism*. In *How Britain Rules Africa*, he endeavoured to emphasize every imaginable misdemeanour carried out by imperialists in Africa. In *Africa and World Peace*, Padmore provided an appraisal of European diplomacy during the 1930s, showing to what extent the scramble for colonies in Africa as a source of raw materials and outlet for monopoly capital affected relationships and coalitions among leading European nations. He recognized that a new struggle for the redivision of the earth was the main aim of Germany and Italy, and a world war seemed imminent to him.

In *How Russia Transformed Her Colonial Empire: A Challenge to the Imperialist Powers*, Padmore examined how the Soviet Union resolved the national and colonial questions it inherited from czarist Russia. He strongly believed that Britain should follow the model provided by the Soviet Union and grant independence to her colonies. In *Africa: Britain's Third Empire*, Padmore indicted imperialism from the perspective of an African in light of the many defenders of empire in the British Labour Party government after World War II. In *The Gold Coast Revolution: The Struggle of an African People for Freedom*, Padmore examined the economic and social conflict that took place in the post-1945 period and the methods of agitation used by political parties and trade unions in the battle for constitutional reform and independence. Padmore hoped that the book would motivate other African nationalists who were fighting colonialism. In *Pan-Africanism or Communism*, his main objective was to record the rise and growth of modern black political movements, namely pan-Africanism and Garveyism.

Padmore's books extended the discussion of the newspaper articles and pamphlets he had written and helped to further propagate his ideas as he exposed the ills of colonialism, promoted self-determination and solidified his commitment to the creation of a United States of Africa free from the encumbrances of colonialism and on a pan-African socialist path of development.

For Padmore, conferences were important organizational tools, and he participated in and organized several international conferences. He participated in the TUUL Convention in 1929 and was one of the main organizers of the 1930 International Conference of Negro Workers, the International of Seamen and Harbour Workers in 1932 and the Congress of the International Labour Defence in the Soviet Union. He was intimately involved in planning the aborted Negro World Conference that was planned for France in 1935. He attended a European socialist conference in Paris (1939) and two Subject Peoples Conferences that took place in London (June and October 1945), was the chief organizer of the historic fifth PAC in Manchester (1945) and attended the British Centre against Imperialism Conference in London (1946) and the Paris Peace Conference (1946). Padmore was the main organizer of the Conference of Independent States (1958) and the All African Peoples Conference (1958), held in Accra. He attended the Guinea-Ghana Conference (1959) and the Ghana-Guinea-Liberia Conference (1959).

The fact that Padmore participated in numerous conferences suggests that conferences were an important aspect of his politics. These conferences provided a forum for dialogue, where like-minded individuals shared information, disseminated ideas, networked and shared experiences. They provided instant and constructive feedback that had not been available to Padmore as a newspaper editor, which, for Padmore, transcended the importance of discussion and voting on resolutions and making presentations. They also assisted in building solidarity and providing inspiration for the task at hand. The conferences that he organized, especially the fifth PAC and the All African People's Conference, were platforms for him to impose his ideas, which he did in the resolutions passed and in the general thrust of the conference discussion.

Padmore had thousands of contacts in Europe, North America, the Caribbean and Africa, many of which he had cultivated as a member of the Comintern. Indeed, he utilized his contacts to assist with the distribution of the *Negro Worker*, to recruit students to send to the Soviet Union, to provide information about political activity taking place, for political agitation and for the dissemination of information about prospective conferences. As a servant of pan-Africanism, he continued to use his contacts in the same manner as when he had been a member of the Comintern.

George Padmore contributed significantly toward the enrichment of pan-African thought and activism, black internationalism and anti-colonial thought. He was a political agitator par excellence who used newspapers, pamphlets, books and conferences to critique colonialism, build solidarity and agitate for the liberation of Africa and the Caribbean from colonial rule. George Padmore was a leading pan-Africanist intellectual and activist who made an invaluable contribution to the struggle against colonialism.

NOTES

INTRODUCTION

1. Peter Abrahams, *The Coyaba Chronicles: Reflections on the Black Experience in the 20th Century* (Kingston: Ian Randle, 2000), 163.
2. Cedric Robinson, *Black Marxism: The Making of the Black Radical Tradition* (1983; repr., Chapel Hill: University of North Carolina Press, 2000), xxx.
3. Ibid.
4. Anthony Bogues, *Caliban's Freedom: The Early Political Thought of C.L.R. James* (Chicago: Pluto, 1997), 4.
5. Ibid., 4–5.
6. Michael West, William Martin and Fanon Wilkins, *From Toussaint to Tupac: The Black International Since the Age of Revolution* (Chapel Hill: University of North Carolina Press, 2009), 1.
7. Ibid.
8. C. Robinson, *Black Marxism*, 22.
9. Michael Dawson, *Black Visions: The Roots of Contemporary African American Political Ideologies* (London: University of Chicago Press, 2001), 173.
10. George Padmore, *Negro Workers and the Imperialist War: Intervention in the Soviet Union* (Hamburg: International Trade Union Committee of Negro Workers, 1931), 16.
11. "Our Aims", *International Negro Workers' Review* 1, no. 1 (1931): 3.
12. Brent Haynes Edwards, *The Practice of Diaspora: Literature, Translation and the Rise of Black Internationalism* (Cambridge: Harvard University Press, 2003), 243.
13. Anthony Bogues, *Black Heretics, Black Prophets: Radical Political Intellectuals* (New York: Routledge, 2003), 13.
14. C. Robinson, *Black Marxism*, 313.
15. Paget Henry, *Caliban's Reason: Introducing Afro-Caribbean Philosophy* (New York: Routledge, 2000), 93.

16. Ibid.
17. C.L.R. James, "The West Indian Intellectual", introduction to *Froudacity: West Indian Fables by James Anthony Froude*, by J.J. Thomas (London: New Beacon Books, 1969), 45.

CHAPTER 1: THE MAKING OF A PAN-AFRICANIST

1. James Hooker, *Black Revolutionary: George Padmore's Path from Communism to Pan-Africanism* (New York: Praeger, 1967), 6.
2. Joyce Moore Turner, *Caribbean Crusaders and the Harlem Renaissance* (Urbana: University of Illinois Press, 2005), 151.
3. Ibid.
4. See Anna Grimshaw, *The C.L.R. James Reader* (Oxford: Blackwell, 1992), 288; C.L.R. James, *At the Rendezvous of Victory* (London: Allison and Busby, 1984), 252.
5. Rukudzo Murapa, "George Padmore and the African Struggle" (paper presented at the Conference on Linkages in the Black Pluriverse: Africa, Afro-America and Afro-Caribbean, State University of New York, Binghamton, New York, 29–31 October 1971), 2, George Padmore Special Collection, Alma Jordan Library, University of the West Indies, St Augustine.
6. Ivar Oxaal, *Black Intellectuals and the Dilemmas of Race and Class in Trinidad* (Cambridge, MA: Schenkman, 1982), 61.
7. Ibid.
8. Murapa, "George Padmore", 2.
9. C.L.R. James, "Notable West Indians", C.L.R. James Special Collection, Box 38, Folder 20, Alma Jordan Library, University of the West Indies, St Augustine.
10. Padmore's attack on Edward Partridge is seen in a note written in the top and side margins of Partridge's obituary in the *Weekly Guardian*. George Padmore Special Collection, SC 97, Box 1, Folder 17, Alma Jordan Library, University of the West Indies, St Augustine.
11. Hooker, *Black Revolutionary*, 4–5.
12. Edward Blyden, *Christianity, Islam and the Negro Race* (1887; repr., Edinburgh: Edinburgh University Press, 1967), 116.
13. Ibid., 116–17.
14. Ibid., 118.
15. Hollis Lynch, *Black Spokesman: Selected Writings of Edward Wilmot Blyden* (London: Frank Cass, 1971), 28.

16. Ibid., 29.
17. Ibid., 200.
18. Ibid.
19. Carl Campbell, "John Jacob Thomas of Trinidad: The Early Career of a Black Teacher and Scholar, 1855–1870", *African Studies Association Bulletin*, no. 8 (1978): 4.
20. J.J. Thomas, *Froudacity*, 51–52.
21. Ibid.
22. Ibid., 92–93.
23. Ibid., 115.
24. Ibid., 160.
25. Ibid., 179.
26. Dennis Benn, *The Growth and Development of Political Ideas in the Caribbean, 1774–1983* (Kingston: Institute of Social and Economic Research, University of the West Indies), 61.
27. Selwyn R. Cudjoe, "C.L.R. James and the Trinidad and Tobago Intellectual Tradition: On Not Learning Shakespeare under a Mango Tree", *C.L.R. James Journal* 10 (Winter 1997): 22–23.
28. Bridget Brereton, "John Jacob Thomas: An Estimate", *Journal of Caribbean History* 8–9 (1976–77): 32.
29. Ras Makonnen, *Pan-Africanism from Within* (New York: Oxford University Press, 1973), 100.
30. Herbert Aptheker, *The Correspondence of W.E.B. Du Bois*, vol. 3, *Selections, 1944–1963* (Amherst: University of Massachusetts Press, 1978), 62. James Hooker (*Black Revolutionary*, 93) claims that Padmore was not related to Henry Sylvester Williams. However, at the Conference on the Life and Times of George Padmore, Black Radicalism in the Twentieth Century, held at the University of the West Indies in Trinidad and Tobago, 2–4 October 2003, a number of Trinidadian historians stated that Williams was a distant relative of Padmore.
31. George Padmore, *Pan-Africanism or Communism* (1956; repr., New York: Doubleday, 1971), 95.
32. Ibid., 95–96.
33. Imanuel Geiss, *The Pan-African Movement*, trans. Anna Keep (London: Methuen, 1974), 82–83.
34. Owen Charles Mathurin, *Henry Sylvester Williams and the Origins of the Pan-African Movement, 1869–1911* (Westport, CT: Greenwood, 1976), 96.

35. Bridget Brereton, *A History of Modern Trinidad, 1783–1962* (London: Heinemann, 1981), 126.
36. Marika Sherwood, *Origins of Pan-Africanism: Henry Sylvester Williams, Africa and the African Diaspora* (London: Routledge, 2011), 220.
37. Mathurin, *Henry Sylvester Williams*, 57.
38. George Padmore, "Jamaica Rejects Sham Democratic Constitution", *New Leader*, 6 September 1941, 7.
39. Brereton, *History of Modern Trinidad*, 156.
40. George Padmore, "Why the RAF Has Dropped the Colour Bar", *New Leader*, 25 January 1941, 7.
41. Brereton, *History of Modern Trinidad*, 156.
42. Padmore, "Why the RAF Has Dropped the Colour Bar", 7.
43. Brereton, *History of Modern Trinidad*, 156.
44. Winston James, *Holding Aloft the Banner of Ethiopia: Caribbean Radicalism in Early Twentieth-Century America* (London: Verso, 1998), 63.
45. W.F. Elkins, *Black Power in the Caribbean: The Beginnings of the Modern National Movement* (New York: Revisionist Press, 1977), 12.
46. Selwyn Ryan, *Race and Nationalism* (Toronto: University of Toronto Press, 1972), 28.
47. Brinsley Samaroo, "The Trinidad Disturbances of 1917–1920: Precursor to 1937", in *The Trinidad Labour Riots of 1937*, ed. Roy Thomas (Port of Spain: Extra-Mural Studies Unit, University of the West Indies, St Augustine, 1987), 31.
48. Padmore, "Why the RAF Has Dropped the Colour Bar", 7.
49. W. James, *Holding Aloft the Banner*, 64.
50. Samaroo, "Trinidad Disturbances", 25.
51. Ibid., 21.
52. Ibid.
53. Mathurin, *Henry Sylvester Williams*, 163.
54. Tony Martin, *The Pan-African Connection: From Slavery to Garvey and Beyond* (Dover, MA: Majority Press, 1983), 13.
55. Ibid.
56. Kelvin Singh, *Race and Class Struggles in a Colonial State: Trinidad 1917–1945* (Kingston: University of the West Indies Press, 1994), 22.
57. Ibid., 234.
58. Brereton, *History of Modern Trinidad*, 161.
59. Ibid.
60. Ryan, *Race and Nationalism*, 29.
61. T. Martin, *Pan-African Connection*, 53.

62. Elkins, *Black Power*, 12.
63. Brereton, *History of Modern Trinidad*, 163.
64. Singh, *Race and Class Struggles*, 35.
65. T. Martin, *Pan-African Connection*, 68.
66. Padmore, "Jamaica Rejects Sham Democratic Constitution".
67. Singh, *Race and Class Struggles*, 97.
68. Makonnen, *Pan-Africanism from Within*, 99.
69. T. Martin, *Pan-African Connection*, 74.
70. Handwritten note on Partridge's obituary in the *Weekly Guardian*, George Padmore Special Collection, SC 97, Box 1, Folder 17, Alma Jordan Library, University of the West Indies, St Augustine.
71. Brinsley Samaroo, "The Trinidad Workingmen's Association and the Origins of Popular Protest in a Crown Colony", *Social and Economic Studies* 21 (1972): 215.
72. C.L.R. James, "C.L.R. James and British Trotskyism", interview with Al Richards, Clarence Chrysostom and Anna Grimshaw, South London, 8 and 16 November 1986, https://www.marxists.org/archive/james-clr/works/1986/11/revhis-interview.htm, 4.

CHAPTER 2: EARLY MARXISM

1. C.L.R. James, "Notes on the Life of George Padmore", undated typescript, Schomburg Center for Research in Black Culture, 6.
2. Herbert Aptheker, "The Fisk Student Strike of 1925", in *A Documentary History of the Negro in the United States, 1910–1932*, ed. Herbert Aptheker (Secaucus, NJ: Citadel, 1973), 494.
3. W. James, *Holding Aloft the Banner*, 76.
4. Makonnen, *Pan-Africanism from Within*, 99.
5. "George Padmore, Mr. Pan-Africa", *People*, 21 March 1959, George Padmore Special Collections, SC 97, Box 1, Folder 2, Alma Jordan Library, University of the West Indies, St Augustine.
6. Murapa, "George Padmore", 5.
7. Hakim Adi, *Pan-Africanism and Communism: The Communist International, Africa and the Diaspora, 1919–1939* (Trenton, NJ: Africa World Press, 2013), 143.
8. See letter written by John Dillingham to W.C. Craver about getting foreign nationals to participate in the conference. George Padmore Special Collection, SC 97, Box 1, Folder 7, Alma Jordan Library, University of the West Indies, St Augustine.

9. Nnamdi Azikiwe, *My Odyssey* (London: C. Hurst, 1970), 138.
10. Mathurin, *Henry Sylvester Williams*, 72.
11. Ibrahim Sundiata, *Brothers and Strangers: Black Zion, Black Slavery, 1914–1940* (Durham, NC: Duke University Press, 2003), 35.
12. Ibid., 99.
13. Ibid., 113.
14. Azikiwe, *My Odyssey*, 138.
15. Ibid. 139.
16. Ibid.
17. Susan Pennybacker, *From Scottsboro to Munich: Race and Political Culture in 1930s Britain* (Princeton: Princeton University Press, 2009), 66.
18. See Hakim Adi and Marika Sherwood, *Pan-African History: Political Figures from Africa and the Diaspora since 1787* (London: Routledge, 2003), 152.
19. "800.00B/ Padmore, George", State Department Decimal Files, 1920–1929, Record Group 59, National Archives and Records Administration, College Park, Maryland.
20. Ibid.
21. Ibid.
22. T. Martin, *Pan-African Connection*, 96–97.
23. "800.00B/ Padmore, George", State Department Decimal Files, 1920–1929, Record Group 59, National Archives and Records Administration, College Park, Maryland.
24. Rupert Lewis, *Marcus Garvey: Anti-Colonial Champion* (Trenton, NJ: Africa World Press, 1988), 139.
25. George Padmore, "Marcus Garvey, Misleader of His Race: Negro Workers Vote Communist", George Padmore Special Collection, SC 97, Box 1, Folder 2, Alma Jordan Library, University of the West Indies, St Augustine.
26. Ibid.
27. Ibid.
28. Hooker, *Black Revolutionary*, 7.
29. Oxaal, *Black Intellectuals*, 67–68.
30. Ibid.
31. Makonnen, *Pan-Africanism from Within*, 101.
32. Ibid.
33. Ibid.
34. C. Alvin Hughes, "The Negro Sanhedrin Movement", *Journal of Negro History*, 69, no. 1 (1984): 3.

35. W. D. Wright, "The Thought and Leadership of Kelly Miller", *Phylon* 39, no. 2 (1978): 191.
36. Ibid.
37. George Padmore, "Negro Art", George Padmore Special Collection, SC 97, Box 1, Folder 14, Alma Jordan Library, University of the West Indies, St Augustine.
38. Robin D.G. Kelley, " 'Afric's Sons with Banner Red': African-American Communists and the Politics of Culture, 1919–1934", in *Imagining Home: Class, Culture and Nationalism in the African Diaspora*, edited by Sidney J. Lemelle and Robin D.G. Kelley (London: Verso 1994), 40.
39. Ibid., 46.
40. Mark Solomon, *The Cry Was Unity: Communist and African Americans, 1917–1936* (Jackson: University of Mississippi Press, 1998), 60.
41. Herbert Aptheker, *A Documentary History of the Negro People in the United States* (Seacaucus, NJ: Citadel, 1973), 657.
42. Solomon, *Cry Was Unity*, 52.
43. George Padmore, "An Appeal to Negro Workers", *Negro Champion*, 17 November 1928, George Padmore Special Collection, SC 97, Box 1, Folder 2, Alma Jordan Library, University of the West Indies, St Augustine.
44. George Padmore, "A Federated West Indies", *Negro Champion*, 8 August 1928, George Padmore Special Collection, SC 97, Box 1, Folder 15, Alma Jordan Library, University of the West Indies, St Augustine.
45. John Mordecai, *The West Indies Federal Negotiations* (London: George Allen and Unwin, 1968), 19.
46. Ibid., 20.
47. Padmore, "Federated West Indies".
48. "Theses of the Second Congress of the Communist International on the National and Colonial Questions", in *Nationalism in Asia and Africa*, ed. Elie Kedourie (New York: New American Library and World Publishing, 1970), 543.
49. V.I. Lenin, *Selected Works in One Volume* (1944; repr., New York: International Publishers, 1971), 160.
50. Theodore Draper, *American Communism and Soviet Russia: The Formative Period – 1960* (London: Macmillan, 1960), 136.
51. Solomon, *Cry Was Unity*, 4.
52. Ibid.
53. "Internationally Known Scribe Dies in London", *Pittsburgh Courier*, 3 October, 1957.
54. George Padmore, "Awakened Negro Youth", *Negro Champion*, 2 June

1928, George Padmore Special Collection, SC 97, Box 1, Folder 15, Alma Jordan Library, University of the West Indies, St Augustine.
55. George Padmore, "An Open Letter to Earl Browder", *Crisis*, October 1935, 302.
56. Hooker, *Black Revolutionary*, 13.
57. Grimshaw, *C.L.R. James Reader*, 289.
58. George Padmore, *How Russia Transformed Her Colonial Empire: A Challenge to the Imperialist Powers* (London: Dennis Dobson, 1946), 83.
59. Padmore, *Pan-Africanism*, 283.
60. Padmore, *How Russia Transformed*, 84.
61. Padmore, *Negro Workers*, 9.
62. George Padmore, "Imperialists Treat Blacks Like Nazis Treat Jews", *New Leader*, 13 September 1941, 7.
63. Ibid.
64. C.L.R. James, "Notes on the Life", 7–8.
65. W. James, *Holding Aloft the Banner*, 182.
66. Harry Haywood, *Black Bolshevik: Autobiography of an Afro-American Communist* (Chicago: Liberator, 1978), 117.
67. George Padmore, "Negro Workers Should Join Workers", *Daily Worker*, September 1928, George Padmore Special Collection, SC 97, Box 1, Folder 15, Alma Jordan Library, University of the West Indies, St Augustine.
68. Mark Naison, *Communists in Harlem during the Depression* (New York: Grove, 1985), 4.
69. Manning Marable, *African and Caribbean Politics: From Kwame Nkrumah to the Grenada Revolution* (London: Verso, 1987), 41.
70. Dawson, *Black Visions*, 183.
71. Naison, *Communists in Harlem*, 3.
72. Padmore, *Pan-Africanism*, 268.
73. C. Robinson, *Black Marxism*, 287–88.
74. Padmore, *How Russia Transformed*, xxiii.
75. Rupert Lewis, "The Question of Imperialism and Aspects of Garvey's Political Activities in Jamaica, 1929–30", in *Garvey: Africa, Europe, the Americas*, ed. Rupert Lewis and Maureen Warner-Lewis (Kingston: Institute of Social and Economic Research, University of the West Indies, 1986), 89.
76. Bogues, *Caliban's Freedom*, 15.
77. Padmore, *How Russia Transformed*, xix.
78. Ibid.
79. Padmore, *Pan-Africanism*, 272.

80. Kevin McDermott and Jeremy Agnew, *The Comintern: A History of International Communism from Lenin to Stalin* (New York: St Martin's, 1997), 3–4.
81. Andrew Heywood, *Political Ideologies*, 4th ed. (London: Macmillan, 2007), 123.
82. Padmore, *Pan-Africanism*, 272.
83. Ibid., 279.
84. V.I. Lenin, *Imperialism: The Highest Stage of Capitalism* (1917; repr. Moscow: Progress, 1983), 12.
85. Ibid., 280–81.
86. Padmore, *Pan-Africanism*, 280.
87. Edward Wilson, *Russia and Black Africa before World War II* (London: Holmes and Meier, 1974), 96–97.
88. Ibid.
89. Padmore, *How Russia Transformed*, xix–xx.
90. C. Robinson, *Black Marxism*, 219.
91. Jane Degras, ed., *Soviet Documents on Foreign Policy*, vol. 1, 1917–19243 (Oxford: Oxford University Press, 1965), 224.
92. R. Lewis, *Marcus Garvey*, 129.
93. Padmore, *How Russia Transformed*, xx.
94. Lenin, *Selected Works*, 598–99.
95. Lenin, *Imperialism*, 84.
96. Padmore, *Pan-Africanism*, 298.
97. Ibid., 284.
98. Ibid., 285.
99. Ibid.
100. Draper, *American Communism*, 349–50.
101. Harvey Klehr, *The Heyday of American Communism: The Depression Decade* (New York: Basic Books, 1984), 325.
102. C. Robinson, *Black Marxism*, 224
103. Padmore, *Pan-Africanism*, 285.
104. Naison, *Communists in Harlem*, 18.
105. C. Robinson, *Black Marxism*, 225.
106. Haywood, *Black Bolshevik*, 253.
107. Alan Wald, "African Americans, Culture, and Communism: National Liberation and Socialism", in *Black Liberation and the American Dream: The Struggle for Racial Justice*, ed. Paul Le Blanc (New York: Humanity Books, 2003), 202.
108. Haywood, *Black Bolshevik*, 661–62.

109. Ibid., 330.
110. Solomon, *Cry Was Unity*, 103.
111. Klehr, *Heyday of American Communism*, 15.
112. Wilson Record, *Race and Radicalism: The NAACP and the Communist Party in Conflict* (Ithaca: Cornell University Press, 1964), 52.
113. George Padmore, "The TUUC and the Negro Masses", *Labor Unity*, 24 August 1929, George Padmore Special Collection, SC 95, Box 1, Folder 15, Alma Jordan Library, University of the West Indies, St Augustine.
114. Hooker, *Black Revolutionary*, 13.
115. George Padmore, "Trade Union Unity Convention and the Negro Worker and the Negro Masses", *Daily Worker*, 27 August 1929.
116. Ibid.
117. Theodore Kornweibel, *No Crystal Stair: Black Life and the Messenger, 1917–1928* (Westport, CT: Greenwood, 1975), 182.
118. Marc Karson and Ronald Radosh, "The American Federation of Labor and the Negro Worker, 1894–1949", in *The Negro and the American Labor Movement*, ed. Julius Jacobson (New York: Anchor, 1968), 157.
119. Padmore, "Trade Union Unity Convention".
120. Solomon, *Cry Was Unity*, 69.
121. Kornweibel, *No Crystal Stair*, 196.
122. Padmore, "Trade Union Unity Convention".
123. Klehr, *Heyday of American Communism*, 16.
124. Ibid.
125. Ibid.
126. Ibid.
127. Ibid., 29.
128. Ibid.
129. Ibid.
130. Solomon, *Cry Was Unity*, 109.
131. "Sending Labour Jury to Charlotte Trial; Picket Two 'Jim Crow' Hotels", *Daily Worker*, 2 May 1929, George Padmore Special Collection, SC 97, Box 1, Folder 16, Alma Jordan Library, University of the West Indies, St Augustine.
132. Ibid.
133. George Padmore, "Gastonia: Its Significance for Negro Labour", *Daily Worker*, 4 October 1929.
134. Padmore, "Gastonia".
135. Ibid.
136. Record, *Race and Radicalism*, 24.

137. Will Herberg, "Marxism and the American Negro", in *Negro: An Anthology*, ed. Nancy Cunard (1934; repr., New York: Frederick Ungar, 1970), 135.
138. Padmore, "Gastonia".
139. Ibid.
140. Ibid.
141. Jane Degras, ed., *The Communist International 1919–1943: Documents*, vol. 3, *1929–1943* (Oxford: Oxford University Press, 1965), 42.

CHAPTER 3: A BLACK INTERNATIONALIST WITHIN THE COMINTERN

1. Moore Turner, *Caribbean Crusaders*, 193.
2. Padmore, *How Russia Transformed*, xi.
3. Padmore, *Pan-Africanism*, 276.
4. Padmore, *How Russia Transformed*, x.
5. "George Padmore, Mr. Pan-Africa", *People*, 21 March 1959, George Padmore Special Collection, SC 97, Box 1, Folder 2, Alma Jordan Library, University of the West Indies, St Augustine.
6. Padmore, *How Russia Transformed*, x.
7. C.L.R. James, "Notes on the Life", 15.
8. Ibid., 15–16.
9. Ibid., 19.
10. See R. Lewis, "Question of Imperialism", 93.
11. W. Arthur Lewis, *Economic Survey, 1919–1939* (New York: Harper and Row, 1969), 52.
12. George Padmore, "The Fight for Bread", *Negro Worker* 3, nos. 6–7 (1933): 1.
13. James Ford, *World Problems of the Negro People: A Refutation of George Padmore* (New York: Harlem Section of the Communist Party, 1935), 16.
14. George Padmore, *What Is the International Trade Union Committee of Negro Workers?* (Hamburg: International Trade Union Committee of Negro Workers, 1931), 3–4.
15. George Padmore, "Way to Win Africans against Nazism", *New Leader*, 3 October 1940, 3.
16. George Padmore, letter to Cyril Ollivierre, 16 April 1930, MG-624, Schomburg Center for Research in Black Culture.
17. Padmore, *What Is*, 23.

18. Holger Weiss, *Framing a Radical African Atlantic: African American Agency, West African Intellectuals and the International Trade Union Committee of Negro Workers* (Boston: Brill, 2014), 247.
19. Weiss, *Framing a Radical African Atlantic*, 245.
20. George Padmore, *The Life and Struggles of Negro Toilers* (1931; repr., Hollywood, CA: Sun Dance, 1971), 6.
21. Padmore, *What Is*, 5.
22. Ford, *World Problems*, 2.
23. Padmore, *What Is*, 7.
24. Padmore, *Negro Workers*, 16.
25. Weiss, *Framing a Radical African Atlantic*, 286.
26. Ibid., 314.
27. Ibid., 313.
28. Demetrio Boersner, *The Bolsheviks and the National and Colonial Question, 1917–1928* (Paris: Minard, 1957), 30.
29. Padmore, *Life and Struggles*, 5.
30. Bill Schwarz, "George Padmore", in *West Indian Intellectuals in Britain* ed. Bill Schwarz (Oxford: Manchester, 2003), 3.
31. Padmore, *Life and Struggles*, 5.
32. Ibid., 6.
33. Ralph Austen, *African Economic History* (London: James Currey, 1987), 199.
34. Padmore, *Life and Struggles*, 5.
35. Ibid., 6.
36. Ibid., 78.
37. Ibid., 103.
38. Ibid., 123–24. See also George Padmore, "Bankruptcy of Negro Leadership", *Negro Worker* 1, no. 12 (December 1931): 5–7.
39. Padmore, *Life and Struggles*, 124.
40. Record, *Race and Radicalism*, 54–55.
41. Padmore, *Life and Struggles*, 125.
42. David Levering Lewis, *W.E.B. Du Bois: The Fight for Equality and the American Century, 1919–1963* (New York: Henry Holt, 2000), 195.
43. Padmore, *Life and Struggles*, 125.
44. Rukundo Murapa, "Padmore's Role in the African Liberation Movement" (PhD diss., University of Illinois, 1974), 23.
45. George Padmore, *Africa: Britain's Third Empire* (New York: Negro Universities Press, 1969), 8.
46. Solomon, *Cry Was Unity*, 170.

47. Ibid.
48. Harold Gosnell, *Negro Politicians: The Rise of Negro Politics in Chicago* (Chicago: University of Chicago Press, 1967), 186.
49. Padmore, *Life and Struggles*, 124.
50. Solomon, *Cry Was Unity*, 54–55.
51. Padmore, *Pan-Africanism*, 288.
52. Padmore, *Life and Struggles*, 125.
53. Edward Roux, *Time Longer than Rope: A History of the Black Man's Struggle for Freedom in South Africa* (Madison: University of Wisconsin Press, 1964) 167.
54. Ibid., 177.
55. Ibid., 184.
56. Ibid., 161–62.
57. Padmore, *Life and Struggles*, 125.
58. Padmore, *Pan-Africanism*, 326–27.
59. George Padmore, "Marcus Garvey, Misleader of His Race: Negro Workers Vote Communist", George Padmore Special Collection, SC 97, Box 1, Folder 16, Alma Jordan Library, University of the West Indies, St Augustine.
60. Jane Degras, ed., *The Communist International 1919–1943: Documents*, vol. 2, *1923–1928* (Oxford: Oxford University Press, 1960), 519.
61. Boersner, *Bolsheviks*, 129.
62. Kelley, "Afric's Sons", 38.
63. Henry Kendal, "A Garveyite Offended", *Negro Worker* 2, no. 8 (1932): 22–23.
64. Ibid., 23.
65. Ibid.
66. Padmore, *Pan-Africanism*, 80.
67. Ibid. 283.
68. Padmore, *How Russia Transformed*, 85.
69. Padmore, *Pan-Africanism*, 283.
70. C.L.R. James, "Notes on the Life", 31a.
71. "What Is the International Trade Union Committee of Negro Workers?", *Negro Worker* 1, nos. 10–11 (1931): 45.
72. Weiss, *Framing a Radical African Atlantic*, 298.
73. Jan Valtin, *Out of the Night* (New York: Alliance, 1941), 309.
74. Ibid., 309.
75. Adi, *Pan-Africanism and Communism*, 104.
76. Edwards, *Practice of Diaspora*, 7–8.

77. V.I. Lenin, *What Is to Be Done*, trans. Joe Fineberg and George Hann (1902; London: Penguin, 1962), 160.
78. Padmore, "Gastonia".
79. Kornweibel, *No Crystal Stair*, 42.
80. Theodore Vincent, *Voices of a Black Nation: Political Journalism in the Harlem Renaissance* (San Francisco: Ramparts, 1973), 15.
81. Weiss, *Framing a Radical African Atlantic*, 557–58.
82. Editorial, "Our Aims", *International Negro Workers' Review* 1, no. 1 (1931): 3.
83. George Padmore, letter to Cyril Ollivierre, 26 September 1932, MG-624, Schomburg Center for Research in Black Culture.
84. Editorial, "Our Aims", *International Negro Workers' Review* 1, no. 1 (1931): 3
85. Weiss, *Framing a Radical African Atlantic*, 561.
86. Adi, *Pan-Africanism and Communism*, 147–48.
87. Weiss, *Framing a Radical African Atlantic*, 559.
88. Ibid., 563.
89. Valtin, *Out of the Night*, 308–9.
90. E. Wilson, *Russia and Black Africa*, 219.
91. Ibid., 214.
92. Ibid., 214–15.
93. Ibid., 214.
94. Ibid., 220.
95. C.L.R. James, "Notes on the Life", 16.
96. Ibid., 17.
97. "The Change in the Name of Our Journal", *Negro Worker* 1, no. 3 (1931): 2.
98. Ibid.
99. Minkah Makalani, *In the Cause of Freedom: Radical Black Internationalism from Harlem to London, 1917–1939* (Chapel Hill: University of North Carolina Press, 2011), 165.
100. Weiss, *Framing a Radical African Atlantic*, 329.
101. Geiss, *Pan-African Movement*, 336.
102. Ibid., 322.
103. Ibid., 336–37.
104. George Padmore, "Hands Off Liberia!" *Negro Worker* 1, nos. 10–11 (1931): 6.
105. Ibid.
106. Sundiata, *Brothers and Strangers*, 134.

107. Padmore, "Hands Off Liberia!", 6–7.
108. Ibid.
109. Sundiata, *Brothers and Strangers*, 128.
110. Padmore, "Hands Off Liberia!", 6–7.
111. Ibid., 7–8.
112. Ibid., 9.
113. Ibid., 9–10.
114. Ibid., 10–11.
115. George Padmore, "How the Empire Is Governed", *Negro Worker* 2, no. 7 (1932): 1.
116. Ibid., 3–4.
117. Ibid.
118. Ibid., 4–5.
119. Ibid., 6.
120. George Padmore, "How the Imperialists Are Civilizing Africa", *Negro Worker* 2, no. 3 (1932): 11–12.
121. McDermott and Agnew, *Comintern*, 98.
122. Padmore, "How the Imperialists Are Civilizing Africa".
123. Ibid., 12.
124. Lenin, *Selected Works*, 165.
125. E. Wilson, *Russia and Black Africa*, 221.
126. Roi Ottley, *No Green Pastures* (New York: Charles Scribner's Sons, 1951), 62.
127. Jeremy Murray-Brown, *Kenyatta* (London: George Allen and Unwin, 1972), 166.
128. Harvey Klehr, John Haynes and Fridrikh Firsov, *The Secret World of American Communism* (New Haven, CT: Yale University Press, 1995), 21.
129. Moore Turner, *Caribbean Crusaders*, 198.
130. George Padmore, letter to Cyril Ollivierre, 5 July 1932, MG-624, Schomburg Center for Research in Black Culture.
131. Ottley, *No Green Pastures*, 62.
132. Moore Turner, *Caribbean Crusaders*, 199.
133. Valtin, *Out of the Night*, 309.
134. Moore Turner, *Caribbean Crusaders*, 199.
135. Samuel Rohdie, "The Gold Coast Aborigines Abroad", *Journal of African History* 6, no. 3 (1965): 393.
136. Ibid., 396.
137. Ibid.
138. Pennybacker, *From Scottsboro to Munich*, 75.
139. Weiss, *Framing a Radical African Atlantic*, 542.

140. C.L.R. James, "Notes on the Life", 23.
141. Weiss, *Framing a Radical African Atlantic*, 591.
142. Ibid., 659.
143. Ibid., 495.
144. Moore Turner, *Caribbean Crusaders*, 212.
145. Hooker, *Black Revolutionary*, 35.
146. Weiss, *Framing a Radical African Atlantic*, 244.
147. Ibid., 330–34.
148. Ibid., 335–36.
149. Pennybacker, *From Scottsboro to Munich*, 86.
150. George Padmore, "Au Revoir", *Negro Worker* 3, nos. 8–9 (1933): 18.
151. Ibid.
152. Ibid.
153. E. Wilson, *Russia and Black Africa*, 260.
154. Valtin, *Out of the Night*, 328.
155. Adi, *Pan-Africanism and Communism*, 156.
156. Weiss, *Framing a Radical African Atlantic*, 599.
157. Adi, *Pan-Africanism and Communism*, 157.
158. George Padmore, letter to Cyril Ollivierre, 28 July 1934, MG-624, Schomburg Center for Research in Black Culture.
159. George Padmore, "Britain Is Still Imperialist", *Socialist Leader*, 9 November 1946, 7.
160. Weiss, *Framing a Radical African Atlantic*, 613.
161. Solomon, *Cry Was Unity*, 180.
162. Jonathan Derrick, *Africa's "Agitators": Militant Anti-Colonialism in Africa and the West, 1918–1939* (New York: Columbia University Press, 2008), 289–90.
163. Weiss, *Framing a Radical African Atlantic*, 602.
164. Derrick, *Africa's "Agitators"*, 291.
165. George Padmore, letter to Cyril Ollivierre, 28 July 1934, MG-624, Schomburg Center for Research in Black Culture.
166. Woodford McClellan, "African and Black Americans in the Comintern Schools, 1925–1934", *International Journal of African Historical Studies* 26, no. 2 (1993): 384.
167. Padmore, *Pan-Africanism*, 304.
168. ICC, "Expulsion of George Padmore from the Revolutionary Movement", *Negro Worker* 4, no. 2 (1934): 14.
169. Ibid., 14.
170. Ibid., 15.

171. Edwards, *Practice of Diaspora*, 251–59.
172. "Expulsion of Kouyate", *Negro Worker* 4, no. 1 (1934): 32.
173. Moore Turner, *Caribbean Crusaders*, 212.
174. Valtin, *Out of the Night*, 44.
175. Sundiata, *Brothers and Strangers*, 216.
176. Weiss, *Framing a Radical African Atlantic*, 609.
177. Paul Trewhela, "The Death of Albert Nzula and the Silence of George Padmore", *Searchlight South Africa* 1, no. 1 (1988): 66.
178. "Remembrances about George Padmore, Part 3, Common Work in Berlin (1931–1932)", C.L.R. James Special Collection, Folder 440, Box 23, Alma Jordan Library, University of the West Indies, St Augustine.
179. Weiss, *Framing a Radical African Atlantic*, 605.
180. Hooker, *Black Revolutionary*, 27.
181. Padmore, "Open Letter", 302.
182. Solomon, *Cry Was Unity*, 181.
183. Hooker, *Black Revolutionary*, 33.
184. Sundiata, *Brothers and Strangers*, 216.
185. George Padmore, *American Imperialism Enslaves Liberia* (Moscow: Centrizdat, 1931), 18.
186. C.L.R. James, *Rendezvous of Victory*, 251.
187. Richard Wright, foreword to *Pan-Africanism or Communism*, by George Padmore (New York: Doubleday, 1971), xxiii.
188. C. Robinson, *Black Marxism*, xxxi.
189. Helen Davis, "The Rise and Fall of George Padmore as a Revolutionary Fighter", *Negro Worker* 4, no. 4 (August 1934): 17.
190. Makalani, *In the Cause of Freedom*, 158.
191. Ford, *World Problems*, 6.
192. Davis, "Rise and Fall", 17.
193. Ibid., 17.
194. Ford, *World Problems*, 6.
195. "James Ford Answers Padmore's Charges", *Negro Liberator*, 4 August 1934, 1, 5; "Ford Analyzes Padmore as Police Spy Agent", *Negro Liberator*, 25 August 1934, 5.
196. Davis, "Rise and Fall", 17.
197. Padmore, "Open Letter", 302.
198. Ibid.
199. Ibid.
200. Ibid.
201. Ibid.

202. Ibid.
203. "James Ford Answers Padmore's Charges"; "Ford Analyzes Padmore".
204. Ibid.
205. Earl Browder, "Earl Browder Replies", *Crisis*, December 1935, 372.
206. Weiss, *Framing a Radical African Atlantic*, 606.
207. Pennybacker, *From Scottsboro to Munich*, 68.
208. "We Resume Publication", *Negro Worker* 4, no. 1 (1934): 1.
209. Record, *Negro and the Communist Party*, 85.
210. Browder, "Earl Browder Replies", 372.
211. George Padmore, "Ethiopia Today", in *Negro: An Anthology*, ed. Nancy Cunard (1934; repr., New York: Frederick Unger Publishing, 1970), 391.
212. Browder, "Earl Browder Replies", 372.

CHAPTER 4: RADICAL PAN-AFRICAN ACTIVISM

1. Hooker, *Black Revolutionary*, 35.
2. Valtin, *Out of the Night*, 190.
3. C.L.R. James, "Notes on the Life", 21.
4. Grimshaw, *C.L.R. James Reader*, 292.
5. Davis, "Rise and Fall", 21.
6. Leslie James, *George Padmore and Decolonization from Below: Pan-Africanism, The Cold War and the End of Empire* (London: Palgrave, 2015), 73.
7. George Padmore, letter to Cyril Ollivierre, 28 July 1934, MG-624, Schomburg Center for Research in Black Culture.
8. George Padmore, letter to Cyril Ollivierre, 26 September 1932, MG-624, Schomburg Center for Research in Black Culture.
9. Abrahams, *Coyaba Chronicles*, 39.
10. Ibid., 86.
11. Hazel Rowley, *Richard Wright: The Life and Times* (New York: Henry Holt, 2001), 347.
12. Edwards, *Practice of Diaspora*, 277.
13. Ibid.
14. Ibid., 279.
15. Ibid., 280.
16. Ibid., 281.
17. Hooker, *Black Revolutionary*, 39–40.
18. Editorial, "Fascist Terror against Negroes in Germany", *Negro Worker* 3, nos. 4–5 (1933): 2. In "The Second World War and the Darker Races"

(*Crisis,* December 1939, 328), Padmore stated that he spent three months in a Nazi prison.
19. Editorial, "Fascist Terror", 1.
20. Ibid.
21. Ibid.
22. Ibid.
23. George Padmore, *Africa and World Peace* (1937; repr., London: Frank Cass, 1972), 107.
24. Ernest Work, *Ethiopia: A Pawn in European Diplomacy* (New Concord, OH: Ernest Work, 1935), 283.
25. Joseph Harris, *African American Reactions to War in Ethiopia, 1936–1941* (Baton Rouge: Louisiana State University Press, 1994), 2.
26. S.K.B. Asante, *Pan-African Protest: West Africa and the Italo-Ethiopian Crisis, 1934–1941* (London: Longman, 1977), 11.
27. Harris, *African American Reactions,* 19–20.
28. George Padmore, "Ethiopia and World Politics", *Crisis,* May 1935, 157.
29. George Padmore, "The Missionary Racket", *Crisis,* July 1935, 214.
30. C.L.R. James, "Notes on the Life", 29.
31. Abrahams, *Coyaba Chronicles,* 38.
32. Padmore, *Pan-Africanism,* 123.
33. C.L.R. James, "Notes on the Life", 29.
34. Ibid., 30.
35. George Padmore, *How Britain Rules Africa* (1936; repr., New York: Negro Universities Press, 1969), 363.
36. Asante, *Pan-African Protest,* 3.
37. Padmore, *Africa and World Peace,* 123.
38. Work, *Ethiopia,* 332.
39. Cited by G.M. Gathorne-Hardy, "Italy and Abyssinia" in *The Ethiopian Crisis: Touchstone of Appeasement?,* ed. Ludwig Schaefer (Boston, MA: D.C. Heath, 1961), 11.
40. Thomas Verich, *The European Powers and the Italo-Ethiopian War, 1935–1936: A Diplomatic Study* (Salisbury: Documentary Publications: 1980), 4.
41. Ibid. 5.
42. Padmore, *Africa and World Peace,* 124–25.
43. Ibid., 152–53.
44. Ibid., 153.
45. See Gaetano Salvemini, "Prelude to World War II", in *The Ethiopian Crisis: Touchstone of Appeasement?,* ed. Ludwig Schaefer (Boston: D.C. Heath, 1961), 34.

46. Luigi Vallari, "The Ethiopia War: An Italian View", in *The Ethiopian Crisis: Touchstone of Appeasement?*, ed. Ludwig Schaefer (Boston: D.C. Heath, 1961), 48.
47. Verich, *European Powers*, 16.
48. Padmore, *Africa and World Peace*, 153.
49. Adi, *Pan-Africanism and Communism*, 180.
50. C.L.R. James, *World Revolution, 1917–1936: The Rise and Fall of the Communist International* (New York: Pioneer, 1937), 388.
51. Roy Medvedev, *Let History Judge: The Origins and Consequences of Stalinism*, trans. George Shriver (New York: Columbia University Press, 1969), 724.
52. Padmore, *Africa and World Peace*, 154.
53. Ibid.
54. Adi, *Pan-Africanism and Communism*, 182.
55. Ibid., 182–83.
56. Robin D.G. Kelley, *Race Rebels: Culture, Politics and the Black Working Class* (New York: Free Press, 1996), 136.
57. Padmore, *Africa and World Peace*, 155.
58. Padmore, *How Britain Rules Africa*, 389.
59. F.A. Ridley, *The Papacy and Fascism: The Crisis of the Twentieth Century* (London: Martin Secker Warburg, 1937), 195.
60. Padmore, "Missionary Racket", 214.
61. Asante, *Pan-African Protest*, 83.
62. Padmore, *How Britain Rules Africa*, 16.
63. Editorial, *International African Opinion* 1, no. 1 (1938): 2.
64. Ibid., 2–3.
65. Padmore, *Pan-Africanism*, 125.
66. Makonnen, *Pan-Africanism from Within*, 117.
67. Editorial, *International African Opinion* 1, no. 1 (July 1938): 2–3.
68. Ibid.
69. Lenin, *What Is to Be Done?*, 83.
70. C.L.R. James, "Notes on the Life", 35.
71. L. James, *George Padmore*, 94.
72. Hooker, *Black Revolutionary*, 46.
73. Makonnen, *Pan-Africanism from Within*, 179.
74. Ibid.
75. Carol Polsgrove, *Ending British Rule in Africa: Writers in a Common Cause* (Manchester: Manchester University Press, 2009), 27.
76. Hooker, *Black Revolutionary*, 49.

77. C.L.R. James, *Rendezvous of Victory*, 257.
78. Ibid.
79. C.L.R, James, "Notes on the Life", 37.
80. Dudley Thompson, *From Kingston to Kenya: The Making of a Pan-Africanist Lawyer* (Dover, MA: Majority Press, 1993), 41.
81. James, "Notes on the Life", 37.
82. C.L.R. James, *Nkrumah and the Ghana Revolution* (London: Allison and Busby, 1977), 56.
83. George Padmore, letter to Cyril Ollivierre, 19 August 1945, MG-624, Schomburg Center for Research in Black Culture.
84. Padmore, *Pan-Africanism*, 126.
85. Ibid., 129.
86. Hakim Adi and Marika Sherwood, *The 1945 Manchester Pan-African Congress Revisited* (London: New Beacon Books, 1995), 13.
87. Padmore, *Pan-Africanism*, 127.
88. Ibid., 132.
89. Polsgrove, *Ending British Rule*, 38.
90. Adi and Sherwood, *1945 Manchester Pan-African Congress*, 60.
91. Herbert Aptheker, ed. *The Correspondence of W.E.B. Du Bois,* vol. 2, *Selections, 1934–1944* (Amherst: University of Massachusetts Press, 1976), 375–83.
92. Aptheker, *Correspondence of W.E.B. Du Bois*, 3:56–57.
93. Ibid., 64.
94. Ibid.
95. Ibid., 62–65.
96. Ibid., 67–68.
97. Ibid., 77.
98. Ibid., 77–78.
99. Ibid., 78.
100. Ibid., 78–79
101. Ibid., 80–81.
102. Ibid., 82–83.
103. Ibid., 87–88
104. Abrahams, *Coyaba Chronicles*, 45–46.
105. Ibid.
106. Kwame Nkrumah, *The Autobiography of Kwame Nkrumah* (Edinburgh: Thomas Nelson and Sons, 1957), 52.
107. Adi and Sherwood, *1945 Manchester Pan-African Congress*, 60.
108. Ibid., 22.

109. George Padmore, letter to Cyril Ollivierre, 19 August 1945, MG-624, Schomburg Center for Research in Black Culture.
110. Adi and Sherwood, *1945 Manchester Pan-African Congress*, 81.
111. Ibid., 55.
112. Ibid.
113. Ibid.
114. Padmore, *Pan-Africanism*, 148.
115. Ibid., 56.
116. Ibid., 149.
117. Ibid., 139.

CHAPTER 5: RADICAL ANTI-IMPERIALIST CRITIQUES

1. Hooker, *Black Revolutionary*, 111.
2. Padmore, *How Britain Rules Africa*, 19.
3. Ibid., 7.
4. Padmore, *Africa*, 47.
5. Ibid., 387.
6. Padmore, *How Britain Rules Africa*, 2–3.
7. Alfred Plummer, *Raw Materials or War Materials?* (London: Victor Gollancz, 1937), 10.
8. Jolanda Ballhaus, "The Colonial Aims and Hitler's Regime, 1933–1939" in *German Imperialism in Africa: From the Beginnings until the Second World War*, ed. Helmuth Stoecker, trans. Bernd Zöllner (London: C. Hurst, 1977), 346.
9. Padmore, *How Britain Rules Africa*, 12.
10. Padmore, *Africa and World Peace*, 228.
11. Ibid., 240.
12. Upthegrove Campbell, *Empire by Mandate: A History of the Relations of Great Britain with the Permanent Mandates Commission of the League of Nations* (New York: Bookman, 1954), 17.
13. Ibid., 17–18.
14. George Padmore, "A New World War for the Colonies", *Crisis,* October 1937, 309.
15. R. Palme Dutt, *World Politics, 1918–1936* (London: Victor Gollancz, 1936), 176.
16. Ibid., 189.
17. Ibid.

18. George Padmore, "A New World War for the Colonies", *Crisis*, October 1937, 309.
19. Leonard Woolf, *Mandates and Empire* (London: British Periodicals, 1920), 7.
20. William Hailey, *The Future of Colonial Peoples* (1944; repr., Oxford: Oxford University Press, 1953), 191.
21. Padmore, *Africa and World Peace*, 185.
22. Ibid., 194.
23. Ibid., 187.
24. James Murray, *The United Nations Trusteeship System* (Urbana: University of Illinois Press, 1957), 13.
25. Padmore, *Africa and World Peace*, 187.
26. Ibid.
27. Slave Trade and Importation into Africa of Firearms, Ammunition and Spirituous Liquors (General Act of Brussels), 2 July 1890, https://www.loc.gov/law/help/us-treaties/bevans/m-ust000001-0134.pdf.
28. George Padmore, "The Old Firm under a New Name", *New Leader*, 23 February 1946, 4.
29. Padmore, *Africa and World Peace*, 190.
30. Ibid., 196.
31. Ibid., 203–4.
32. Rodney Davenport and Christopher Saunders, *South Africa: A Modern History* (London: Macmillan, 2000), 292.
33. Ruth First, *South West Africa* (London: Penguin, 1975), 101–3.
34. Padmore, *Africa and World Peace*, 205.
35. Ibid., 194.
36. Ibid., 192.
37. Ibid.
38. Ibid., 206.
39. George Padmore, "Trusteeship: The New Imperialism", *Crisis*, October, 1946, 313.
40. W.R. Crocker, *Self-Government for the Colonies* (London: Allen and Unwin, 1949), 12.
41. Padmore, "Trusteeship".
42. Ibid.
43. Ibid.
44. Padmore, *Africa*, 130.
45. Ibid.
46. Ibid., 131.

47. Ibid., 132.
48. Padmore, *How Britain Rules Africa*, 311.
49. Ibid., 315.
50. Padmore, *Africa*, 111.
51. Padmore, *How Britain Rules Africa*, 315.
52. Padmore, *Africa*, 112.
53. Ibid.
54. Ibid., 112.
55. Ibid., 114.
56. George Padmore, "British Indirect Rule", *Crisis*, October, 1945, 107.
57. George Padmore, "British Brand of Fascism", *New Leader*, 13 March 1943, 4.
58. Padmore, *Africa*, 113.
59. Ibid., 129.
60. Padmore, *How Britain Rules Africa*, 317.
61. Margery Perham, *The Colonial Reckoning* (London: Collins, 1961), 58.
62. Mahmood Mamdani, "Indirect Rule, Civil Society and Ethnicity: The African Dilemma", in *Out of One, Many Africas*, ed. William G. Martin and Michael West (Chicago: University of Illinois Press, 1999), 190.
63. Padmore, *How Britain Rules Africa*, 317.
64. Ibid.
65. Mamdani, "Indirect Rule", 191.
66. Padmore, *How Britain Rules Africa*, 318.
67. Padmore, "British Indirect Rule", 120.
68. Ibid.
69. Ibid.
70. Ibid.
71. Padmore, *Africa*, 114.
72. Ibid., 128.
73. Margery Perham, *Africans and British Rule* (London: Oxford University Press, 1949), 69.
74. Arthur Lewis, Michael Scott, Martin Wright and Colin Legum, *Attitude to Africa* (Harmondsworth, UK: Penguin, 1951), 33.
75. Padmore, *Africa*, 128.
76. George Padmore, "Not Nazism, Not Imperialism! But Socialism!" *New Leader*, 27 December 1941, 4–5.
77. Ibid.
78. Ibid.

79. Frantz Fanon, *The Wretched of the Earth*, trans. Constance Farrington (Harmondsworth, UK: Penguin, 1985), 28.
80. Hannah Arendt, *The Origins of Totalitarianism* (London: George Allen and Unwin, 1958), 185.
81. Mahmood Mamdani, *When Victims Become Killers: Colonialism, Nativism and the Genocide in Rwanda* (Princeton, NJ: Princeton University Press, 2001), 12.
82. Horst Drecher, "The Conquest of Colonies: The Establishment and Extension of German Colonial Rule: South West Africa, 1885–1907", in *German Imperialism in Africa: From the Beginnings until the Second World War,* ed. Helmuth Stoecker, trans. Bernd Zöllner (London: C. Hurst, 1977), 58.
83. Mamdani, *When Victims Become Killers,* 12.
84. Ibid.
85. Clarence Lusane, *Hitler's Black Victims: The Historical Experiences of Afro-Germans, European Blacks, Africans and African Americans in the Nazi Era* (New York: Routledge, 2003), 51.
86. Padmore, *How Britain Rules Africa,* 59.
87. Ibid., 160.
88. Nigel Worden, *The Making of Modern South Africa* (Oxford: Blackwell, 1994), 65.
89. Padmore, *How Britain Rules Africa,* 160.
90. Roger Beck, *The History of South Africa* (Westport, CT: Greenwood, 2000), 113–14.
91. Padmore, *How Britain Rules Africa,* 163.
92. Padmore, *Africa,* 17.
93. Ibid., 23.
94. Padmore, *How Britain Rules Africa,* 189–90.
95. Stanley Payne, *History of Fascism, 1914–1945* (Madison: University of Wisconsin Press, 1995), 338.
96. George Padmore, "The British Empire Is the Worst Racket Yet Invented by Man", *New Leader,* 15 December 1939, 3.
97. Beck, *History of South Africa,* 114.
98. George Padmore, "White Rule in Africa: A Terrible Indictment", *Forward,* December 1938, 9.
99. Padmore, *Africa,* 30.
100. Padmore, "Not Nazism".
101. Ibid.
102. Padmore, *How Britain Rules Africa,* 124.

103. Padmore, *Africa*, 64.
104. Padmore, *How Britain Rules Africa*, 123.
105. Ibid., 59–60.
106. Ibid., 101.
107. Ibid., 124.
108. Ibid., 129.
109. Ibid.
110. Ibid., 130.
111. Ibid., 97.
112. Ibid.
113. LaRay Denzer, "Wallace-Johnson and the Sierra Leone Labour Crisis of 1939", *African Studies Review* 25 nos. 2/3 (1982): 159.
114. George Padmore, "Fascism Invades West Africa", *Crisis*, October 1939.
115. George Padmore, "Democracy Not for the Coloured Race", *Crisis,* January 1940.
116. Padmore, "Democracy Not for the Coloured Race".
117. Padmore, "Fascism Invades West Africa".
118. Leo Spitzer and LaRay Denzer, "I.T.A. Wallace-Johnson and the West African Youth League", *International Journal of African Historical Studies* 6, no. 3 (1973): 426.
119. John Hammond Moore, "The Angelo Herdon Case, 1932–1937", *Phylon* 32, no. 1 (1971): 62.
120. Charles Martin, "Communists and Blacks: The ILD and the Angelo Herndon Case", *Journal of Negro History* 64, no. 2 (1979): 131.
121. Padmore, "Fascism Invades West Africa".
122. George Padmore, "Fascism in the West Indies", *Crisis,* March 1938, 78–79.
123. Lenin, *Selected Works*, 159.
124. Padmore, *How Russia Transformed*, 150.
125. Nancy Cunard and George Padmore, *The White Man's Duty* (London: W.H. Allen, 1945), 12.
126. Henry Wilson, *African Decolonization* (London: Edward Arnold, 1994), 54.
127. Dane Kennedy, *Britain and Empire 1880–1945* (London: Longman, 2002), 84.
128. Cunard and Padmore, *White Man's Duty*, 15.
129. Ibid., 19.
130. Ibid.
131. George Padmore, "Whither the West Indies?", *New Leader,* 29 March 1941, 5.

132. Arthur Lewis, *Labour in the West Indies* (London: New Beacon Books, 1977), 53.
133. W. Arthur Lewis, "The 1930s Social Revolution", in *Caribbean Freedom: Economy and Society from Emancipation to the Present*, ed. Hilary Beckles and Verene Shepherd (Kingston: Ian Randle, 1993), 392.
134. Padmore, "Whither the West Indies?".
135. Cunard and Padmore, *White Man's Duty*, 20.
136. A. Lewis, *Labour in the West Indies*, 53.
137. Cunard and Padmore, *White Man's Duty*, 20.
138. George Padmore, "To Defeat Nazism We Must Free Colonials", *New Leader*, 25 July 1940, 5.
139. Ibid.
140. Padmore, *How Russia Transformed*, 35.
141. Ibid., 33.
142. Ibid., 49.
143. Ibid., 39.
144. Ibid.
145. Ibid., 44.
146. Ibid., 33.

CHAPTER 6: PAN-AFRICAN THEORIZING

1. Padmore, *Pan-Africanism*, xiv.
2. C.L.R. James, *Rendezvous of Victory*, 262.
3. George Padmore, "A Guide to Pan-African Socialism", in *African Socialism*, ed. William H. Friedland and Carl G. Rosberg (Palo Alto, CA: Stanford University Press, 1964), 223.
4. W. Scott Thompson, *Ghana's Foreign Policy, 1957–1966: Diplomacy, Ideology and the New State* (Princeton: Princeton University Press, 1969), 22.
5. Azinna Nwafor, "The Revolutionary as Historian: Padmore and Pan-Africanism", introduction to *Pan Africanism or Communism*, by George Padmore (New York: Doubleday, 1971), xxv.
6. Geiss, *Pan-African Movement*, 507.
7. Walter Rodney, "Aspects of the International Class Struggle in Africa, the Caribbean and America", https://www.marxists.org/subject/africa/rodney-walter/works/internationalclassstruggle.htm.
8. Horace Campbell, "Walter Rodney and Pan-Africanism Today" (paper presented at the African Studies Research Center, Cornell University, 28 September 2005), 15.

9. Richard Gibson, *African Liberation Movements: Contemporary Struggles against White Minority Rule* (New York: Oxford University Press, 1972), 84.
10. Paul Trewhela, "George Padmore: A Critique: Pan-Africanism or Marxism?" *Searchlight South Africa* 1, no. 1 (1988): 42.
11. Padmore, *Pan-Africanism*, 322.
12. Marable, *African and Caribbean Politics*, 115.
13. Dennis Austin, *Politics in Ghana, 1940–1960* (1964; repr., London: Oxford University Press, 1970), 170.
14. Trevor Munroe, *The Cold War and the Jamaican Left, 1950–55: Reopening the Files* (Kingston: Kingston Publishers, 1992), 104–5.
15. Colin Legum, "Pan-Africanism and Communism", in *The Soviet Bloc, China and Africa*, ed. Sven Hamrell and Carl Gösta Widstrand (Uppsala: Scandinavian Institute of African Studies, 1964), 9.
16. Padmore, *Pan-Africanism*, xiii.
17. A. Lewis et al., *Attitude to Africa*, 27.
18. Padmore, *Pan-Africanism*, xiii.
19. Ibid., xv.
20. Wright, foreword, xxi.
21. C.L.R. James, "Notes on the Life", 14.
22. Padmore, *Africa and World Peace*, 4.
23. C.L.R. James, "Notes on the Life", 38.
24. Ibid., 39–41. See also C.L.R. James, *Nkrumah*, 66.
25. George Padmore, "Hands Off the Soviet Union", *Left*, February 1940, 41, http://marxists.anu.edu.au/archive/padmore/1940/hands-off-soviets.htm.
26. Padmore, *How Russia Transformed*, ix.
27. George Padmore, "Socialist Attitude to the Invasion of the USSR", *Left* 60 (September 1941), http://Marxists.anu.edu.au/archive/padmore/1941/invasion-ussr.htm.
28. George Novack, "The First and Second Internationals", in *The First Three Internationals: Their History and Lessons,* by George Novack, Dave Frankel and Fred Feldman (New York: Pathfinder, 1974,), 9.
29. "Tribute by Professor Arthur Lewis", *Evening News,* 4 October 1959, George Padmore Special Collection, SC97, Box 2, Folder 16, Alma Jordan Library, University of the West Indies, St Augustine.
30. C.L.R. James, "Notes on the Life", 38.
31. Makonnen, *Pan-Africanism from Within*, 263.
32. Aptheker, *Correspondence of W.E.B. Du Bois*, 3:373–74.
33. Cheddi Jagan, *The West on Trial: The Fight for Guyana's Freedom* (Berlin: Seven Seas, 1980), 123–24.

34. Padmore, *Pan-Africanism*, 323.
35. George Padmore, "The Crisis: A Review of Constitutional Development: British Guiana Supplement", *Socialist Leader*, 31 October 1953, 7.
36. Jagan, *West on Trial*, 119.
37. Padmore, *Pan-Africanism*, xv.
38. Ibid., 320.
39. Horace Campbell, *Pan-Africanism: The Struggle against Imperialism and Neo-Colonialism* (Toronto: Afro-Carib Publications, 1974), 53.
40. Ibid., 348.
41. Ibid., xv.
42. Henry Winston, *Strategy for a Black Agenda: A Critique of New Theories* (New York: International Publishers, 1975), 148.
43. Padmore, *Pan-Africanism*, xv.
44. Marika Sherwood, "George Padmore and Kwame Nkrumah: A Tentative Outline of Their Relationship", in *George Padmore: Pan-African Revolutionary*, ed. Fitzroy Baptiste and Rupert Lewis (Kingston: Ian Randle, 2009), 170.
45. Padmore, *The Gold Coast Revolution* (London: Dennis Dobson, 1953), 213.
46. Padmore, *Pan-Africanism*, 317.
47. Nwafor, "Revolutionary as Historian", xxxvi.
48. Padmore, *Gold Coast Revolution*, 3.
49. Padmore, *Pan-Africanism*. 317.
50. Ibid., 317–18.
51. A.W. Singham and Shirley Hune, *Non-Alignment in an Age of Alignments* (London: Zed Books, 1986), 67.
52. George Padmore, "Pan-Africanism and Ghana", *United Asia* 9, no. 1 (February 1957): 52.
53. C.L.R. James, "Notes on the Life", 41.
54. Kwame Nkrumah, *The Struggle Continues* (London: PANAF Books, 1973), 7.
55. Padmore, *Pan-Africanism*, xvi.
56. Peter Willetts, *The Non-Aligned Movement* (London: Frances Pinter, 1982), 20.
57. Marable, *African and Caribbean Politics*, 109.
58. Nwafor, "Revolutionary as Historian", xxx–xxxi.
59. Legum, "Pan-Africanism", 26.
60. Ali Mazrui, *Towards a Pax Africana: A Study of Ideology and Ambition* (Chicago: University of Chicago Press, 1967), 165.

61. Padmore, *Pan-Africanism*, 356.
62. Padmore, "A Guide to Pan-Africa Socialism", 228–29.
63. Padmore, *Pan-Africanism*, 356.
64. Ibid., xix.
65. Fanon, *Wretched of the Earth*, 128.
66. Reginald Green and Ann Seidman, *Unity or Poverty? The Economics of Pan-Africanism* (London: Penguin, 1968), 12–13.
67. Padmore, *How Russia Transformed*, 58.
68. Ibid.
69. W.S. Thompson, *Ghana's Foreign Policy*, 22.
70. Nkrumah, *Revolutionary Path*, 125.
71. See Dorothy Padmore's comments in Adi and Sherwood, *1945 Manchester Pan-African Congress*, 166.
72. See "George Padmore Appointed Advisor to Nkrumah", National Archives and Records Administration, Maryland, 745J. 13/11-1457.
73. W.S. Thompson, *Ghana's Foreign Policy*, 29.
74. C.L.R. James, "Notes on the Life", 2.
75. Ibid., 58.
76. Padmore, *Gold Coast Revolution*, 1.
77. Hooker, *Black Revolutionary*, 117.
78. See "Kwame Nkrumah Funeral Oration on the Occasion of the Interment of the Ashes of the Late George Padmore, at Christiansburg Castle, Osa, Accra, 4 October 1959", in C.L.R. James, "Notes on the Life".
79. St Clair Drake, "Diaspora Studies and Pan-Africanism", in *Global Dimensions of the African Diaspora*, ed. Joseph Harris, 2nd ed. (Washington, DC: Howard University Press, 1982), 460.
80. June Milne, *Kwame Nkrumah: A Biography* (London: PANAF Books, 1999), 134.
81. Abrahams, *Coyaba Chronicles*, 71.
82. L. James, *George Padmore*, 170.
83. W.S. Thompson, *Ghana's Foreign Policy*, 33–39.
84. Ibid., 22.
85. Ibid., 58.
86. Aptheker, *Correspondence of W.E.B. Du Bois*, 3:373.
87. W.S. Thompson, *Ghana's Foreign Policy*, 58.
88. Kwame Nkrumah, *Revolutionary Path* (London: PANAF Books, 1973), 130.
89. W.S. Thompson, *Ghana's Foreign Policy*, 60.

90. V.B. Thompson, *Africa and Unity: The Evolution of Pan-Africanism* (London: Longmans, 1969), 353.
91. Ibid., 358.
92. Makonnen, *Pan-Africanism from Within*, 269.
93. Drake, "Diaspora Studies and Pan-Africanism", 468–69.
94. Immanuel Wallerstein, "Pan-Africanism as Protest", in *The Revolution in World Politics*, ed. Morton A. Kaplan (New York: John Wiley and Sons, 1962), 147.
95. L. James, *George Padmore*, 182.
96. "George Padmore, Mr. Pan-Africa".
97. Padmore, *Pan-Africanism*, xvi.
98. Kermit E. McKenzie, *Comintern and World Revolution 1928–1943: The Shaping of Doctrine* (New York: Columbia University Press, 1964), 113–91.
99. George Fredrickson, *Black Liberation: A Comparative History of Black Ideologies in the United States and South Africa* (New York: Oxford University Press, 1995), 181.
100. Medvedev, *Let History Judge*, 354–99.
101. Padmore, *Pan-Africanism*, xvi.
102. W.S. Thompson, *Ghana's Foreign Policy*, 22.
103. Marable, *African and Caribbean Politics*, 110.
104. Padmore, *Pan-Africanism*, xvi–xvii.
105. Ibid., xvii.
106. This letter is cited in Polsgrove, *Ending British Rule*, 146.
107. Cited in Fitzroy Baptiste, "The African Conference of Governors and Indigenous Collaborators, 1947–1948: A British Strategy to Blunt the 1945 Manchester Pan-African Congress", in *George Padmore: Pan-African Revolutionary*, ed. Fitzroy Baptiste and Rupert Lewis (Kingston: Ian Randle, 2009), 59.
108. Nwafor, "Revolutionary as Historian", xxxvi.
109. Ibid., xxxvii.
110. Padmore, *Pan-Africanism*, xix.
111. Ibid., 307.
112. Ibid.
113. Hooker, *Black Revolutionary*, 128–29.
114. Adi, *Pan-Africanism and Communism*, 162.
115. Padmore, *Pan-Africanism*, 349.
116. Ibid.
117. Ibid.

118. Ibid.
119. Kiven Tunteng, "George Padmore's Impact on Africa: A Critical Appraisal", *Phylon* 35, no. 1 (1974): 42.
120. Ibid.
121. Padmore, *Africa*, 216.
122. Ibid.
123. V.B. Thompson, *Africa and Unity*, 357.
124. Padmore, *Pan-Africanism*, 350–51.
125. Cited in Ian Duffield, "Pan-Africanism, Rational and Irrational", *Journal of African History* 18, no. 4 (1977): 598.
126. Bruce Berman, Dickson Eyoh and Will Kymlicka, "Introduction: Ethnicity and the Politics of Democratic Nation-Building in Africa", in *Ethnicity and Democracy in Africa*, ed. Bruce Berman, Dickson Eyoh and Will Kymlicka (Oxford: James Currey, 2004), 3–4.
127. Padmore, *Pan-Africanism*, 352.
128. Ibid.
129. Ibid.
130. Cited in Polsgrove, *Ending British Rule*, 161.
131. Winston, *Strategy for a Black Agenda*, 48.
132. Ibid., 53.
133. Marable, *African and Caribbean Politics*. 282.
134. Immanuel Wallerstein, *Africa: The Politics of Unity: An Analysis of a Contemporary* Movement (London: Pall Mall, 1968), 44.
135. A.M. Babu, *African Socialism or Socialist Africa?* (Dar es Salaam: Tanzania Publishing House, 1981), 106.
136. William Friedland and Carl Rosberg, "Introduction: The Anatomy of African Socialism", in *African Socialism*, ed. William Friedland and Carl Rosberg (Palo Alto, CA: Stanford University Press, 1964), 11.
137. David Apter, *Ghana in Transition*, 2nd ed. (Princeton, NJ: Princeton University Press, 1972), xvii.
138. W.S. Thompson, *Ghana's Foreign Policy*, 22.
139. Padmore, "Guide to Pan-African Socialism", 226.
140. Ibid., 227.
141. Ibid., 229.
142. Ibid.
143. Ibid., 230.
144. Ibid., 231.
145. Ibid.
146. Ibid., 231–32.

147. Ibid., 233–34.
148. Ibid., 234.
149. Ibid., 234–35.

BIBLIOGRAPHY

ARCHIVAL SOURCES

George Padmore Collection, Alma Jordan Library, University of the West Indies, St Augustine, Trinidad and Tobago.
C.L.R. James, Collection, Alma Jordan Library, University of the West Indies, St Augustine, Trinidad and Tobago.
George Padmore Collection, the Schomburg Center for Research in Black Culture, New York Public Library.
The National Archives and Records Administration, College Park, Maryland.

WORKS BY GEORGE PADMORE

Books and Pamphlets

Padmore, George. *How Britain Rules Africa*. 1936. Reprint, New York: Negro Universities Press, 1969.
———. *Africa and World Peace*. 1937. Reprint, London: Frank Cass, 1972.
———. *Africa: Britain's Third Empire*. 1949. Reprint, New York: Negro Universities Press, 1969.
———. *Pan-Africanism or Communism*. 1956. Reprint, New York: Doubleday, 1971.
———. *The Gold Coast Revolution*. London: Dennis Dobson, 1953.
———. *American Imperialism Enslaves Liberia*. Moscow: Centrizdat, 1931.
———. *The Life and Struggles of Negro Toilers*. 1931. Reprint, Hollywood, CA: Sun Dance, 1971.
———. *Negro Workers and the Imperialist War: Intervention in the Soviet Union*. Hamburg: International Trade Union Committee of Negro Workers, 1931.
———. *What Is the International Trade Union Committee of Negro Workers?* Hamburg: International Trade Union Committee of Negro Workers, 1931.

———. *Hands Off the Protectorates*. Manchester: International African Service Bureau, 1938.

———, ed. *The Voice of Coloured Labour: Speeches and Reports of Colonial Delegates to the World Trade Union Conference – 1945*. Manchester: PANAF Books, 1945.

———, ed. *Colonial and Coloured Unity: A Programme of Action: History of the Pan-African Congress*. London: Hammersmith Bookshop, 1963.

Padmore, George, and Nancy Cunard. *The White Man's Duty*. London: W.H. Allen, 1942.

Padmore, George, and Dorothy Pizer. *How Russia Transformed Her Colonial Empire: A Challenge to the Imperialist Powers*. London: Dennis Dobson, 1946.

Articles

———. "Gastonia: Its Significance for Negro Labour". *Daily Worker*, 4 October 1929.

———. "Bankruptcy of Negro Leadership". *Negro Worker* 1, no. 12 (1931): 4–7.

———. "The Change in the Name of Our Journal". *Negro Worker* 1, no. 3 (1931): 2.

———. "Hands Off Liberia!" *Negro Worker* 1, nos. 10–11 (1931): 5–11.

———. "How the Imperialists Are Civilizing Africa". *Negro Worker* 2, no. 3 (1932): 11–14.

———. "Liberia and the Dirty Work of the Negro Reformists". *Negro Worker* 1, no. 8 (1931): 1.

———. "Our Aims". *International Negro Workers' Review* 1, no. 1 (1931): 3.

———. "The Revolutionary Movement in Africa". *Negro Worker* 1, no. 6 (1931): 3–5.

———. "Fifteen Years of Soviet Russia". *Negro Worker* 2, nos. 11–12 (1932): 28–31.

———. "How the Empire Is Governed". *Negro Worker* 2, no. 7 (1932): 1–6.

———. "An Open Letter to the I.L.D.". *Negro Worker* 2, no. 7 (1932): 6.

———. "The War Is Here". *Negro Worker* 2, nos. 1–2 (1932): 4–10.

———. "The World Today". *Negro Worker* 2, no. 8 (1932): 1.

———. "Au Revoir". *Negro Worker* 3, nos. 8–9 (1933): 18.

———. "Fascist Terror against Negroes in Germany". *Negro Worker* 3, nos. 4–5 (1933): 1–2.

———. "The Fight for Bread". *Negro Worker* 3, nos. 6–7 (1933): 1–4.

———. "Negro Toilers Speak at the World's Congress of I.L.D.". *Negro Worker* 3, no. 2 (1933): 1.

———. "Notes and Comments". *Negro Worker* 3, nos. 8–9 (1933): 9–16.

———. "Ethiopia Today". In *Negro: An Anthology*, edited by Nancy Cunard, 386–92. 1934. Reprint, New York: Frederick Ungar, 1970.

———. "White Man's Justice in Africa". In *Negro: An Anthology*, edited by Nancy Cunard, 457–60. 1934. Reprint, New York: Frederick Ungar, 1970.

———. "Ethiopia and World Politics". *Crisis*, May 1935, 138–39, 156–57.

———. "The Missionary Racket in Africa". *Crisis*, May 1935, 214.

———. "An Open Letter to Earl Browder". *Crisis*, October 1935, 302, 315.

———. "Hitler, Mussolini and Africa". *Crisis*, September 1937, 262–63, 274.

———. "A New World for the Colonies". *Crisis*, October 1937, 302–4, 309, 318.

———. "An African's View on German Colonies". *Forward*, 19 November 1938, 4.

———. "Cocoa War on the Gold Coast". *Crisis*, February 1938, 52.

———. "Fascism in the West Indies". *Crisis*, March 1938, 78–79.

———. "The Government's Betrayal of the Protectorates". *Controversy*, 21 June 1938, https://www.marxists.org/archive/padmore/1938/government-betrayal.htm.

———. "Labour Unrest in Jamaica". *International African Opinion* 1, no. 1 (1938): 6–7, 13.

———. "Manifesto against War". *International African Opinion* 1, no. 4 (1938): https://www.marxists.org/archive/padmore/1938/manifesto-iasb.htm.

———. "An Outrageous Report". *Controversy*, 18 March 1938, http://marxists.anu.edu.au/archive/padmore/1938/outrageous-report.htm.

———. "Truth about Cocoa Slaves". *Forward*, 7 May 1938, 3.

———. "West Africans, Watch Your Land". *International African Opinion* 1, no. 3 (1938): 11, 16.

———. "White Rule in Africa". *Forward*, 31 December 1938, 9.

———. "White Workers and Black". *Controversy*, 20 May 1938, http://marxists.anu.edu.au/archive/padmore/1938/white-workers-black.htm.

———. "Why Moors Help Franco". *New Leader*, 20 May 1938, 4–5.

———. "The British Empire Is the Worst Racket Yet Invented by Man". *New Leader*, 15 December 1939, 3.

———. "Fascism Invades West Africa". *Crisis*, October 1939, 297–98.

———. "Franco-Italian Conflict over Tunis". *Crisis*, March 1939, 84–85.

———. "Police Swoop on Workers' Leaders in Colonies". *New Leader*, 20 October 1939, http://marxists.anu.edu.au/archive/padmore/1939/police-swoop.htm.

———. "The Second World War and the Darker Races". *Crisis*, November 1939, 327–28.

———. "Why I Oppose Conscription". *New Leader*, 2 June 1939, 4.

———. "African Students Present their Demands to Lord Lloyd". *New Leader*, 17 October 1940, 4–5.

———. "Democracy: Not for the Coloured Race". *Crisis*, January 1940, 13, 25.

———. "Democracy Runs Amok in the Colonies". *New Leader*, 31 October 1940, 4-5.

———. "England's West Indian Slums". *Crisis*, October 1940, 317–18, 322.

———. "Hands Off the Soviet Union". *Left*, February 1940, https://www.marxists.org/archive/padmore/1940/hands-off-soviets.htm.

———. "To Defeat Nazism We Must Free the Colonies". *New Leader*, 25 July 1940, 5.

———. "Way to Win Africans against Nazism". *New Leader*, 3 October 1940, 3.

———. "We Gave Them Copper – They Gave Us Lead!" *New Leader*, 18 April 1940, 4–5.

———. "West Indies Reply to Churchill and Roosevelt". *New Leader*, 19 September 1940, 3.

———. "Answers to a Questionnaire on the War". *Left*, November 1941, http://marxists.anu.edu.au/archive/padmore/1941/questionaire.htm.

———. "Colonials Demand Britain War Aims". *New Leader*, 15 February 1941, 2.

———. "Empire 'Gauleiters' Greet Each Other". *Left* , January 1941, http://marxists.anu.edu.au/archive/padmore/1941/gauleiters.htm.

———. "Imperialists Treat Blacks like Nazis Treat Jews". *New Leader*, 13 September 1941, 7.

———. "Jamaica Rejects Sham 'Democratic' Constitution". *New Leader*, 6 September 1941, 7.

———. "Lift the Veil of Censorship over the Colonies". *New Leader*, 5 July 1941, 7.

———. "Not Nazism, not Imperialism but Socialism". *New Leader*, 27 December 1941, 4–5.

———. "The Socialist Attitude to the Invasion of the USSR". *Left*, September 1941, http://marxist.anu.edu.au/archive/padmore/1941/invasion-ussr.htm.

———. "Warning from the West Indies". *New Leader*, 3 May 1941, 4–5.

———. "What's the Game in Abyssinia?" *New Leader*, 8 March 1941, 4–5.

———. "Whither the West Indies?" *New Leader*, 29 March 1941, 4–5.

———. "Why the RAF Has Dropped the Colour Bar". *New Leader*, 25 January 1941, 7.

———. "Colored U.S. Troops May Defend African Life Line". *Pittsburgh Courier*, 23 May 1942.
———. "Crisis in the British Empire". *Crisis*, July 1942, 216–20.
———. "Nigeria Questions Intent of Atlantic Charter". *Chicago Defender*, 31 January 1942, 12.
———. "No Atlantic Charter for Colonies". *New Leader*, 24 January 1942, 3.
———. "Padmore Finds Colorful Characters the Second AEF". *Pittsburgh Courier*, 15 August 1942, 1.
———. "Padmore Tells How Panzer's Invasion of the Suez Was Checked". *Pittsburgh Courier*, 12 September 1942.
———. "Padmore Visits Troops in Britain: Men Being Trained in 'Blitz' Tactics". *Pittsburgh Courier*, 15 August 1942, 1, 4.
———. "Race Issue Takes Spotlight in Great Britain". *Chicago Defender*, 23 May 1942, 1.
———. "Race Relations, Soviet and British". *Crisis*, November 1942, 345–47.
———. "Russia Asks for African Freedom: Soviet Union Tells Stand to UNO Assembly". *Chicago Defender*, 2 February 1942, 1, 7.
———. "Stalinists Assassinate Negro Labour Leader". *New Leader*, 29 August 1942, 6.
———. "Twenty Million Africans Ask Churchill to explain the Atlantic Meaning". *Pittsburgh Courier*, 7 February 1942, 12.
———. "Uncle Sam's Black Ward". *Tribune*, 23 October 1942, 6, 7.
———. "Blue Print of Post-War Anglo American Imperialism". *Left*, October 1943, 197–202.
———. "Britain Follows Mussolini". *New Leader*, 17 July 1943, 2.
———. "British Brand of Fascism: What Indirect Rule in the Empire Means". *New Leader*, 13 March 1943, 4.
———. "British Indirect Rule". *Crisis*, April 1943, 106–8, 120, 124.
———. "How Colonies Are Ruled". *New Leader*, 6 March 1943, 4.
———. "New Jim Crow Ban Brings Fresh Crisis to S. Africa". *Chicago Defender*, 1 May 1943, 9.
———. "New Patterns of Imperialism". *New Leader*, 4 December 1943, 4–5.
———. "Pan-African Confab Looms: White Settlers Initiate Their Plans". *Pittsburgh Courier*, 12 June 1943, 12.
———. "Wall Street Prepares to Cash In". *New Leader*, 11 December 1943, 4.
———. "African Troops Go into Battle on the Burmese Front". *Chicago Defender*, 1 May 1944.
———. "Anglo-American Plan for Control of the Colonies". *Crisis*, November 1944, 357–59.

———. "Half Million Join Africa Bus Boycott". *Chicago Defender*, 9 December 1944, 2.

———. "Imperialism: The Basis of Labour Party Crisis". *Left*, June 1944, http://Marxists.anu.edu.au/archive/padmore/1944/labour-crisis.htm.

———. "Mob Burns Newspaper Office in African Riot". *Chicago Defender*, 11 November 1944, 1.

———. "Padmore Sees Wall St. Invasion of Liberia". *Chicago Defender*, 18 November 1944, 2.

———. "See Revival of Post-War Trade with Ethiopians". *Chicago Defender*, 9 December 1944.

———. "African Troops Lead Advance on Burma Japs". *Chicago Defender*, 6 January 1945.

———. "Amazing Jamaican Labor Blitz at Polls". *Chicago Defender*, 3 February 1945.

———. "American Mission, Plans to Modernize Liberia". *Pittsburgh Courier*, 17 February 1945, 5.

———. "British Indirect Rule". *Crisis*, October 1945, 106–8, 120, 124.

———. "British Labour and the Colonies". *Crisis*, October 1945, 291–94.

———. "British Queen Worried over U.S. Race Riots: Unionist Told She Hopes for End of Violence: World Labor Parley Gives Support to Colonials". *Chicago Defender*, 24 February 1945, 1.

———. "Call for Pan-African Confab in Paris Drafted by British Colonial Leaders". *Chicago Defender*, 17 March 1945, 12.

———. "Fares Reduced: African Win Transit Fight". *Pittsburgh Courier*, 3 February 1945.

———. "Gandhi Urges Justice for Colored Peoples: Indian Leader Lashes Imperialist Rule over Colonies". *Chicago Defender*, 28 April 1945, 1.

———. "Gandhi Urges Unity of all Dark Races". *Chicago Defender*, 20 January 1945, 1.

———. "No Colonies for Italians after War, Says Eden". *Chicago Defender*, 24 February 1945.

———. "A Political Review of the Colonies". *Left*, February 1945, https://www.marxists.org/archive/padmore/1945/review-colonies.htm.

———. "South Africa Wins Two-Month Transit Strikes". *Chicago Defender*, 3 February 1945.

———. "South Africans Strike against Trolley Lines: Protest Native's Death in Johannesburg Race Riots". *Chicago Defender*, 13 January 1945, 1.

———. "Two Colonials in WTU Group". *Pittsburgh Courier*, 3 October 1945, 1.

———. "The Voice of Africa". *Forward*, 14 April 1945, 3.

———. "World Labor Parley Hears Colonial Plea". *Chicago Defender*, 3 February 1945, 1, 4.
———. "Big Three Compromise on Colonial Question". *New Leader*, 9 February 1946, 4.
———. "Britain Is Still Imperialist". *Socialist Leader*, 9 November 1946, 7.
———. "British Fight Russ Threat to Imperialism: Bevin Asks Foreign Ministers to Okay Abyssinian Grab". *Chicago Defender*, 11 May 1946, 1.
———. "Keep to the Point, Padley". *Socialist Leader*, 9 November 1946, 6.
———. "The Old Firm under a New Name". *New Leader*, 23 February 1946, 4.
———. "Review of the Paris Peace Conference". *Crisis*, November 1946, 331–33, 347.
———. "Starvation and Sadism, Famine Grows in South Africa". *Chicago Defender*, 3 February 1946, 5.
———. "There's No Real Difference". *New Leader*, 9 March 1946, 4.
———. "They Have Come to Speak for the Sudanese". *Socialist Leader*, 23 November 1946, 3.
———. "Trusteeship: The New Imperialism". *New Leader*, 2 February 1946, 3.
———. "Trusteeship: The New Imperialism". *Crisis*, October 1946, 312–15, 318
———. "UNO Debates Colonies". *New Leader*, 16 February 1946, 4.
———. "UNO Gets South African Appeal". *Chicago Defender*, 16 February 1946, 5.
———. "Madagascar Fights for Freedom". *Left*, October 1947, https://marxists.catbull.com/archive/padmore/1947/madagascar.htm.
———. "Economics of Race Riots in South Africa". *Socialist Leader*, 26 February 1949, 6, 7.
———. "Bloodless Revolution in the Gold Coast". *Crisis*, March 1952, 172–77, 197–99.
———. "Behind the Mau Mau". *Phylon* 14, no. 4 (1953): 355–72.
———. "The Crisis: A Review of Constitutional Development: British Guiana Supplement". *Socialist Leader*, 31 October 1953, 5–8.
———. "The Buganda Crisis". *Socialist Leader*, 19 December 1953, 5–8.
———. "Pan-Africanism and Ghana". *United Asia* 9, no. 1 (1957): 50–54.
———. "The Press Campaign against Ghana". *Socialist Leader*, 28 September 1957, 4–5.
———. "A Guide to Pan-African Socialism". In *African Socialism*, edited by William H. Friedland and Carl Rosberg, 223–37. Palo Alto, CA: Stanford University Press, 1964.

GENERAL BIBLIOGRAPHY

Abrahams, Peter. *The Coyaba Chronicles: Reflections on the Black Experience in the 20th Century.* Kingston: Ian Randle, 2000.
———. *A Wreath for Udomo.* London: Faber and Faber, 1956.
Adewale, Toks. *Pan-Africanism in Polarity.* Chicago: Research Associates and Frontline Distribution, 1995.
Adi, Hakim. *Pan-Africanism and Communism: The Communist International, Africa and the Diaspora, 1919–1939.* Trenton, NJ: Africa World Press, 2013.
———. *West Africans in Britain, 1900–1960: Nationalism, Pan-Africanism, and Communism.* London: Lawrence and Wishart, 1998.
Adi, Hakim, and Marika Sherwood, eds. *The 1945 Manchester Pan-African Congress Revisited.* London: New Beacon Books, 1995.
———. *Pan-African History: Political Figures from Africa and the Diaspora since 1787.* London: Routledge, 2003.
Agyeman, Opoku. "The Supermarxists and Pan-Africanism". *Journal of Black Studies* 8, no. 4 (1978): 489–510.
Ajayi, J.F., and Margaret Vogt, eds. *Proceedings of the First Pan-African Conference on Reparations.* Abuja, Nigeria: Research and Documentation Committee of the OAU Group of Eminent Persons for Reparation, 1994.
Alleyne, Brian. "Classical Marxism, Caribbean Radicalism and the Black Atlantic Intellectual Tradition". *Small Axe*, no. 3 (1998): 157–69.
———. *Radicals against Race: Black Activism and Cultural Politics.* New York: Oxford, 2002.
Alpers, Edward, and Pierre-Michel Fontaine. *Walter Rodney: Revolutionary and Scholar.* Los Angeles: University of California Center for Afro-American Studies and African Studies, 1982.
Anderson, Benedict. *Imagined Communities: Reflections on the Origin and Spread of Nationalism.* London: Verso, 1983.
Andrain, Charles. "The Pan-African Movement: The Search for Organization and Community". *Phylon* 23, no. 1 (1962): 5–13.
Appolus, Emil. *The Resurgence of Pan-Africanism.* London: Kalahari, 1974.
Apter, David. *Ghana in Transition.* Princeton, NJ: Princeton University Press, 1972.
Aptheker, Herbert, ed. *The Correspondence of W.E.B. Du Bois.* Vol. 2, *Selections, 1934–1944.* Amherst: University of Massachusetts Press, 1976.
———, ed. *The Correspondence of W.E.B. Du Bois.* Vol. 3, *Selections, 1944–1963.* Amherst: University of Massachusetts Press, 1978.

———, ed. *A Documentary History of the Negro People in the United States, 1910–1932*. Secaucus, NJ: Citadel, 1973.
Arendt, Hannah. *The Origins of Totalitarianism*. London: George Allen and Unwin, 1958.
Asante, S.K.B. *Pan-African Protest: West Africa and the Italo-Ethiopian Crisis, 1934–1941*. London: Longman, 1977.
Assensoh, A.B. *African Political Leadership: Jomo Kenyatta, Kwame Nkrumah, and Julius Nyerere*. Malabar, FL: Krieger, 1998.
Austen, Ralph. *African Economic History*. London: James Currey, 1987.
Austin, Dennis. *Politics in Ghana, 1946–1960*. 1964. Reprint, London: Oxford University Press, 1970.
Azikiwe, Nnamdi. *My Odyssey*. London: C. Hurst, 1970.
Babu, A.M. *African Socialism or Socialist Africa?* Dar es Salaam: Tanzania Publishing House, 1981.
Baldwin, Kate. *Beyond the Colour Line and the Iron Curtain: Reading Encounters between Black and Red, 1922–1963*. London: Duke University Press, 2002.
Ballhaus, Jolanda. "The Colonial Aims and Preparations of the Hitler Regime, 1933–1939". In *German Imperialism in Africa: From the Beginnings until the Second World War*, edited by Helmuth Stoecker; translated by Bernd Zöllner, 337–65. London: C. Hurst, 1977.
Baptiste, Fitzroy. *The United States and West Indian Unrest, 1918–1939*. Kingston: Institute of Social and Economic Research, University of the West Indies, 1978.
———. "The African Conference of Governors and Indigenous Collaborators, 1947–1948: A British Strategy to Blunt the 1945 Manchester Pan-African Congress". In *George Padmore: Pan-African Revolutionary*, edited by Fitzroy Baptiste and Rupert Lewis, 37–65. Kingston: Ian Randle, 2009.
Baptiste, Fitzroy, and Rupert Lewis. *George Padmore: Pan-African Revolutionary*. Kingston: Ian Randle, 2009.
Beck, Roger. *The History of South Africa*. Westport, CT: Greenwood, 2000.
Benn, Denis. *The Growth and Development of Political Ideas in the Caribbean, 1774–1983*. Kingston: Institute of Social and Economic Research, University of the West Indies, 1983.
Bennett, George. *Kenya: A Political History: The Colonial Period*. London: Oxford University Press, 1963.
Berman, Bruce, Dickson Eyoh and Will Kymlicka. "Introduction: Ethnicity and the Politics of Democratic Nation-Building in Africa". In *Ethnicity and*

Democracy in Africa, edited by Bruce Berman, Dickson Eyoh and Will Kymlicka, 1–21. Oxford: James Currey, 2004.

Bernstein, Michael. *The Great Depression*. Cambridge: Cambridge University Press, 1987.

Blyden, Edward. *Christianity, Islam and the Negro Race*. 1887. Reprint, Edinburgh: Edinburgh University Press, 1967.

———. *West Africa before Europe and other Addresses Delivered in England in 1901 and 1903*. London: C.M. Phillips, 1905.

Boahen, A. Adu, ed. *General History of Africa: Africa under Colonial Domination, 1880–1935*. Abridged ed. Paris: United Nations Educational, Scientific and Cultural Organization, 1990.

Boersner, Demetrio. *The Bolsheviks and the National and Colonial Question, 1917–1928*. Paris: Libraire Minard, 1957.

Bogues, Anthony. *Black Heretics: Black Prophets*. New York: Routledge, 2003.

———. *Caliban's Freedom: The Early Political Thought of C.L.R. James*. Chicago: Pluto, 1997.

———. "C.L.R. James, Black Radicalism and Critical Theory: A Response". *Small Axe*, no. 3 (1998): 170–73.

———. "Investigating the Radical Caribbean Intellectual Tradition". *Small Axe*, no. 4 (1998): 29–45.

———. "Shades of Black and Red: Freedom and Socialism". *Small Axe*, no. 1 (1997): 65–75.

Borkenau, Franz. *World Communism: A History of the Comintern*. New York: W.W. Norton, 1939.

Botwinick, Rita. *A History of the Holocaust: From Ideology to Annihilation*. Trenton, NJ: Prentice Hall, 2001.

Boyd, Herb. "Radicalism and Resistance: The Evolution of Black Radical Thought". *Black Scholar* 28, no. 1 (1998): 43–53.

Brereton, Bridget. *A History of Modern Trinidad, 1783–1962*. London: Heinemann, 1981.

———. "John Jacob Thomas: An Estimate". *Journal of Caribbean History* 8–9 (1976–77): 22–42.

Brockway, Fenner. *The Colonial Revolution*. London: Hart-Davis MacGibbon, 1973.

Broderick, Francis, and August Meier, eds. *Negro Protest Thought in the Twentieth Century*. Indianapolis: Bobbs and Merrill, 1965.

Browder, Earl. "Earl Browder Replies". *Crisis*, December 1935, 372.

Buell, Raymond. *Liberia: A Century of Survival, 1847–1947*. Philadelphia: University of Pennsylvania Press, 1947.

Buhle, Paul. *C.L.R. James: The Artist as Revolutionary*. London: Verso, 1988.
———, ed. *C.L.R. James: His Life and Work*. London: Allison and Busby, 1986.
Campbell, Carl. "John Jacob Thomas of Trinidad: The Early Career of a Black Leader and Scholar, 1855–1870". *African Studies Bulletin* 10 (1978): 4–17.
Campbell, Horace. *Pan-Africanism: The Struggle against Imperialism and Neo-Colonialism*. Toronto: Afro-Carib Publications, 1974.
———. "Walter Rodney and Pan-Africanism Today". Paper presented at the Africana Studies Research Center, Cornell University, September 2005.
Campbell, Horace, and Rodney Worrell. *Pan-Africanism, Pan-Africanists, and African Liberation in the 21st Century*. Washington, DC: New Academia Publishing, 2006.
Campbell, Upthegrove. *Empire by Mandate: A History of the Relations of Great Britain with the Permanent Mandates Commission of the League of Nations*. New York: Bookman, 1954.
Carr, E.H. *Twilight of the Comintern, 1930–1935*. New York: Pantheon, 1982.
Cobley, Alan. *Class and Consciousness: The Black Petty Bourgeoisie in South Africa, 1924 to 1950*. Westport, CT: Greenwood, 1990.
Cohen, Benjamin. *The Question of Imperialism: The Political Economy of Dominance and Dependence*. New York: Basic Books, 1973.
Conquest, Robert. *The Great Terror: Stalin's Purge of the Thirties*. New York: Collier, 1973.
Cox, Oliver. *Caste, Class and Race: A Study in Social Dynamics*. New York: Monthly Review Press, 1970.
Crocker, W.R. *Self-Government for the Colonies*. London: George Allen and Unwin, 1949.
Crowder, Michael. *Senegal: A Study of French Assimilation*. London: Methuen, 1967.
———. *West Africa under Colonial Rule*. London: Hutchinson, 1968.
Crowder, Michael, and Obaro Ikime, eds. *West African Chiefs*. Translated by Brenda Packman. Teaneck, NJ: Africana Publishing Corporation, 1970.
Cruse, Harold. *The Crisis of the Negro Intellectual*. New York: William Morrow, 1967.
———. *Rebellion or Revolution*. New York: William Morrow, 1968.
Cudjoe, Selwyn. "C.L.R. James and the Trinidad and Tobago Intellectual Tradition: On Not Learning Shakespeare under a Mango Tree". *C.L.R. James Journal* 10 (Winter 1997): 4–43.
Cunard, Nancy, ed. *Negro: An Anthology*. 1934. Reprint, New York: Frederick Ungar, 1970.

Davenport, Rodney, and Christopher Saunders. *South Africa: A Modern History*. London: Macmillan, 2000.

Davidson, Basil. *Africa in History*. New York: Macmillan, 1991.

Davis, Helen. "The Rise and Fall of George Padmore as a Revolutionary Worker". *Negro Worker* 4, no. 4 (1934): 15–17, 21.

Dawson, Michael. *Black Visions: The Roots of Contemporary African-American Political Ideologies*. London: University of Chicago Press, 2001.

De Allen, Gertrude. "Charles Mills' *From Class to Race: Essays in White Marxism and Black Radicalism*". Review. *Philosophia Africana* 8 (2005): 83–86.

Degras, Jane, ed. *The Communist International 1919–1943: Documents*. Vol. 2, *1923–1928*. Oxford: Oxford University Press, 1960.

———. *The Communist International 1919–1943: Documents*. Vol. 3, *1929–1943*. Oxford: Oxford University Press, 1965.

———. *Soviet Documents on Foreign Policy*. Vol. 1, *1917–1924*. Oxford: Oxford University Press, 1951.

Denzer, LaRay. "Wallace-Johnson and the Sierra Leone Labour Crisis of 1939". *African Studies Review* 25, nos. 2–3 (1982): 159–83.

Derrick Jonathan. *Africa's "Agitators": Militant Anti-Colonialism in Africa and the West, 1918–1939*. London: Hurst, 2008.

Diop, Anta Cheikh. *Precolonial Black Africa*. Translated by Harold Salemson. Chicago: Lawrence Hill, 1987.

Doro, Marxon, and Newell Stultz, eds. *Governing in Black Africa*. Englewood Cliffs, NJ: Prentice Hall, 1970.

Drake, St Clair. *Black Metropolis*. New York: Harcourt, Brace and World, 1970.

———. "Diaspora Studies and Pan-Africanism". In *Global Dimensions of the African Diaspora*, edited by Joseph Harris, 451–514. Washington, DC: Howard University Press, 1982.

Draper, Theodore. *American Communism and Soviet Russia*. London: Macmillan, 1960.

———. *The Roots of American Communism*. New York: Octagon, 1977.

Drecher, Horst. "The Conquest of Colonies: The Establishment and Extension of German Colonial Rule: South West Africa, 1885–1907". In *German Imperialism in Africa: From the Beginnings until the Second World War*, edited by Helmith Stoecker; translated by Bernd Zöllner, 136–47. London: C. Hurst, 1977.

Drew, Allison. *Discordant Comrades*. Pretoria: Unisa, 2002.

Du Bois, W.E.B. *The World and Africa*. 1947. Reprint, New York: International Publishers, 1981.

Duffield, Ian. "Pan-Africanism, Rational and Irrational". *Journal of African History* 18, no. 4 (1977): 597–620.
Dutt, R. Palme. *The Crisis of Britain and the British Empire*. London: Lawrence and Wishart, 1953.
———. *World Politics, 1918–1936*. London: Victor Gollancz, 1936.
Edgar, Robert. "Notes on the Life and Death of Albert Nzula". *International Journal of African Historical Studies* 16, no. 4 (1983): 675–79.
Edwards, Brent Haynes. "The Autonomy of Black Radicalism". *Social Text* 19, no. 2 (2001): 1–13.
———. "Pebbles of Consonance: A Reply to Critics". *Small Axe*, no. 17 (2005): 134–49.
———. *The Practice of Diaspora: Literature, Translation and the Rise of Black Internationalism*. Cambridge: Harvard University Press, 2003.
Eisenberg, Bernard. "Kelly Miller: The Negro Leader as a Marginal Man". *Journal of Negro History* 45, no. 3 (1960): 182–97.
Ekekwe, Eme. *Class and State in Nigeria*. London: Longman, 1986.
Elkins, W.F. *Black Power in the Caribbean: The Beginnings of the Modern Nationalist Movement*. New York: Revisionist Press, 1977.
———. "Hercules and the Society of Peoples of African Origin". *Caribbean Studies* 11, no. 4 (1971): 47–59.
Emerson, Rupert, and Martin Kilson, eds. *The Political Awakening of Africa*. Englewood Cliffs, NJ: Prentice Hall, 1965.
d'Encausse, Hélène. *The Great Challenge: Nationalities and the Bolshevik State, 1917–1930*. Translated by Nancy Festinger. New York: Holmes and Meier, 1992.
Eudin, Xenia, and Robert Slusser, eds. *Soviet Foreign Policy, 1928–1934*. University Park: Pennsylvania State University Press, 1966.
Falola, Toyin. *Nationalism and Africa Intellectuals*. Rochester, NY: University of Rochester Press, 2001.
Fanon, Frantz. *The Wretched of the Earth*. Translated by Constance Farrington. Harmondsworth, UK: Penguin, 1985.
Fernando, Claudin. *The Communist Movement from Comintern to Cominform*. Translated by Brain Pearce. New York: Monthly Review Press, 1975.
First, Ruth. *South West Africa*. London: Penguin, 1975.
Ford, James. *World Problems of the Negro People: A Refutation of George Padmore*. New York: Harlem Section of the Communist Party, 1935.
Fredrickson, George. *Black Liberation: A Comparative History of Black Ideologies in the United States and South Africa*. New York: Oxford University Press, 1995.

Friedland, William, and Carl Rosberg. "Introduction: The Anatomy of African Socialism". In *African Socialism*, edited by William Friedland and Carl Rosberg, 1–11. Palo Alto, CA: Stanford University Press, 1964.

Furlong, Patrick. *Between Crown and Swastika: The Impact of the Radical Right on the Afrikaner Nationalist Movement in the Fascist Era*. Hanover, MA: University Press of New England, 1991.

Fyfe, Christopher. "Race, Empire and the Historians". *Race and Class* 33, no. 4 (1992): 15–32.

Gaines, Kevin. *American Africans in Ghana: Black Expatriates and the Civil Rights Era*. Chapel Hill: University of North Carolina Press, 2006.

Galbraith, John. *The Great Crash, 1929*. Boston: Riverside, 1954.

Gann, L.H., and Peter Duignan. *Burden of Empire: An Appraisal of Western Colonialism in Africa South of the Sahara*. London: Pall Mall, 1968.

———. *The Rulers of Belgian Africa, 1884–1914*. Princeton, NJ: Princeton University Press, 1979.

———. *The Rulers of British Africa, 1870–1914*. Palo Alto, CA: Stanford University Press, 1978.

———. *The Rulers of German Africa, 1884–1914*. Palo Alto, CA: Stanford University Press, 1977.

Gathorne-Hardy, G.M. "Italy and Abyssinia". In *The Ethiopian Crisis: Touchstone of Appeasement?*, edited by Ludwig Schaefer, 1–16 Boston: D.C. Heath, 1961.

Geary, Dick. *Hitler and Nazism*. London: Routledge, 1993.

Geiss, Imanuel. *The Pan-African Movement*. Translated by Anna Keep. London: Methuen, 1974.

Gibson, Richard. *African Liberation Movements: Contemporary Struggles against White Minority Rule*. New York: Oxford University Press, 1972.

Gifford, Prosser, and Roger Louis. *Britain and Germany in Africa: Imperial Rivalry and Colonial Rule*. New Haven, CT: Yale University Press, 1967.

———, eds. *The Transfer of Power in Africa: Decolonization, 1940–1960*. New Haven, CT: Yale University Press, 1982.

Gilroy, Paul. *There Ain't no Black in the Union Jack: The Cultural Politics of Race and Nation*. London: Hutchinson, 1987.

———. *The Black Atlantic: Modernity and Double Consciousness*. London: Verso, 1993.

Goonetilleke, D.C.R.A., ed. *Heart of Darkness*. Toronto: Broadview Literary Texts, 1995.

Gordon, Lewis. "The Problem of Biography in the Study of the Thought of Black Intellectuals". *Small Axe*, no. 4 (1998): 47–63.

Gosnell, Harold. *Negro Politicians in the Rise of Negro Politics in Chicago.* Chicago: University of Chicago Press, 1967.
Green, Reginald, and Ann Seidman. *Unity or Poverty? The Economics of Pan-Africanism.* London: Penguin, 1968.
Gregor, James A. *The Ideology of Fascism.* New York: Free Press, 1969.
Griffin, Roger. *The Nature of Fascism.* London: Routledge, 1991.
Grimshaw, Anna, ed. *The C.L.R. James Reader.* Oxford: Blackwell, 1992.
Gundara, Jagdish, and Ian Duffield, eds. *Essays on the History of Blacks in Britain.* Aldershot, UK: Avebury, 1992.
Hailey, William. *The Future of Colonial Peoples.* 1944. Reprint, Oxford: Oxford University Press, 1953.
Hammond Moore, John. "The Angelo Herndon Case, 1932–1937". *Phylon* 32, no. 1 (1971): 60–71.
Hamrell, Sven, and Carl Gösta Widstrand, eds. *The Soviet Bloc, China and Africa.* Uppsala: Scandinavian Institute of African Studies, 1964.
Hanchard, Michael. "Translation, Political Community, and Black Internationalism: Some Comments on Brent Hayes Edwards's *The Practice of Diaspora*". *Small Axe*, no. 17 (2005): 112–19.
Hannaford, Ivan. *The History of an Idea in the West.* Baltimore, NJ: Johns Hopkins University Press, 1996.
Hansen, Emanuel. *Frantz Fanon: Social and Political Thought.* Norman, OH: Ohio State University Press, 1977.
Harding, Neill. *Lenin's Political Thought.* Vol. 1, *Theory and Practice in the Democratic Revolution.* London: Macmillan, 1977.
Harris, Joseph, ed. *African American Reactions to the War in Ethiopia, 1936–1941.* Baton Rouge: Louisiana State University Press, 1994.
———, ed. *Global Dimensions of the African Diaspora.* 2nd ed. Washington, DC: Howard University Press, 1982.
Haywood, Harry. *Black Bolshevik: Autobiography of an Afro-American Communist.* Chicago: Liberator Press, 1978.
Held, David, ed. *Political Theory Today.* Palo Alto, CA: Stanford University Press, 1991.
Hennessy, Alister, ed. *Intellectuals in the Twentieth-Century Caribbean.* Vol. 1. London: Macmillan, 1992.
Henry, Paget. *Caliban's Reason: Introducing Afro-Caribbean Philosophy.* New York: Routledge, 2000.
———. "Philosophy and the Caribbean Intellectual Tradition". *Small Axe*, no. 4 (1998): 3–28.

Herberg, Will. "Marxism and the American Negro". In *Negro: An Anthology*, edited by Nancy Cunard, 131–34. 1934. Reprint, New York: Frederick Ungar, 1970.
Herndon, Angelo. *Let Me Live*. New York: Random House, 1937.
Heywood, Andrew. *Political Ideologies*. 4th ed. London: Macmillan, 2007.
Hobson, J.A. *Imperialism: A Study*. 1902. Reprint, London: Unwin, 1988.
Hochschild, Adam. *King Leopold's Ghost: A Story of Greed, Terror, and Heroism in Colonial Africa*. New York: Houghton Mifflin, 1998.
Hodgkin, Thomas. *Nationalism in Colonial Africa*. London: Muller, 1956.
Hogsbjerg, Christian. *Mariner, Renegade and Castaway: Chris Braithwaite, Seamen's Organiser, Socialist and Militant Pan-Africanist*. London: Socialist History Society and Redwords, 2014.
Hollander, Paul. *Political Pilgrims: Travels of Western Intellectuals to the Soviet Union, China and Cuba, 1928–1978*. New York: Harper and Row, 1983.
Holt, Thomas. *The Problems of Freedom*. Kingston: Ian Randle, 1992.
Hooker, James. "Africa for Afro-Americans: Padmore and the Black Press". *Radical America* 2, no. 4 (1968): 14–19.
———. *Black Revolutionary: George Padmore's Path from Communism to Pan-Africanism*. New York: Praeger, 1967.
———. *Henry Sylvester Williams: Imperial Pan-Africanist*. London: Rex Collings, 1975.
hooks, bell, and Cornel West. *Breaking Bread: Insurgent Black Intellectual Life*. Boston: South End, 1991.
Hopkins, A.G. *An Economic History of West Africa*. London: Longman, 1973.
Howe, Stephen. *Empire: A Very Short Introduction*. Oxford: Oxford University Press, 2002.
Hudson, Hosea. *Black Worker in the Deep South*. New York: International Publishers, 1972.
Hughes, Alvin. C. "The Negro Sanhedrin Movement". *Journal of Negro History* 69, no. 1 (1984): 1–13.
Hutchinson, Earl. *Blacks and Reds: Race and Class Conflict, 1919–1990*. East Lansing: Michigan State University Press, 1995.
Jacobson, Julius, ed. *The Negro and the American Labor Movement*. New York: Anchor, 1968.
Jaffe, Hosea. *European Colonial Despotism*. London: Karnak House, 1994.
Jagan, Cheddi. *The West on Trial: The Fight for Guyana's Freedom*. Berlin: Seven Seas, 1980.
James, C.L.R. "C.L.R. James and British Trotskyism". Interview with Al Rich-

ards, Clarence Chrysostom and Anna Grimshaw. 8 and 16 November 1986, South London. https://www.marxists.org/archive/james-clr/works/1986/11/revhis-interview.htm.

———. *The Life of Captain Cipriani: An Account of the British Government in the West Indies.* Lancashire, UK: Nelson, 1932.

———. *Nkrumah and the Ghana Revolution.* London: Allison and Busby, 1977.

———. *At the Rendezvous of Victory.* London: Allison and Busby, 1984.

———. "The West Indian Intellectual". Introduction to *Froudacity: West Indian Fables by James Anthony Froude,* by J.J. Thomas, 23–49. London: New Beacon Books, 1969.

———. *World Revolution, 1917–1936: The Rise and Fall of the Communist International.* New York: Pioneer, 1937.

James, Leslie. *George Padmore and Decolonization from Below: Pan-Africanism, the Cold War, and the End of Empire.* New York: Palgrave Macmillan, 2015.

James, Winston. *Holding Aloft the Banner of Ethiopia: Caribbean Radicalism in Early Twentieth-Century America.* London: Verso, 1998.

Johnson, J.R. *Why Negroes Should Oppose the War.* New York: Pioneer, 1940.

Jones, Arthur. *New Fabian Colonial Essays.* London: Hogarth, 1959.

Joseph, C.L. "The British West Indies Regiment, 1914–1918". *Journal of Caribbean History* 2 (1971): 94–124.

Kadalie, Modibo. *Internationalism, Pan-Africanism, and the Struggle of Social Classes.* Savannah, GA: One Quest, 2000.

Kaplan, Morton, ed. *The Revolution in World Politics.* New York: John Wiley and Sons, 1962.

Karson, Marc, and Ronald Radosh. "The American Federation of Labor and the Negro Worker, 1894–1949". In *The Negro and the American Labor Movement,* edited by Julius Jacobson, 155–87. New York: Anchor, 1968.

Kedourie, Elie, ed. *Nationalism in Asia and Africa.* New York: New American Library and World Publishing, 1970.

Kelley, Robin D.G. " 'Afric's Sons with Banner Red': African-American Communists and the Politics of Culture, 1919–1934". In *Imagining Home: Class Culture and Nationalism in the African Diaspora,* edited by Sidney J. Lemelle and Robin D.G. Kelley, 35–55. London: Verso 1994.

———. *Hammer and Hoe: Alabama Communists during the Great Depression.* Chapel Hill: University of North Carolina Press, 1990.

———. *Freedom Dreams: The Black Radical Imagination.* Boston: Beacon, 2002.

———. *Race Rebels*. New York: Free Press, 1994.
Kennedy, Dane. *Britain and Empire, 1880–1945*. London: Longman, 2002.
Killingray, David, ed. *Africans in Britain*. London: Frank Cass, 1994.
Kimble, David. *A Political History of Ghana, 1850–1928*. Oxford: Clarendon, 1963.
Kiros, Teodros, ed. *Explorations in African Political Thought*. New York: Routledge, 2001.
Kitchen, Martin. *The British Empire and Commonwealth*. London: Macmillan, 1996.
Klehr, Harvey. *The Heyday of American Communism: The Depression Decade*. New York: Basic Books, 1984.
Klehr, Harvey, John Haynes and Fridrikh Firsov. *The Secret World of American Communism*. New Haven, CT: Yale University Press, 1995.
Knei-Paz, Baruch. *The Social and Political Thought of Leon Trotsky*. Oxford: Clarendon, 1978.
Kornweibel, Theodore. *No Crystal Stair: Black Life and the Messenger, 1917–1928*. Westport, CT: Greenwood, 1975.
Kouyatè, G. "Black and White Seamen Organize for Struggle". *Negro Worker* 1, no. 2 (1931): 19–20.
———. "Solidarity between White and Coloured Sailors". *Negro Worker* 2, no. 3 (1932): 27.
La Guerre, John. *Enemies of Empire*. Port of Spain: Extra-Mural Studies Unit, University of the West Indies, 1984.
———. *The Social and Political Thought of the Colonial Intelligentsia*. Kingston: Institute of Social and Economic Research, University of the West Indies, 1982.
Langley, J. Ayodele, ed. *Ideologies of Liberation in Black Africa, 1856–1970: Documents of Modern African Political Thought from Colonial Times to the Present*. London: Rex Collings, 1979.
———. *Pan-Africanism and Nationalism in West Africa, 1900–1945*. Oxford: Clarendon, 1973.
Lapping, Brian. *End of Empire*. London: Granada, 1985.
Laybourn, Keith. *The Rise of Socialism in Britain, 1881–1951*. Herndon, UK: Sutton, 1997.
Le Blanc, Paul, ed. *Black Liberation and the American Dream: The Struggle for Racial Justice*. New York: Humanity Books, 2003.
Lee Moon, Henry. "Pan-African Conference Set for Paris in Fall". *Chicago Defender*, 10 March 1946, 2.

Legum, Colin. *Pan-Africanism: A Short Political Guide*. London: Pall Mall, 1962.

———. "Pan-Africanism and Communism". In *The Soviet Bloc, China and Africa*, edited by Sven Hamrell and Carl Gösta Widstrand, 9–29. Uppsala: Scandinavian Institute of African Studies, 1964.

Lemelle, Sidney J., and Robin D.G. Kelley, eds. *Imagining Home: Class, Culture and Nationalism in the African Diaspora*. London: Verso, 1994.

Lenin, V.I. *Imperialism, the Highest Stage of Capitalism*. 1917. Reprint, Moscow: Progress, 1983.

———. *Selected Works in One Volume*. 1944. Reprint, New York: International Publishers, 1971.

———. *The State and Revolution*. 1918. Reprint, New York: International Publishers, 1943.

———. *What Is to Be Done?* Translated by Joseph Fineberg and Georg Hann. 1902. Reprint, London: Penguin, 1962.

Levenstein, Harvey. *Communism, Anti-Communism and the CIO*. Westport, CT: Greenwood, 1981.

Lewis, W. Arthur. *Economic Survey, 1919–1939*. New York: Harper and Row, 1969.

———. "The 1930s Social Revolution". In *Caribbean Freedom: Economy and Society from Emancipation to the Present,* edited by Hilary Beckles and Verene Shepherd, 376–92. Kingston: Ian Randle, 1993.

Lewis, Arthur, Michael Scott, Martin Wight and Colin Legum. *Attitude to Africa*. Harmondsworth, UK: Penguin, 1951.

Lewis, David Levering. *W.E.B. Du Bois: The Fight for Equality and the American Century, 1919–1963*. New York: Henry Holt, 2000.

Lewis, Gordon. *Main Currents in Caribbean Thought*. Kingston: Heinemann, 1983.

Lewis, Linden. "Richard B. Moore: The Making of a Caribbean Organic Intellectual". *Journal of Black Studies* 25, no. 5 (1995): 589–609.

Lewis, Rupert. "J.J. Thomas and Political Thought in the Caribbean". *Caribbean Quarterly* 36, nos. 1–2 (1990): 46–58.

———. *Marcus Garvey: Anti-Colonial Champion*. Trenton, NJ: Africa World Press, 1988.

———. "The Question of Imperialism and Aspects of Garvey's Political Activities in Jamaica, 1929–30". In *Garvey, Europe, the Americas,* edited by Rupert Lewis and Maureen Warner-Lewis, 89–110. Kingston: Institute of Social and Economic Research, University of the West Indies, 1986.

---. *Walter Rodney's Intellectual and Political Thought*. Kingston: University of the West Indies Press, 1998.

---. "The Writing of Caribbean Political Thought". *Caribbean Quarterly* 36, nos. 1–2 (1990): 153–65.

Lewis, Rupert, and Maureen Warner-Lewis, eds. *Garvey: Africa, Europe, Americas*. Kingston: Institute of Social and Economic Research, University of the West Indies, 1986.

Leys, Norman. *The Colour Bar in Kenya*. London: Hogarth, 1941.

Linebaugh, Peter, and Marcus Rediker. *The Many-Headed Hydra*. Boston: Beacon, 2000.

Losovsky, A. "Greetings to Negro Workers". *Negro Worker* 1, no. 1 (1931): 7–13.

Louis, Roger. *Ends of British Imperialism: The Scramble for Empire, Suez and Decolonization*. London: I.B. Tauris, 2006.

Low, D. Anthony, and R. Cranford Pratt. *Buganda and British Overrule, Two Studies*. London: Oxford University Press, 1970.

Lowy, Michael. *Fatherland or Mother Earth? Essays on the National Question*. London: Pluto, 1998.

Lugard, Lord. *The Dual Mandate in British Tropical Africa*. 5th ed. London: Frank Cass, 1965.

Lukacs, Georg. *Lenin*. Translated by Nicholas Jacob. London: NLB, 1971.

Lusane, Clarence. *Hitler's Black Victims: The Historical Experiences of Afro-Germans, European Blacks, Africans and African Americans in the Nazi Era*. London: Routledge, 2002.

Lynch, Hollis, ed. *Black Spokesman: Selected Published Writings of Edward Wilmot Blyden*. London: Frank Cass, 1971.

---. "Edward W. Blyden: Pioneer West African Nationalist". *Journal of African History* 6, no. 3 (1965): 373–88.

---. *Edward Wilmot Blyden: Pan-Negro Patriot, 1832–1912*. London: Oxford University Press, 1967.

Mackenzie, Alan. "Radical Pan-Africanism in the 1930s: A Discussion with C.L.R. James". *Radical History Review* 24, no. 1 (1980): 68–75.

Macmillan, W.M. *Warning from the West Indies: A Tract for Africa and Empire*. London: Faber and Faber, 1936.

Magubane, Bernard. *The Political Economy of Race and Class in South Africa*. New York: Monthly Review Press, 1979.

---. *The Ties That Bind: African-American Consciousness of Africa*. Trenton, NJ: Africa World Press, 1987.

Makalani Minkah. *In the Cause of Freedom: Radical Black Internationalism from Harlem to London, 1917–1939*. Chapel Hill: University of North Carolina Press, 2011.

Makonnen, Ras. *Pan-Africanism from Within*. New York: Oxford University Press, 1973.

Mamdani, Mahmood. "Indirect Rule, Civil Society and Ethnicity: The African Dilemma". In *Out of One, Many Africas*, edited by William G. Martin and Michael West, 189–96. Chicago: University of Illinois Press, 1999.

———. *When Victims Become Killers: Colonialism, Nativism and the Genocide in Rwanda*. Princeton, NJ: Princeton University Press, 2001.

Mannheim, Karl. *Ideology and Utopia*. London: Routledge, 1939.

Marable, Manning. *African and Caribbean Politics: From Kwame Nkrumah to the Grenada Revolution*. London: Verso, 1987.

Markovitz, Irving. *Power and Class in Africa*. Englewoods Cliffs, NJ: Prentice Hall, 1977.

Marshall, Ray. *The Negro Worker*. Toronto: Random House, 1967.

Martin, Charles. "Communists and Blacks: The ILD and the Angelo Herndon Case". *Journal of Negro History* 64, no. 2 (1979): 131–41.

Martin, Tony. *The Pan-African Connection: From Slavery to Garvey and Beyond*. Dover, MA: Majority Press, 1983.

———. *Race First: The Ideological and Organizational Struggles of Marcus Garvey and the Universal Negro Improvement Association*. Dover, MA: Majority Press, 1976.

Martin, William, and Michael West, eds. *Out of One, Many Africans*. Urbana: University of Illinois Press, 1999.

Martin, William, Michael West and Fanon Che Wilkins, eds. *From Toussaint to Tupac: The Black International since the Age of Revolution*. Chapel Hill: University of North Carolina Press, 2009.

Mathurin, Owen Charles. *Henry Sylvester Williams and the Origins of the Pan-African Movement, 1869–1911*. Westport, CT: Greenwood, 1976.

Mazrui, Ali. *Towards a Pax Africana: A Study of Ideology and Ambition*. Chicago: University of Chicago Press, 1967.

McClellan Woodford. "Africans and Black Americans in the Comintern Schools, 1925–1934". *International Journal of Historical Studies* 26, no. 2 (1993): 371–90.

McDermott, Kevin, and Jeremy Agnew. *The Comintern: A History of International Communism from Lenin to Stalin*. New York: St Martin's, 1997.

McKay, Claude. *A Long Way from Home*. New York: Harcourt Brace, 1970.

McKay, Vernon. *Africa in World Politics*. New York: Harper and Row, 1963.

McKenzie, Kermit E. *Comintern and World Revolution 1928–1943: The Shaping of Doctrine*. New York: Columbia University Press, 1964.
McLellan, David. *Ideology*. Minneapolis: University of Minnesota Press, 1986.
McLemee, Scott. *C.L.R. James on the "Negro Question"*. Jackson: University Press of Mississippi, 1996.
Medvedev, Roy. *Let History Judge: The Origins and Consequences of Stalinism*. Translated by George Shriver. New York: Columbia University Press, 1989.
Memmi, Albert. *Racism*. Minneapolis: University of Minneapolis Press, 2000.
Miller, James, Susan Pennybacker and Eve Rosenhaft. "Mother Ada Wright and the International Campaign to Free the Scottsboro Boys, 1931–1934". *American Historical Review* 106, no. 2 (2001): 387–430.
Miller, Norman. *Kenya: The Quest for Prosperity*. Boulder: Westview, 1984.
Mills, Charles. *Blackness Visible: Essays on Philosophy and Race*. London: Cornell University Press, 1998.
———. *From Class to Race: Essays on White Marxism and Black Radicalism*. New York: Rowman and Littlefield, 2003.
Milne, June. *Kwame Nkrumah*. London: PANAF Books, 1999.
Mockler, Anthony. *Haile Selassie's War*. Oxford: Signal, 2003.
Moore Turner, Joyce. *Caribbean Crusaders and the Harlem Renaissance*. Urbana: University of Illinois Press, 2005.
Mordecai, John. *The West Indies: The Federal Negotiations*. London: George Allen and Unwin, 1968.
Morrow, John. *A History of Political Thought*. New York: New York University Press, 1998.
Moses, Jeremiah, ed. *Classical Black Nationalism: From the American Revolution to Marcus Garvey*. New York: New York University Press, 1996.
Mullen, Bill, and James Smethurst, eds. *Left of the Color Line: Race, Radicalism and Twentieth-Century Literature of the United States*. London: University of North Carolina Press, 2003.
Munroe, Trevor. *The Cold War and the Jamaican Left, 1950–55: Reopening the Files*. Kingston: Kingston Publishers, 1992.
Murapa, Rukundo. "Padmore's Role in the African Liberation Movement". PhD dissertation, University of Illinois, 1974.
Murray, James. *The United Nations Trusteeship System*. Urbana: University of Illinois Press, 1957.
Murray-Brown, Jeremy. *Kenyatta*. London: Fontana, 1974.
Naison, Mark. *Communists in Harlem during the Depression*. New York: Grove, 1985.

Nantambu, Kwame. "Pan-Africanism versus Pan-African Nationalism: An Afrocentric Analysis". *Journal of Black Studies* 28, no. 5 (1998): 561–74.
Nembhard, Lenford. *Trials and Triumphs of Marcus Garvey*. New York: Kraus, 1940.
Nkrumah, Kwame. *Africa Must Unite*. London: PANAF Books, 1998.
———. *The Autobiography of Kwame Nkrumah*. Edinburgh: Thomas Nelson and Sons, 1957.
———. *Class Struggle in Africa*. New York: International Publishers, 1970.
———. *Revolutionary Path*. London: PANAF Books, 1973.
———. *The Struggle Continues*. London: PANAF Books, 1973.
Nnoli, Okwudiba. *Ethnic Politics in Nigeria*. Lagos: Fourth Dimension, 1978.
Novack, George, Dave Frankel and Fred Feldman. *The First Three Internationals: Their History and Lessons*. New York: Pathfinder, 1974.
Nwafor, Azinna. "The Revolutionary as Historian: Padmore and Pan-Africanism". Introduction to *Pan Africanism or Communism*, by George Padmore, xxv–xlii. New York: Doubleday, 1971.
Nwamaka, Danielle. "Anthony Bogues' *Black Heretics, Black Prophets: Radical Political Analysis*". Review of *Black Heretics, Black Prophets: Radical Political Analysis*, by Anthony Bogues. *Philosophia Africana* 7, no. 2 (2004): 81–87.
Nyerere, Julius. *UJAMAA: Essays on Socialism*. London: Oxford University Press, 1968.
Nzongola-Ntalaja, Georges. *Revolution and Counter-Revolution in Africa: Essays in Contemporary Politics*. London: Zed Books, 1987.
Okafor, S.O. *Indirect Rule: The Development of Central Legislature in Nigeria*. Lagos: Thomas Nelson and Sons, 1981.
Ottley, Roi. *No Green Pastures*. New York: Charles Scribner and Sons, 1951.
Owens-Watkins, Irma. *Blood Relations: Caribbean Immigrants and the Harlem Community, 1900–1932*. Bloomington: Indiana University Press, 1996.
Oxaal, Ivar. *Black Intellectuals Come to Power: The Rise of Creole Nationalism in Trinidad and Tobago*. Cambridge, MA: Schenkman, 1968.
———. *Black Intellectuals and the Dilemmas of Race and Class in Trinidad*. Cambridge, MA: Schenkman, 1982.
Pal Singh, Nikhil. *Black Is a Country*. Cambridge: Harvard University Press, 2005.
Parsons, Talcott, and Edward Shils. *Toward a General Theory of Action*. Harvard, CT: Cambridge University Press, 1962.
Patterson, William. "Helping Britain to Rule Africa", parts 1–3. *Negro Worker* 6, no. 9 (1936): 5, 7; 7, no. 1 (1937): 8–9, 15; 7, no. 2 (1937): 12–13, 16.

Payne, Stanley. *Fascism: Comparison and Definition*. Madison: University of Wisconsin Press, 1980.

———. *History of Fascism, 1914–1945*. Madison: University of Wisconsin Press, 1995.

Pennybacker, Susan. *From Scottsboro to Munich: Race and Political Culture in 1930s Britain*. Princeton: Princeton University Press, 2009.

Pepper, John. *American Negro Problems*. New York: Negro Project Workers Library, 1928.

Perham, Margery. *Africans and British Rule*. 6th ed. London: Oxford University Press, 1949.

———. *The Colonial Reckoning*. London: Collins, 1961.

———. *Native Administration in Nigeria*. London: Oxford University Press, 1937.

Plamenatz, John. *On Alien Rule and Self-Government*. London: Longmans, 1960.

Plummer, Alfred. *Raw Materials or War Materials?* London: Victor Gollancz, 1937.

Polsgrove, Carol. *Ending British Rule in Africa: Writers in a Common Cause*. Manchester: Manchester University Press, 2009.

Rathborne, Richard. *Nkrumah and the Chiefs: The Politics of Chieftaincy in Ghana, 1951–1960*. Oxford: James Currey, 2000.

Record, Wilson. *The Negro and the Communist Party*. New York: Atheneum, 1971.

———. *Race and Radicalism: The NAACP and the Communist Party in Conflict*. Ithaca: Cornell University Press, 1964.

Ridley, F.A. *The Papacy and Fascism: The Crisis of the Twentieth Century*. London: Martin Secker and Warburg, 1937.

Robinson, Cedric. "The African Diaspora and the Italo-Ethiopian Crisis". *Race and Class* 27, no. 12 (1985): 51–65.

———. *An Anthropology of Marxism*. Hampshire, UK: Ashgate, 2001.

———. *Black Marxism: The Making of the Black Radical Tradition*. 1983. Reprint, Chapel Hill: North Carolina University Press, 2000.

Robinson, Ronald, John Gallagher and Alice Denny. *Africans and the Victorians: The Official Mind of Imperialism*. London: Macmillan, 1974.

Rodney, Walter. "Aspects of the International Class Struggle in Africa, the Caribbean and America". https://www.marxists.org/subject/africa/rodney-walter/works/internationalclassstruggle.htm.

———. *How Europe Underdeveloped Africa*. Washington, DC: Howard University Press, 1982.

Rohdie, Samuel. "The Gold Coast Aborigines Abroad". *Journal of African History* 6, no. 3 (1965): 389–411.
Rowley, Hazel. *Richard Wright: The Life and Times*. New York: Henry Holt, 2001.
Roux, Edward. *Time Longer than Rope: A History of the Black Man's Struggle for Freedom in South Africa*. Madison: University of Wisconsin Press, 1964.
Ryan, Selwyn. *Race and Nationalism*. Toronto: University of Toronto Press, 1972.
Rydell, Robert. *The Reason why the Colored American Is Not in the World's Columbian Exposition*. 1893. Reprint, Urbana: University of Illinois Press, 1999.
Sabine, George. *A History of Political Theory*. Fort Worth, TX: Harcourt Brace, 1978.
Said, Edward. *Representations of the Intellectual*. New York: Pantheon, 1994.
Salvemini, Gaetano. "Prelude to World War II". In *The Ethiopian Crisis: Touchstone of Appeasement?*, edited by Ludwig Schaefer, 32–47. Boston: D.C. Heath, 1961.
Samaroo, Brinsley. "The Trinidad Disturbances of 1917–1920: Precursor to 1937". In *The Trinidad Labour Riots of 1937*, edited by Roy Thomas, 21–56. Port of Spain: Extra-Mural Studies Unit, University of the West Indies, St Augustine, 1987.
———. "The Trinidad Workingmen's Association and the Origins of Popular Protest in a Crown Colony". *Social and Economic Studies* 21 (1972): 205–22.
Santiago-Valles, W.F. "Africana Studies and the Research Collective". *Race and Class* 47, no. 2 (2005): 100–110.
———. "C.L.R. James: Asking Questions of the Past". *Race and Class* 45, no. 1 (2003): 61–81.
Sartre, Jean-Paul. *Colonialism and Neocolonialism*. London: Routledge, 2001.
Schaefer, Ludwig, ed. *The Ethiopian Crisis Touchstone of Appeasement?* Boston: D.C. Heath, 1961.
Schwarz, Bill, ed. *West Indian Intellectuals in Britain*. Oxford: Manchester, 2003.
Scobie, Edward. *Global African Presence*. New York: A & B Books, 1994.
Sharpley-Whiting, T. "Erasures and the Practice of Diaspora Feminism". *Small Axe*, no. 17 (2005): 129–33.
Shepperson, George. "Pan-Africanism: Some Historical Notes". *Phylon* 23, no. 4 (1962): 346–58.
Sherwood, Marika. "George Padmore and Kwame Nkrumah: A Tentative

Outline of Their Relationship". In *George Padmore: Pan-African Revolutionary*, edited by Fitzroy Baptiste and Rupert Lewis, 162–82. Kingston: Ian Randle, 2009.

———. *Kwame Nkrumah: The Years Abroad, 1935–1937*. Accra: Freedom Publications, 1966.

———. *Origins of Pan-Africanism: Henry Sylvester Williams, Africa and the African Diaspora*. London: Routledge, 2011.

———. "Race, Empire and Education: Teaching Racism". *Race and Class* 42, no. 3 (2001): 1–28.

Singh, Kelvin. *Race and Class Struggles in a Colonial State: Trinidad, 1917–1945*. Kingston: University of the West Indies Press, 1994.

Singham, A.W., and Shirley Hune. *Non-Alignment in an Age of Alignments*. London: Zed Books, 1986.

Skidmore, Max. *Ideologies: Politics in Action*. 2nd ed. Fort Worth, TX: Harcourt Brace, 1993.

Small, Richard. "Caliban's Freedom: Its Significance". *Small Axe*, no. 3 (1998): 143–56.

Smith, Faith. *Creole Recitations: John Jacob Thomas and Colonial Formation in the Late Nineteenth-Century Caribbean*. Charlottesville: University of Virginia Press, 2002.

———. "A Man Who Knows His Roots: J.J. Thomas and Current Discourses of Black/Nationalism and Canon Formation". *Small Axe*, no. 5 (1999): 1–13.

Snyder, Louis, ed. *The Imperialism Reader*. Princeton, NJ: D. Van Nostrand, 1962.

Solomon, Mark. *The Cry Was Unity: Communist and African Americans, 1917–1936*. Jackson: University Press of Mississippi, 1998.

Spielvogel, Jackson. *Hitler and Nazi Germany: A History*. Upper Saddle River, NJ: Prentice Hall, 1988.

Spitzer, Leo, and LaRay Denzer. "I.T.A. Wallace-Johnson and the West African Youth League". *International Journal of African Historical Studies* 6, no. 3 (1973): 413–52.

Stalin, Joseph. *Foundations of Leninism*. 1924. Reprint, New York: International Publishers, 1970.

———. *Marxism and the National and Colonial Question*. New York: International Publishers, 1935.

Stephens, Michelle. "Black Transnationalism and the Politics of National Identity: West Indian Intellectuals in Harlem in the Age of War and Revolution". *American Quarterly* 50, no. 3 (1998): 592–608.

———. "Disarticulating Black Internationalisms: West Indian Radicals and the Practice of Diaspora". *Small Axe*, no. 17 (2005): 100–111.
Stoecker, Helmuth, ed. *German Imperialism in Africa: From the Beginnings until the Second World War*. Translated by Bernd Zöllner. London: C. Hurst, 1986.
Sundiata, Ibrahim. *Brothers and Strangers: Black Zion, Black Slavery, 1914–1940*. Durham, NC: Duke University Press, 2003.
Suret-Canale, Jean. *French Colonialism in Tropical Africa*. Translated by Till Gottheimer. New York: Pica, 1971.
Tatum, Travis. "Reflections on Black Marxism". *Race and Class* 47, no. 2 (2005): 71–76.
Temple, Christel. *Literary Pan-Africanism*. Durham, NC: Carolina Academic Press, 2005.
Thomas, J.J. *Froudacity: West Indian Fables*. 1869. Reprint, Port of Spain: New Beacon Books, 1969.
Thomas, Roy, ed. *The Trinidad Labour Riots of 1937: Perspectives 50 Years Later*. Port of Spain: St Augustine, Trinidad: Department of Extra-Mural Studies, University of the West Indies, 1987.
Thompson, Alvin. *Economic Parasitism: European Rule in West Africa, 1880–1960*. Cave Hill, Barbados: Department of History and Philosophy, University of the West Indies, 2006.
Thompson, Dudley. *From Kingston to Kenya: The Making of a Pan-Africanist Lawyer*. Dover, MA: Majority Press, 1993.
Thompson, Leonard. *The Political Mythology of Apartheid*. New Haven, CT: Yale University Press, 1985.
Thompson, Scott W. *Ghana's Foreign Policy, 1957–1966: Diplomacy, Ideology and the New State*. Princeton, NJ: Princeton University Press, 1969.
Thompson, Vincent. *Africa and Unity: The Evolution of Pan-Africanism*. London: Longmans, 1969.
Thomson, David. *Political Ideas*. London: Penguin, 1990.
Tinker, Hugh. *Men Who Overturned Empires: Fighters, Dreamers and Schemers*. London: Macmillan, 1987.
Toynbee, Arnold. *The Impact of the Russian Revolution, 1917–1967*. London: Oxford University Press, 1967.
Trewhela, Paul. "The Death of Albert Nzula and the Silence of George Padmore". *Searchlight South Africa* 1, no. 1 (1988): 64–69.
———. "George Padmore: A Critique: Pan-Africanism or Marxism?" *Searchlight South Africa* 1, no. 1 (1988): 42–63.

Trotsky, Leon. *Leon Trotsky on Black Nationalism and Self-Determination*, edited by George Breitman. 1939. Reprint, New York: Pathfinder, 1978.
Tucker, Robert. *The Lenin Anthology*. New York: W.W. Norton, 1974.
Turner, W. Burghardt, and Joyce Moore Turner. *Richard B. Moore: Caribbean Militant in Harlem*. Bloomington: Indiana University Press, 1998.
Tunteng, P. Kiven. "George Padmore's Impact on Africa: A Critical Appraisal". *Phylon* 35, no. 1 (1974): 33–44.
Uzoigwe, G.N. *Britain and the Conquest of Africa*. Ann Arbor: University of Michigan Press, 1974.
Vaizey, John. *Capitalism*. London: Weidenfeld and Nicolson, 1971.
Van Enckevort, Maria. "The Life and Work of Otto Huiswoud: Professional Revolutionary and Internationalist, 1893–1961". PhD dissertation, University of the West Indies, Mona, 2000.
Vallari, Luigi. "The Ethiopia War: An Italian View". In *The Ethiopian Crisis: Touchstone of Appeasement?*, edited by Ludwig Schaefer, 48–62. Boston: D.C. Heath, 1961.
Valtin, Jan. *Out of the Night*. New York: Alliance, 1941.
Verich, Thomas. *The European Powers and the Italo-Ethiopian War, 1935–1936*. Salisbury, UK: Documentary Publications, 1980.
Vincent, Theodore. *Voices of a Black Nation: Political Journalism in the Harlem Renaissance*. San Francisco: Ramparts, 1973.
Von Albertini, Rudolf. *Decolonization: The Administration and Future of the Colonies, 1919–1960*. Translated by Francisca Garvie. New York: Doubleday, 1971.
Von Eschen, Penny. *Race against Empire: Black Americans and Anti-Colonialism, 1937–1957*. Ithaca: Cornell University Press, 1997.
Wald, Alan. "African Americans, Culture, and Communism: National Liberation and Socialism". In *Black Liberation and the American Dream: The Struggle for Racial Justice*, edited by Paul Le Blanc, 194–221. New York: Humanity Books, 2003.
Wallerstein, Immanuel. *Africa: The Politics of Unity – An Analysis of a Contemporary Movement*. London: Pall Mall, 1968.
——. "Pan-Africanism as Protest". In *The Revolution in World Politics*, edited by Morton A. Kaplan, 137–51.New York: John Wiley and Sons, 1962.
Weiss, Holger. *Framing a Radical African Atlantic: African American Agency, West African Intellectuals and the International Trade Union Committee of Negro Workers*. Boston: Brill, 2014.
Weisborg, Robert. "British West Indian Reaction to the Italian-Ethiopian War: An Episode in Pan-Africanism". *Caribbean Studies* 10, no. 1 (1970): 34–41.

Wellington, John. *South West Africa and its Human Issues*. Oxford: Clarendon, 1967.
Wesson, Robert. *Why Marxism? The Continuing Success of a Failed Theory*. New York: Basic Books, 1976.
Willetts, Peter. *The Non-Aligned Movement*. London: Frances Pinter, 1982.
Williams, Eric. *History of the People of Trinidad and Tobago*. London: Andre Deutsch, 1964.
Wilson, Edward. *Russia and Black Africa before World War II*. London: Holmes and Meier, 1974.
Wilson, Henry. *African Decolonization*. London: Edward Arnold, 1994.
Winston, Henry. *Class, Race and Black Liberation: A Critique of New Theories of Liberation in the United States and Africa*. New York: International Publishers, 1977.
———. *Strategy for a Black Agenda*. New York: International Publishers, 1975.
Woodis, Jack. *Africa: The Roots of Revolt*. London: Lawrence and Wishart, 1960.
Woolf, Leonard. *Economic Imperialism*. London: Swarthmore Press, 1920.
———. *Empire and Commerce in Africa: A Study in Economic Imperialism*. London: Allen and Unwin, 1968.
———. *Mandates and Empire*. London: British Periodicals, 1920.
Worden, Nigel. *The Making of Modern South Africa*. Oxford: Blackwell, 1994.
Work, Ernest. *Ethiopia: A Pawn in European Diplomacy*. New Concord, OH: Ernest Work, 1935.
Woronoff, Jon. *Organizing African Unity*. Metuchen, NJ: Scarecrow, 1970.
Worsley, Peter. *Marx and Marxism*. London: Routledge, 2000.
Wright, Richard. *Black Power*. New York: Harper and Brothers, 1954.
———. Foreword to *Pan Africanism or Communism*, by George Padmore, xxi–xxiv. New York: Doubleday, 1971.
Young, Crawford. *The African Colonial State in Comparative Perspective*. New Haven, CT: Yale University Press, 1994.

INDEX

Aboriginal Rights Protection Society, 74
Abrahams, Peter, 1–2, 93, 109, 158–59
Adjei, Ako, 159
Africa: Bandung Conference brought together independent territories from Asia and, 153–54; Berlin Act of 1885, 122; Blyden championed as birthplace of human civilization, 10–11; colonial rule and hostility toward British, 142; conditions of black workers in, 53–54, 119; discussed as site for fifth Pan-African Congress, 110–11; independence and pan-Africanism, 164–65; Russian foreign policy and, 90; self-determination for, 138–43; socialism for as delineated by Padmore, 170–72
Africa and the World (publication of IASB), 104
Africa and World Peace (Padmore), 118, 147–48, 182; uses a Marxist-Leninist framework to analyse imperialism and colonialism, 176
Africa: Britain's Third Empire (Padmore), 56, 118, 182; chapter entitled "Colonial Fascism in South Africa", 130

African Americans: and ideological disputes in US compared to Britain, 112; and student pan-African association, 24; urged by Padmore to uphold black international struggle, 137–38
African Association, and call for first pan-African conference (1900), 13–14
African Blood Brotherhood, 33
African colonials and fifth Pan-African Congress, 114
African diaspora, 13, 54; in Harlem, 30
African Empires and Civilizations (PAF pamphlet), 109
African independence movements, 147
African Marxists, 65–66
African nationalism: Blyden and, 11; Conference of Independent States and, 159–60; and tensions with communism, 7, 147–53
African Progressive Association, supported proposal for PAF, 108
African Sentinel (publication of IASB), 104
African socialism, political, economic and social aspects of, 172
African Standard (newspaper), 135

249

Index

Africans struggling against imperialism, 13
African Telegraph (newspaper), 17
African Union, supported proposal for PAF, 108
"African utopia", Liberia as, 23
African Youth League, supported proposal for PAF, 108
Afrikaners, 133
agriculture, diversification of in Ghana, 173
All African People's Conference, Accra (1958), 158, 159–61, 183; tribalism as main issue, 167
All African People's Conference (1960), 161
All-American Anti-Imperialist League, 26
American consul in Trinidad, 18
American Federation of Labor (AFL), 40, 46; discriminatory practices in, 41–42
American Imperialism Enslaves Liberia, (Padmore), 63, 67, 83, 93, 181; classified as agitational or propagandistic, 175–76
American Negro Labor Congress (ANLC), 28–30, 57, 160; Padmore a field organizer of, 26
American Negro Problem (PAF pamphlet), 109
Amsterdam International (International Federation of Trade Unions), 58
Anglo-Ethiopian treaty (1897), 97
Angola, 122, 146
anti-colonialism, 2, 146
apartheid legalized in South Africa, 132–33

"An Appeal to Negro Workers! Help Build Your Paper" (Padmore), 29
Appiah, Joe, 107
Argos (newspaper), 17–18
Arendt, Hannah, and roots of totalitarianism, 131
Ashanti Confederacy, 158
Asia, anti-colonial struggles in, 153–54
Association of Haitian Writers, 102
Association of Students of African Descent, supported proposal for PAF, 108
Atlantic Charter (1941), and self-government clause, 139
Azikiwe, Benjamin Nnamdi, 22, 24, 67, 107

Back to Africa project (Garvey), 83
Ballinger, William, 57
Baltimore Afro-America (newspaper), 83
Bandung Conference (1955), and non-alignment policy, 153–54
Bathhurst Trade Union (Gambia), 75
Belgian Congo, 64, 122
Belgian Labour Party, 72
Belgian socialists, 72
Belle Plantation (Barbados), 8
Berlin Act (1885), 122
Berlin Conference (1885), 130
Bioko (Fernando Pó), Liberians exported to, 67
Bismark, Otto von, 130
Black Belt (US), racial oppression in, 52–53
Black Belt thesis, critique of, 6, 38–40

Index 251

black civil rights, communist party and relationship with, 163
black communists. *See* black Marxists
black internationalism, 2–5, 52, 62, 66, 94–95, 156
Black Man (journal), 67
black Marxists, 3–4, 33–35
black nationalism, 13, 33, 92
black radical tradition, 2–5
Blacks and Whites (film), 80
black trade unions, 57
black workers: exploited as a class and a race, 33; and Great Depression, 49; and response to crisis of capitalism, 54–61. *See also* "Negro toilers"
black world conference. *See* Negro World Conference (1935)
Blyden, Edward Wilmot, 5, 6, 9, 10–11, 23, 92; Padmore's continental pan-Africanism built on ideas of, 155
Boer War, 127; and extermination of Hottentot tribes, 131
Bolshevik Revolution, 3, 6, 47; black Marxists and attraction of the, 33–35
Bondelzwarts, bombing of, 123
Briggs, Cyril, 30, 33, 34
Britain, 5, 100; imperialist tactics used by, 69–70; indirect rule by, 127–29; mandatory system increased colonial empire of, 121; pan-Africanism viewed as benign, 165; used racially charged language in Africa, 134
British Central Intelligence Department, 73

British Centre against Imperialism Conference, London (1946), 183
British Empire, 48; colonial peoples of and fifth Pan-African Congress, 112, 113
British Foreign Office and pan-Africanism, 165
British Guiana, 17, 64, 140; British troops sent in to remove Jagan, 150; East Indian Muslim and Hindu populations in, 140
British Independent Labour Party (ILP), 58
British investment in Volga River project, Padmore's apprehension about, 169
British Labour Party, 71, 120
British West Africa, 65, 135
British West Indies Regiment, racism in the, 15–16
Brotherhood of Sleeping Car Porters (BSCP), 42, 57
Browder, Earl, 86–89
Brussels Conference Act (1890), 122
Buckle, Desmond, 110
Burma, 142, 153, 154; Russia offered aid to, 169

Cambridge Senior Certificate, completed by Padmore, 9
Campbell, Horace, 151; and critique of Padmore's *Pan-Africanism or Communism*, 145
Campbell, Robert, 23
capitalism, 3–4, 27–28, 34, 103; black workers and response to crisis of, 54–61; class interests under, 32–33; as contrasted with socialism, 172; crisis of, 53–54;

Campbell, Robert (*continued*)
and justification of exploitation in Africa, 71; Padmore against, 31; pan-Africanism and rejection of, 154; and racial oppression, 52–53
Carey-Bernard, Brigadier, 16
Caribbean: intellectual tradition, 5–7; writings by Padmore on colonialism in, 181
Caribbean colonies, 54, 90; crown colonies/direct rule practised in differed from that in Africa, 125; intellectual tradition in, 5; self-determination for, 138–43
Carlyle, Thomas, 12
Castle, William, 68
Catholic Standard (newspaper), 19
Champion, A.W.G., 57–58
Chicago Defender (newspaper), 110
China, liberated by peasants, 153
Christian, Jacobus, 123
Christian church and imperialism, 103
Christianity, Islam and the Negro Race (Blyden), 9
Churchill, Winston, 71, 139
Cipriani, Captain A.A., 16
class, tension between race and, 32–33, 45
class struggle, 44–45, 166; and national liberation, 144; Negro Workers Committee as a class organization, 51
Cleveland conference 1929 (TUUL), 40
Cold War: propaganda during, 147; non-alignment during, 174
Colonial Commission of the Confèdération Générale du travail unitaire, 78
Colonial and Coloured Unity: A Programme of Action–History of the Pan-African Congress (ed. by Padmore), 181
colonial fascism, 7, 143; crown colony government as, 129–31; in Kenya, 134; Padmore developed concept of, 177; in South Africa, 132; in Trinidad, 138; in West Africa, 136
colonialism: and capitalism, 53–54; contradictory attitude of many socialists toward, 52; exploitation in Africa, 7, 119, 179; *Life and Struggles of Negro Toilers* a critique of, 51–52; opposed by ILP, 105–6; potential power vacuum after, 152
colonial nationalism, 36–37, 153
"colour caste system", 70
Coloured Workers' Association, supported proposal for PAF, 108
Comintern (Communist International), 1, 49; fourth Congress and establishment of a Negro Commission, 3; hostility against Garvey, Du Bois, and pan-Africanism sanctioned by sixth Congress, 146; Padmore's break with, 4, 74–76, 80–81; 86–87; Padmore's career with the, 6, 72–73, 92–93; position on the Negro Question, 28; sixth congress of the, 40, 59; strategies concerning social-democratic parties, 162–63
Comintern Commission, Padmore a member of, 48

Comintern Universalism, 4
communism: African nationalism and tensions with, 7, 147–53; Cold War propaganda crediting communism for inspiring African nationalism, 147; and nationalists, 112
Communist International (Comintern). *See* Comintern
Communist International of Youth, 26
Communist Party of Great Britain (CPGB), 149, 150, 153; racism in, 158
Communist Party of the United States (CPUSA), 3, 6, 31–32, 42, 43–44; abandoned "boring-from-within" approach, 41, 55; blacks in, 33–35; dismissal of Tuskegee University, 56; and Harlem Tenants League, 30; and "Negro Question", 59; Padmore joined, 25; racism in 158; and sympathy towards Garvey's deportation, 26
communists, tensions between nationalists and, 151–52
Communist University of the Toilers of the East (KUTV), 75, 93; Padmore as lecturer at, 48
Community of Independent African States, 162
Conference of Independent African States (1958), 156–57, 159, 183
Congo: decimation of population, 131; looting of, 72
Congress of the International Labour Defence (Soviet Union), 92, 183

Conservative Party (Britain), 71
continental pan-Africanism, 7, 155–62
Controversy (newspaper), 106
Convention People's Party (Ghana), 146, 158
Courier (newspaper), 68
Coyaba Chronicles (Abrahams), 1–2
Cri des nègres, 73; Padmore published in, 82, 92
Crisis (journal of NAACP), 32, 55, 56, 97
crown colony government, 12; and direct rule, 125–26; as form of colonial fascism, 177
Crown Lands Ordinance of 1915 (Kenya), 135
Crummell, Alexander, 23

Daily Worker (newspaper), 41, 43; Padmore wrote for, 92
Davies, Phillip, 24
Davis, Helen. *See* Huiswoud, Hermina
de Bourg, John Sydney, 18
Deportation Ordinance, 137
De Priest, Oscar, 55; anti-communism of, 57
Dillingham, John, 22
direct rule and crown colony governments, 7, 125–26
dockworker's strike (1919), 18
Du Bois, W.E.B., 32, 55–56, 91, 109, 164; communist attack on, 146; correspondence with Padmore, 6, 83, 95, 159; correspondence with Padmore regarding fifth Pan-African Congress, 110–14

Dutch East Indies, 142
Dutch imperialism, 153
Dutch socialists, 72

east central Africa, indirect rule practised in, 126
economic reconstruction in Africa, 172–74
Eden, Anthony, 100
Egypt, 15, 159; Russia offered aid to, 169
Emergency Powers Act (Sierra Leone), 136
equatorial Africa, indirect rule in, 128
Ethiopia, 5, 23, 53, 159; betrayed by League of Nations, 99–103; commercial treaty between Japan and, 89; history of written by Homer, 11; Italian invasion of, 97–99
Étoile nord-africaine, 102
European colonizers in Africa, 53–54; Germany and Italy as, 182
European communists, arrogance of, 151
European socialist movements, 36

Fanon, Frantz, 131, 156
fascism: in Europe, 128; Padmore a victim of, 96; roots located in imperialism in Africa, 130, 142–43. *See also* colonial fascism
federation of the West Indies, idea of, 29–30
fifth Pan-African Congress (1945), 1, 5, 6, 56, 154, 166; and building of a black international, 156; in Manchester, 115–17; Padmore as chief organizer of, 183; planning of, 110–14; pledges of solidarity with India, Indonesia and Vietnam, 153
Finance Corporation of America (Firestone subsidiary), 23–24
Finland, 142; invasion by Soviet Union, 148
Firestone Company, 67; Padmore's proposal for buying out, 83
Firestone Plantation Company, 23–24; Liberians exploited on, 68
Fisk Herald (student newspaper), 22
Fisk University, Padmore at, 6, 21
Forced Labour in Africa (Padmore), 63, 93, 181
Ford, James, 49, 50, 62, 85–86; editor of *Negro Worker,* 63
"Ford Analyses Padmore as Police Agent and Spy" (Ford), 87
Foster, William Z., 39, 40
France, 50, 53, 64; in equatorial Africa, 130; mandatory system increased colonial empire of, 121; minister of the colonies of and fifth Pan-African Congress, 111
Franco-Ethiopian treaty (1897), 97
French Communist Party, 102
French communists, 82
French imperialism, 153
French socialists, 71
Friends of African Freedom Society, supported proposal for PAF, 108
Froude, James Anthony, 12–13
Froudacity: West Indian Fables by James Anthony Froude (Thomas), 12–13

Gambia, 50, 64, 141, 155
Gandhian "doctrine of non-violence", 154

Garvey, Amy Ashwood (first wife of Marcus Garvey), 98
Garvey, Amy Jacques (widow of Marcus Garvey), 109
Garvey, Marcus, 5, 85, 91; anti-communism of, 31–32; and black nationalism, 16, 58–59; blocked from relocating headquarters to Liberia, 23; communist attack on, 146; deportation from US and Canada, 26; heckled by Padmore and James, 60–61; Padmore and praise for, 60
Garveyism, 31–32; influence on self-determination for the Black Belt, 38; Padmore's attack on, 58–59; *Pan-Africanism or Communism* records rise of, 182; strong among US and Caribbean workers, 60
"Gastonia: Its Significance for Negro Labour" (Padmore), 43
Gastonia textile strike, 6, 40, 43–47
Geiss, Imanuel, 66–67, 168; on Padmore's *Pan-Africanism or Communism*, 145
Germany: as Aryan state, 96; and atrocities committed against Jews, 177; and link between colonial methods of savagery in Africa and Holocaust, 131; mandatory system and, 120, 121; slaughter of Herero and Nama people, 131; in South West Africa, 130
Ghana: economic reconstruction, 172–74; independence of, 144; indirect rule in, 128; two conferences on pan-Africanism held in (1958), 156–57; Volta River project in, 168–69. *See also* Gold Coast
Ghana-Guinea-Liberia Conference (1959), 183
Ghana-Guinea Union (1958); Nkrumah and Touré formed, 162
Gold Coast, 50, 64, 129, 141, 153, 155; indirect rule practised in, 126; Fanti and democratic practices, 127; Volta River project in the, 168–69. *See also* Ghana
Gold Coast Revolution (Padmore), 158, 182
Great Britain, 53
Great Depression, 49
Grenada Gazette (newspaper), 12
Guérin, Daniel, 166; critique of Padmore's *Pan-Africanism or Communism*, 170
"Guide to Pan-African Socialism" (Padmore), 170–71
Guinea-Ghana Conference (1959), 183

Habitual Idlers Ordinance of 1918, 18
Haile Selassie, 99
Hailey, Lord, 121
Haiti, 3, 53, 64
Hamburg Committee, 61–62
Hamburg Conference 1930 (International Conference of Negro Workers), 6, 49–51, 92
"Hands Off Liberia" (Padmore), 67, 83; published by PAF, 109
Hands Off the Protectorates (Padmore), 181
Harlem (NYC), 30–31, 34
Harlem Renaissance, 28

Harlem Tenants League, 30–31

Hayford, Casely, 56; Padmore's continental pan-Africanism built on ideas of, 155

Henderson, Arthur, 71

Hercules, F.E.M., banned from Trinidad, 17

Herndon, Angelo, 89; charged with attempt to incite insurrection, 137–38

historical materialism, as framework for analysis of African society, 162, 178

History of the Russian Revolution (Trotsky), 145

Hitler, Adolf, 79, 96, 141, 163; anti-Semitic laws of compared to apartheid laws, 133

Hobson, J.A., writings of as influential on Padmore, 118

Hooker, James, 8, 83

Hoover, Herbert, 57

Howard, Sir Esmé, 25–26

Howard University, 6, 25–28, 87

How Britain Rules Africa (Padmore), 118, 119, 182; and "Colonial Fascism", 130; uses a Marxist-Leninist framework to analyse imperialism and colonialism, 176

How Russia Transformed Her Colonial Empire (Padmore), 141, 148–49, 182; use of a Marxist-Leninist framework to analyse imperialism and colonialism, 176

"How the Empire Is Governed" (Padmore), 69

"How the Imperialists Are Civilizing Africa" (Padmore), 70–71

Huggins, G.F., 17–18

Huiswoud, Hermina (Helen Davis), 8, 85–86, 92

Huiswoud, Otto (Charles Woodson), 30, 34, 59, 78, 81, 82, 88

humanist approach, 2

imperialism: *Africa: Britain's Third Empire* implicated Labour Party, 182; and African emancipation, 148; black people united against, 25, 113; capitalism and, 33, 53, 142; crimes associated with, 119, 179; Lenin against, 37; *Life and Struggles of Negro Toilers* as a critique of, 51–52; mandatory system as part of, 124; Padmore and critique of, 7, 25–26, 118; roots of fascism in, 130; and totalitarianism, 131; tribalism used against nationalist struggles, 167

Imperialism: A Study (Hobson), 118

Independent African States Conference, 159

Independent Labour Party (ILP), 105, 148

India, 142, 153, 154; Russia offered aid to, 169

indirect rule, 7, 126–29; as form of colonial fascism, 177; local chiefs as colonial administrators, 127–28

Indonesia, 72, 153; Japanese invasion of, 142

Industrial Commercial Union (ICU), 57–58

industrialization in Africa, 173

International African Friends of Abyssinia/Ethiopia, 98, 107

International African Opinion

(publication of IASB), edited by C.L.R. James, 104–5
International African Service Bureau (IASB), 1, 6, 103–8; Leninist political organization of Padmore seen in, 179; repudiation of Stalinist policies, 149; supported proposal for PAF, 108, 110
International Anti-Imperialist Youth League, Padmore secretary of, 25, 26
International Club, Howard University, 25
International Committee for Mutual Aid to Negro Workers, 74
International Conference of Negros and Arabs (1936), 102
International Conference of Negro Workers, Hamburg (1930), 6, 183. See also Hamburg Conference (International Conference of Negro Workers)
International Control Commission (ICC): charges against Padmore, 82, 83; expulsion of Padmore from Communist Party, 80–81
International Federation of Trade Unions (Amsterdam International), 58
internationalism, 37; verses race unity, 91–92
International Negro Workers' Review, 85; name changed to *Negro Worker*, 63, 66
International Red Aid World Congress, Moscow (1932), 92
International of Seamen and Harbour Workers, 76, 82; Conference in Hamburg (1932), 92, 183

International Stuttgart Congress, second, of 1907, 52
International Trade Union Committee of Negro Workers (ITUCNW), 1, 78, 102; Hamburg Committee and concentration in Africa and Caribbean, 62; objectives of, 61; Padmore as executive secretary of, 4, 6, 48; Padmore as prolific writer for, 62–63; provisional committee planning Negro workers conference, 49–50
Italiaander, Rolf, 76
Italian Communist Party, 102
Italo-Ethiopian conflict, 103
Italo-Ethiopia Treaty (1928), 99
Italy, 53; and invasion of Abyssinia, 5, 6, 130

Jagan, Cheddi, removal of by British, 150
Jamaica, 17, 64; Garvey deported to, 32; purging of Marxists in PNP, 146
James, C.L.R., 5, 20, 66, 91, 98, 106, 148, 154, 158
"James Ford Answers Padmore's Charges" (Ford), 87
Jantuah, Dr (acting high commissioner for Ghana in London), 158
Japan: imperialist propaganda of, 89; invasion of Indonesia, 142
Jews: Nazis used racially charged language against, 134; atrocities committed by Germans against, 177
Jim Crow craft unions, 46
Jim Crow laws (US), 21–22, 29, 38
Johnson, Charles, 68

Jones, Chris, founding member of IASB, 103–4
Jones, William, 83
Jouhaux, Léon, 71
journalism, 63; political journalism of Padmore, 92, 98, 180
Junco, Sandalio, 51

Kadalie, Clements, founder of ICU, 57
Kambana, Oscar, 144
Kendal, Henry, 60
Kenya, 64; colonial fascism in, 134–36, 177; repressive racist legislation in, 134
Kenya, Land of Conflict (PAF pamphlet), 108–9
Kenyatta, Jomo (Johnstone), 50, 65, 98, 107; founding member of IASB, 103–4
Kikuyu Central Association: declared illegal in 1940, 134; supported proposal for PAF, 108
King, C.B., administration of, 68
King George V, support for a British West Indies Regiment, 15
Kouyatè, Tiemoko Garan, 4, 65, 73, 78, 81, 94; close comrade of Padmore, 82
Ku Klux Klan, 25
KUTV. *See* Communist University of the Toilers of the East (KUTV)
Kuusinen, 38–39

Labour Action (Musties), 42
Labour Imperialism and East Africa (Padmore), 63, 93, 181
Labour Monthly, 64
land: and economic reconstruction in Africa, 172; as foundation for independent Africa, 179
Latin America, racism in, 54 Laval, P., 101
League against Imperialism and Colonial Oppression, 26, 49, 102
League of Coloured Peoples, 102
League of Nations: article 16, 100; article 22, 122; Mandates Commission, 124; Permanent Mandates Commission and bombing of Bondelzwarts, 123–24
Left (journal), 106
Lenin, Vladimir, 72, 105, 172; impact of on Padmore, 6, 30, 35–38, 47, 138–39, 156; and political journalism, 180; and self-determination for nations of former Russian empire, 141–42; and vanguard party, 93, *What Is to Be Done?* 63
Leninism, 35–38
Lewis, Arthur, 49, 140, 147, 149, 169
Liberia, 50, 53, 81, 159, 164; as site of black diaspora, 22–23; Blyden migrated to, 10; Firestone Plantation Company in, 23–24; imperialism in, 67–69; importance of for Padmore, 83
Life and Struggles of Negro Toilers, (Padmore), 6, 63, 76, 88, 93, 160, 166, 181; classified as agitational or propagandistic, 175–76; critique of colonialism and imperialism, 51–53, 89–90, 118, 176
Ligue de défense de la race nègre, 73, 102
Lochard, Metz, 27

Locke, Alain, 28
London, as coordinating site for fifth Pan-African Congress, 111
Loray Mills, Gastonia, NC (site of textile strike), 43
Loughton, C., 17
Lugard, Lord, 126–27
Lum, George Aldric Lee, 17

Mabella Coaling Company (Sierra Leone), strike at, 135
MacDonald, Ramsay (British PM), 49, 71
Makonnen, Ras, 13, 19, 27, 98, 106, 150, 161; founding member of IASB, 103–4
Mamdani, Mahmood, 128, 131
mandatory system (under article 22 League of Nations covenant), 7, 119–24; as form of colonial fascism, 177; imperialistic nature of, 121; as a trusteeship, 122
Manning, Sam, 98
Mao Tse Tung, 48, 171
Marable, Manning, 154, 164, 169–70
"Marcus Garvey, Misleader of His Race" (Padmore), 58
Marryshow, T. Albert, 98
Marxism, 2; importance of for Africans, 170–71; Lenin and deviation from, 37; Padmore continued to identify with, 113; students attracted to, 165–66
Marxist-Leninist thought, 2, 16; Padmore and, 175, 176
Masters and Servants Ordinance (Kenya), 135
Maughan, R.C.F., 69

Menelik (Ethiopian ruler), 97
Messenger (newspaper), 57
Miller, Kelly, 27–28
Milliard, Peter, 98
Mines and Works Act (1911), 132
Mirror (newspaper), 14
Moody, Harold, 109, 112; ideology of, 113
Moore, Richard B., 30, 34
Moscow City Soviet, Padmore elected to, 48
Moscow Daily News (newspaper), Padmore wrote for, 92
Moscow Soviet, Padmore as deputy to, 48
Moton, Robert, 55; politically conservative, 56
Mussolini, Benito, 100; and Stresa Conference, 101

National African Socialist Students' Organization, 159
National Association for the Advancement of Colored People (NAACP), 32, 41, 55–56, 97, 111
nationalists, tensions between communists and, 151
National Miners Union, 43
National Negro Congress, 102
National Peace Council, 121
national question, 37
Nationalsozialistiche Monatshefte (newspaper), 96
National Textile Workers Union, 43
Native Authority Ordinance (Kenya), 134
Native Lands Act (1913), 132
Native Problem in South Africa (PAF pamphlet), 109

Native Representation Act (1936), 133
Native Republic model in South Africa, 40
Native Trust and Land Act (1936), 132
Native (Urban Areas) Act (1923), 132
Nazis: anti-black sentiment of, 96; comparison to European colonizers in Africa, 133–34; involvement in colonial racist experiments, 131
"Negro Art in America" (Padmore), 28
Negro Association, supported proposal for PAF, 108, 110
Negro Bureau of the Red International of Labour Unions (RILU), 1, 51; Padmore as chair of, 48
Negro Champion (newspaper), 46, 26, 29, 92
Negro Commission of the Comintern, 3
Negro Factories Corporation, 32
Negro in the Caribbean (PAF pamphlet), 109
Negro Liberator (newspaper), 87
"Negro Question", 59; Theses on the, 37
Negro Sanhedrin (black organizations), 27
Negro Textile Workers, 43
"Negro Toilers", 51–54. See also black workers
Negro Welfare Centre, supported proposal for PAF, 108, 110
Negro Worker (journal), 1, 55, 60, 82, 86, 87, 92, 118; mission of, 4; Padmore and resignation as editor of, 76–80; Padmore as editor of, 4, 48, 62–72, 160, 176, 180; themes prescribed by Russian leadership, 65
Negro Workers and the Imperialist War: Intervention in the Soviet Union (Padmore), 63, 93, 181; classified as agitational or propagandistic writing, 175–76
Negro Workers Committee: formed at Hamburg Conference, 51; Moscow, 48
Negro World (UNIA), 9, 17
Negro World Conference, 6, 49, 156; planned and aborted, 94–96
Negro World Unity Conference, 82–83
Negro World Unity Congress, 91, 95
New Leader (journal of ILP), 105
New Negro (anthology of poetry and plays), 28
New York, as coordinating site for fifth Pan-African Congress, 111
New York University, 25
New York Workers School, 31
Nigeria, 64, 141, 155; indirect rule practised in, 126–27; *Negro Worker* banned in, 65; warrant chiefs in, 128
Nkrumah, Kwame, 1, 107, 114, 144, 152, 164, 158; detested issue of racism, 158; emancipation through non-violence, 154; held two conferences on pan-Africanism, 156–57; on trial by PAF, 149–50; Padmore appointed advisor to, 157
non-alignment policy, 7, 174; adopted by newly independent countries, 153–55

Index 261

non-violence, Nkrumah and principle of, 154
North China, 89
Nurse, Alphonso (grandfather of George Padmore), 8
Nurse, Anna (mother of George Padmore), 8
Nurse, Blyden (daughter of George Padmore), 10
Nurse, James (father of George Padmore), 8–9; self-identified as Muslim, 9; influenced by writings of Blyden, 10
Nurse, Malcolm. *See* Padmore, George
Nwafor, Azinna, 152, 165
Nyasaland, crown colonies/direct rule practised in, 125
Nzula, Albert, 65, 82

Ollivierre, Cyril, 50, 64, 78, 93, 107
Ormsby-Gore, W.G., 69
Osservatore Romano (newspaper), 103
Ottley, Roi, 72
Owen, Chandler, 57
Oxaal, Ivar, 27

Padmore, Dorothy. *See* Pizer, Dorothy
Padmore, George: advisor on African Affairs to Nkrumah in Ghana, 1, 157, 161–62; advocated a "Marshall Aid programme for Africa", 168; on African nationalism, 147; against crown colonies/direct rule, 125–26; against indirect rule, 127–29; ANLC, 26; anti-colonial critique of imperialism, 7, 25–26, 118; arrest and deportation from Hamburg, 73; Atlantic Charter and self-government clause, 139; avoidance of radical activity in early years, 19; black radical and black international traditions of, 2–5; Caribbean intellectual tradition of, 5–7; colour-blindness of, 159; conferences important for, 183; critical of Black Belt thesis, 39–40; critical of British communists, 153; critical of Jagan and People's Progressive Party, 150; critical of Stalinism, 148; critical of tribalism, 166–67; critique of colonial fascism, 130; critique of colonialism, 51–52, 93; critique of communism, 165; critique of the mandatory system, 121–24; critique of racial oppression, 52–53; downplayed class struggle, 166; early years of, 9–10, 19–20; editor of *Negro Worker*, 4, 48, 62–72; encounters with Jim Crow laws, 21–22; at Fisk University, 21–24, 56; founding member of IASB, 103–4; on Gastonia textile strike, 43–47; Hamburg Conference, 49–51; historical materialism as framework for analysis of African society, 162, 178; Hobson and influence on, 118; at Howard University, 6, 25–28; ideological shifts of, 2; inspired nationalist movements, 147; as intellectual descendant of J.J. Thomas, 5; as an internationalist, 180; ITUCNW member, 93; Lenin and influence on, 6,

Padmore, George (*continued*)
35–38, 47, 118, 138–39, 156; and Marxism, 3, 148, 170–72; and political journalism, 92, 180–81; political praxis of, 7, 179–84; praised Garvey, 60; problems with Leninism, 148; as pseudonym for Malcolm Nurse, 8; publications post-Comintern, 181; resignation as editor of *Negro Worker*, 76–80; as revolutionary pragmatist, 175; role in organizing and influencing All African Conference, 159–61; on self-determination for nations of former Russian empire, 141–42; on self-determination for US Blacks, 39–40; shaping of Ghana's foreign policy by, 159; and social democracy, 148; on socialism and Marxism, 170–72; support of ILP, 105–6; support for Soviet Union, 147–48; support of West Indies political federation, 139–40; trade unionism as alternative to tribalism, 167; trip to Russia (1929), 40; Wallace-Johnson a long-time comrade of, 137; wrote under byline "The Negro Socialist Leader", 105

Padmore, George, and communism: anti-communist activity, 149–50; as Comintern operative, 48, 72–73; attacked by communists, 85–90; attraction to, 34; break with Comintern, 4, 74–76, 84; critical of British communists, 153; critical of Stalinism, 148; critique of communism, 165; elected to Moscow City Soviet, 48; expulsion from Comintern, 80–81, 91–92; Lenin and influence on, 6, 35–38, 47, 118, 138–39, 156; Marxism and, 3, 148, 170–72; member of CPUSA, 6, 93–94; problems with Leninism, 148; propagandist for Comintern, 92–93; resignation from Comintern, 76; trip to Russia (1929), 40

Padmore, George, and W.E.B. Du Bois: association with, 55–56; correspondence with, 6, 83; correspondence regarding fifth Pan-African Congress, 110–14

Padmore, George, and pan-Africanism, 4–7, 91–117; All African People's Conference and involvement in, 159–62; attack on communism as a pan-Africanist, 146; continental pan-Africanism, 155–57; and socialism, 170–74

pamphlets, importance of for Padmore, 181–82

Pan-African Association (1900), 14

Pan-African Congress (PAC), 55. *See also* fifth Pan-African Congress (1945)

Pan-African Federation (PAF), 1, 6, 108–10; Leninist political organization of Padmore seen in, 179; pamphlets published by, 108–9; rejected Stalinism, 149–50

pan-Africanism, 1, 2, 94–95; building upon ideas of Du Bois, 164; communist attack on, 146; economics of, 170–71; as ideological alternative to communism, 178; mission of, 66–67; *Negro Worker* contributing to, 67; Padmore in the service of, 6, 83; and non-alignment, 153–55; on behalf of Ethiopia, 97–98; political and social objectives of, 7; student movements within, 22, 24, 92; verses communism, 162–66. *See also* continental pan-Africanism; Pan-African socialism

Pan-Africanism or Communism (Padmore), 7, 144–45, 158, 160, 161, 182; omitted discussion of class struggle in, 166

Pan-African Secretariat, Padmore as director of, 161

pan-African socialism, 170–74, 178–79, 182; political and social objectives of, 7

Paris Peace Conference (1946), 183

Parti Communiste Français, 94

Partridge, Edward J., 10, 19; Padmore's attack on, 186n10

pass laws in South Africa, 133

Paul-Boncour, Joseph, 71

Peace and the Colonial Problem conference (1935), 121

People's National Party (Jamaica), purging of Marxists in, 146

People's Progressive Party (British Guiana), 150

Peters, Carl, and murders in German Southeast Africa, 131

Philippines, resistance to Japanese invasion, 142

Phipps, R.E., 14

Pierre, A. Pulcherrie, 14

Pizer (Padmore), Dorothy, 157, 159.

Poland, 129, 130, 142; and colonial experience under Germany, 131; Nazis used racially charged language against, 134

Pope Pius, 103

Popular Front period (1934–39), 107, 163

Port of Spain Gazette (newspaper), 19

Portugal, 53; in Angola, 130

positive neutrality, principle of, 154

Potekin, Ivan, 65

protest of oil and asphalt workers (1917), 16–17

Pullman Company, 42

Queen's Royal College (secondary school), 9

Racamond, Julien, 83

race, tension between class and, 32–33

Race Nègre, 73

racial oppression and capitalism, 52–53

Racial Problems in South Africa (Friends House, London), 133

racial solidarity, 155–56; contrasting with primacy of class, 32–33; contrasting with proletarian internationalism, 91–92

racism: of the British, 134; in the British West Indies Regiment, 15–16; and discrimination at hotels, 44; European genocidal impulses justified on terms of, 131; as handmaiden of the European colonizing project, 177; Nkrumah detested issue of, 158; political economy and, 34; in South Africa, 132

Randolph, A. Philip, 42, 57

Rate Payers Association, 14

Record, Wilson, 44–45, 88
Red International of Labour Unions (RILU), 28, 47, 48; Negro Bureau of, 51, 62
religious separatism, 167
reparations: Padmore's call for, 168–70; political and social objectives of, 7
repatriation to Liberia, 24
Resolution on Frontiers, Boundaries and Federations, 160–61
restitution, Padmore's call for, 168–69. *See also* reparations
Rhodesia, crown colonies/direct rule practised in northern, 125; colonial fascism in, 177
Ridley, F.A., 103, 118
RILU. *See* Red International of Labour Unions (RILU)
Robinson, Cedric, 2, 4, 39, 84
Rodney, Walter, and critique of Padmore, 145
Roosevelt, President Franklin, 139, 170
Roy, M.K., 37
Russia, 169
Russian Revolution, 6; as example for Africans, 171
Russwurm, John Brown, 23

Said, Mohammed, 98
Salmon, Ven Edward Seiler, 18
Salter, Sir Arthur, 120
Save Liberia project, 91; proposal for, 83
Schuyler, George, 68
Scottsboro Boys' case, 89; Padmore and internationalization of, 94, 137

Seditious Publications Ordinance, aimed at *Negro World,* 17, 18, 19
Sekyi, Kobina, 74–75
self-determination: for US Blacks, 39–40; communist party and relationship with groups advocating, 163; for Africa and Caribbean colonies, 38, 138–43, 182
Semper, Julia, 10
Sierra Leone, 50, 64, 141, 155, 164; indirect rule practised in, 126; supported proposal for PAF, 108
Sierra Leone Trade Union Congress, 136
Slavin, Grigorij Naumovic, 51, 85
Small, Edward, 65, 75
social democrats, 71; Padmore moving toward, 148
socialists against colonial rule, 142
Society of People of African Origin, 17
South Africa, 50, 64; apartheid legalized, 132–33; colonial fascism in, 132–34, 177; influence of Padmore's *Pan-Africanism or Communism,* 145; Native Republic model, 40; racially discriminatory legislation in, 132
Southern textile workers, 44
South West Africa, mandatory system denied rights in, 123
Soviet Union, 4, 48, 79; foreign policy shift in 1934, 80; joined League of Nations 1934, 105; Padmore and, 147–49; racial discrimination prohibited in, 37; response to Ethiopia crisis, 101–2; and self-determination for nations of former Russian empire, 141–42,

182; trials against Stalin's opponents, 163
Spanish Civil War, 101–2
St George's Chronicle (newspaper), 12
St Mary's College (secondary school), 9
St Thomas, Blyden born on, 10
Stalin, Joseph, 78; and the national question, 38–39
Stalin Ball Bearing Works, Padmore as representative for, 48
Stalinism, 158; rejection of by PAF, 149–50
Stresa Conference (1935), 101
strikes, 17; dockworker's strike Port of Spain (1919), 18
Storer College, 22
student activism: at Howard University, 25–28; protests at Fisk University, 21
student movements within pan-Africanism, 22, 24; Padmore involved in creation of, 92
Subject Peoples Conference, attended by Padmore, 183
Sudan, 153, 159; Russia offered aid to, 169

Tanganyika, 64, 121; crown colonies/direct rule practised in, 125; indirect rule practised in, 126; mandatory system denied rights in, 123
Taranto, Italy, revolt by black soldiers in, 15–16
Thomas, J.J., 5, 6, 11–13; influenced by writings and black nationalism of Blyden, 10, 13
Thorez, Maurice, 82

totalitarianism, 131
Touré, Sekou, 162
Trade Union Congress, 121
Trade Union Educational League, dissolution of, 40
Trade Union International, 110
trade unionism, 167
Trade Union Unity League (TUUL), 42; Cleveland conference (1929), 6, 40, 41, 44, 46, 183
Transvaal Mine Clerks Association, 58
tribalism, 166–68
Trinidad and Tobago, 8, 20, 48, 64; calls for constitutional reforms prior to WWI, 14–15; colonial fascism in, 138; East Indian Muslim and Hindu populations in, 140; environment and landscape of, 5–6; impact of WWI on, 16–20; *Negro Worker* banned in, 65; strikes in 1919, 17–18
Trinidad Guardian (newspaper), 19; Padmore as reporter for, 10
Trinidadian middle class, writings of Blyden and influence on, 10
Trinidad Lake Asphalt Company, 1917 workers protest at, 16–17
Trinidad Working Men's Association, 16
Tranquillity School, 9
tribalism, political and social objectives of, 7
Trotskyism, 112, 148
trusteeship, 7, 122
Tubman, William (Liberian president), 162
Tunisia, 159; second All African Conference in, 161

Tunteng, Kiven, critical of Padmore's position on tribalism, 167
Turkish colonial territories, mandatory system and, 120, 121
Turner, Bishop Henry McNeal, 23
Tuskegee University, 56

Uganda, 64; crown colonies/direct rule practised in, 125; indirect rule practised in, 126
UNIA. *See* Universal Negro Improvement Association (UNIA)
Union nationale malagache, 102
Union of Soviet Socialist Republics (USSR). *See* Soviet Union
united and popular front strategy of communist party, 163
United Committee of Coloured and Colonial Peoples' Association, supported proposal for PAF, 108
United Nations Trusteeship, 124–25
United States (US), 64; ideological disputes and African Americans in, 112; Padmore advocated a "Marshall Aid programme for Africa", 168; Padmore pursued a university education in, 6; racism in, 54; recognition of Soviet government, 80; West Indian student activism in, 20
United States of Africa, Padmore's concept of, 155, 178
Universal Negro Improvement Association (UNIA), 32, 41, 59, 146

Valtin, Jan (Richard Krebs), 62, 65, 77, 82, 91
Vandervelde, Emile, 72
vanguard party, 93

Voice of Coloured Labour (PAF pamphlet), edited by Padmore, 109, 181
Voice of the New Negro (PAF pamphlet), 109
Volta River project in the Gold Coast/Ghana, 168–69

Wallace-Johnson, I.T.A., 65, 75, 107; charged for libel, 136–37; editor of *African Sentinel*; editor of *African Standard*, 135; founding member of IASB, 103–4
Wallerstein, Immanuel, 161, 170
Ward, Arnold, 73
War Department Defence Works (Sierra Leone), strike at, 135
Washington, Booker T., 56
West Africa, 140; colonial fascism in, 136–38; crown colonies/direct rule practised in, 125; self-government for, 140–41
West Africa Frontier Force, 135
West African Students' Union, 111
West African Youth League, 136
West Indian ideology, WWI as turning point for, 16
West Indian soldiers, political awareness of, 16
West Indies, 72; "colour caste system" in, 70; Padmore a supporter of political federation, 29–30, 139–41
West Indies Labour Congress (1938), 140
West Indies Today (PAF pamphlet), 108
What Is the ITUCNW? (Padmore), 55, 60, 62–63, 93, 181; classified

as agitational or propagandistic, 175–76
What Is to Be Done? (Lenin), 63
white chauvinism, 51
White Man's Duty (PAF pamphlet), co-authored by Padmore and Nancy Cunard, 109, 155, 181
Wickins, Captain W. 135
Williams, Henry Sylvester, 5, 6, 13–14, 187n30; influenced by writings of Blyden, 10
Winston, Henry, 151–52, 169
Wood, E.F.L., 16
Wood, Major Edward, 18
Woodson, Charles. *See* Huiswould, Otto
Workers Party of America, 26
working class, 149

World Federation of Trade Unions, 109, 111, 116
World Trade Union Conference, London, 110, 113–14
World War I, impact of on Trinidad and Tobago, 16–17; roots of fascism traced to, 130
World War II, 106
Wright, Richard, 84, 147; Padmore's correspondence with, 152; visit with Padmore, 94

Young Workers' League of America, 26

Ziese, Max, 76
Zusmanovich, Alexander, 74, 76, 77, 88, 91

www.ingramcontent.com/pod-product-compliance
Lightning Source LLC
Chambersburg PA
CBHW021350300426
44114CB00012B/1157